ADDRESSING FRANK KERMODE

WARWICK STUDIES IN THE EUROPEAN HUMANITIES

General Editor: Tom Winnifrith, Chairman of the Department of English and Comparative Literary Studies, University of Warwick

This series is designed for publications deriving from the European Humanities Research Centre at the University of Warwick, which was founded to promote interdisciplinary and comparative research in the European Humanities. The Centre's aims, pursued through research projects, conferences, seminars and visiting fellowships, include the dissemination of research findings; this series is the Centre's primary means to this end.

Nicholas Hewitt (*editor*)
THE CULTURE OF RECONSTRUCTION

J. R. Mulryne and Margaret Shewring (*editors*)
WAR, LITERATURE AND THE ARTS IN SIXTEENTH-CENTURY EUROPE
THEATRE OF THE ENGLISH AND ITALIAN RENAISSANCE

Brian Rigby and Nicholas Hewitt (*editors*)
FRANCE AND THE MASS-MEDIA 1945–67

Tom Winnifrith and Cyril Barrett (*editors*)
THE PHILOSOPHY OF LEISURE

Margaret Tudeau-Clayton and Martin Warner (*editors*)
ADDRESSING FRANK KERMODE: ESSAYS IN CRITICISM AND INTERPRETATION

Further titles in preparation

Series Standing Order

If you would like to receive future titles in this series as they are published, you can make use of our standing order facility. To place a standing order please contact your bookseller or, in case of difficulty, write to us at the address below with your name and address and the name of the series. Please state with which title you wish to begin your standing order. (If you live outside the UK we may not have the rights for your area, in which case we will forward your order to the publisher concerned.)

Standing Order Service, Macmillan Distribution Ltd,
Houndmills, Basingstoke, Hampshire, RG21 2XS, England.

ADDRESSING FRANK KERMODE

ESSAYS IN CRITICISM AND INTERPRETATION

Edited by

Margaret Tudeau-Clayton
Faculté des lettres, University of Lausanne

and

Martin Warner
*Centre for Research in Philosophy and Literature,
University of Warwick*

MACMILLAN

Chapter 1 © John Stokes 1991; Chapter 2 © A. D. Nuttall 1991; Chapter 3 © Bernard Harrison 1991; Chapter 4 © Patrick Parrinder 1991; Chapter 5 © George Hunter 1991; Chapter 6 © Frank Kermode 1991; Chapter 7 © Dominic Baker-Smith 1991; Chapter 8 © Lisa Jardine 1991; Chapter 9 © Alastair Fowler 1991; Chapter 10 © Richard Poirier 1991; Chapter 11 © John Hollander 1991

ISBN 0–333–53137-X (hardcover)

First published 1991

Published by
MACMILLAN ACADEMIC AND PROFESSIONAL LTD
Houndmills, Basingstoke, Hampshire RG21 2XS
and London Companies and representatives
throughout the world

Phototypeset by Input Typesetting Ltd, London
Printed in Hong Kong

British Library Cataloguing in Publication Data
Addressing Frank Kermode: essays in criticism and interpretation
    1. Literature. Criticism
    I. Tudeau-Clayton, Margaret II. Warner, Martin, 1940–
801.95

ISBN 0–333–53137-X

Contents

Notes on the Contributors

Frank Kermode is an Honorary Fellow of King's College, Cambridge, and a Fellow of both the British Academy and the Royal Society of Literature and an Officer of the Order of Arts and Sciences in France. He has held named Chairs in English Literature at the Universities of Manchester, Bristol, London and Cambridge and been a visiting Professor at Columbia and Charles Eliot Norton Professor of Poetry at Harvard. In 1989 he was Senior Visiting Fellow at the University of Warwick's Centre for Research in Philosophy and Literature where versions 'of the papers comprising Part One of this volume were first presented and discussed. He is General Editor of The Oxford Authors and of Fontana's *Masterguides* and *Modern Masters* Series, and has been co-editor of *Encounter*. Of his many publications, those discussed or referred to in the text are listed in the Bibliography.

Dominic Baker-Smith is Professor of English Literature at the University of Amsterdam; he was previously University Lecturer in English at Cambridge and Professor at University College, Cardiff. He has published on a variety of topics in Renaissance literature and thought, and has edited (with J. A. van Dorsten) *Sir Philip Sidney: 1586 and the Creation of a Legend* (1986). A study of *Utopia* is forthcoming and he is currently working on humanist exegesis.

Alastair Fowler is Regius Professor Emeritus of the University of Edinburgh and Visiting Professor at the University of Virginia. His most recent book was *A History of English Literature* (1987); he is currently working on *The New Oxford Book of Seventeenth Century English Verse* and on *Country House Poems: An Anthology of Seventeenth Century Estates Poems and Related Items*.

Bernard Harrison is Professor of Philosophy at the University of Sussex. He is the author of a number of books on the philosophy of language and on philosophy and literature. The latter include *Henry Fielding's Tom Jones: The Novelist as Moral Philosopher* (1975) and *Narrative and Reality: Literature and the Limits of Theory* (forthcoming).

John Hollander is A. Bartlett Giamatti Professor of English at Yale University, and was co-editor, with Frank Kermode, of *The Oxford Anthology of English Literature* (1973). He is a poet and critic whose most recent volumes are *Harp Lake* (1988) and *Melodious Guile: Fictive Pattern in Poetic Language* (1989).

George Hunter was the founding Professor of English and Comparative Literature at the University of Warwick; he is now Emily Sanford Professor of English and Chairman of the Graduate Program in Renaissance Studies at Yale University.

Lisa Jardine is Professor of English at Queen Mary and Westfield College, University of London. Her publications include *Francis Bacon: Discovery and the Art of Discourse* (1974), *Still Harping on Daughters: Women and Drama in the Age of Shakespeare* (1983); she is co-author of *From Humanism to the Humanities* (1986) and *What's Left? Women in Culture and the Labour Movement* (1989). She is currently working on a book on Erasmus, and is a general editor of the new edition of the complete works of Francis Bacon.

A. D. Nuttall has been Professor of English and Pro-Vice-Chancellor at the University of Sussex; he is now Fellow of New College, Oxford. His publications include *Two Concepts of Allegory* (1967), *A Common Sky* (1974), *Overheard by God* (1980), *Pope's Essay on Man* (1984), and *The Stoic in Love* (1989).

Patrick Parrinder is Professor of English at the University of Reading. He is the author of studies of James Joyce and H. G. Wells, and of *Science Fiction: Its Criticism and Teaching* (1980); he has also published *The Failure of Theory* (1987), a collection of essays, and a history of Anglo-American criticism, *Authors and Authority: English and American Criticism 1750–1990* (1991).

Richard Poirier is the editor of *Raritan Quarterly*, a founder of The Library of America, and Marius Bewly Professor of English at Rutgers University, and was co-editor, with Frank Kermode, of *The Oxford Reader* (1971). His publications include *A World Elsewhere* (1967), *The Performing Self* (1971), *Robert Frost: The Work of Knowing* (1977) and *The Renewal of Literature* (1987).

John Stokes is Lecturer in the Department of English and Comparative Literature at the University of Warwick. He has written widely on the culture of the *fin-de-siècle* and is the author of *In the Nineties* (1989).

Margaret Tudeau-Clayton is a former undergraduate and graduate of King's College, Cambridge, where she was supervised by Frank Kermode, and now teaches English Language and Literature at the University of Lausanne. She has published several articles and is preparing for publication a revised version of her thesis, entitled *Jonson, Shakespeare and the Figure of Vergil*.

Martin Warner is Senior Lecturer in the Department of Philosophy at the University of Warwick and was the founding Programme Director of the University's Centre for Research in Philosophy and Literature; with John Goode he arranged the occasion which formed the foundation for this volume. His publications include *Philosophical Finesse: Studies in the Art of Rational Persuasion* (1989) and (as editor) *The Bible as Rhetoric: Studies in Biblical Persuasion and Credibility* (1990).

Introduction

Margaret Tudeau-Clayton and Martin Warner

For the English critic John Carey he is 'easily the most intelligent critic now writing'; for the American critic J. Hillis Miller he is representative of the current major developments in English (as distinct from American or Canadian) criticism (Carey 1989: G3; Salusinszky 1987: 239). In recognition of his stature a conference on the work of Frank Kermode was held at the University of Warwick in March 1989 under the auspices of its Centre for Research in Philosophy and Literature. Part One of this volume consists in a selection of the papers given on this occasion. Addressed at the time to the person of Frank Kermode, they also address (in the sense of examining) the body of texts that carry his signature. In each a perceived intellectual itinerary of Kermode's through one, or several, of these texts is plotted and interrogated. The essays are thus essays in criticism in the straightforward sense of being 'about', or moving within, this body of critical texts, but also in the sense of attempting critically to engage with them, and to measure their significance.

In so far, of course, as the critical act presupposes an act of interpretation, these essays are also essays in interpretation. We have, however, chosen to use this title rather for the essays in Part Two. The authors here do not so much engage with the work of Frank Kermode as acknowledge, more or less directly, its influence on their own intellectual itineraries and, specifically, on the formation of the interpretative strategies which they then deploy in order to (re)read chosen literary texts, or, in the case of John Hollander, a particular linguistic form. Here again our categories overlap, notably in the essays by Richard Poirier and Alastair Fowler, which both invite a revision of critical opinion concerning the texts they interpret. Our categories should not, therefore, be taken as absolute or mutually exclusive, but rather as general guides to the main orientation of each group of essays.

The discourses in both parts – those which define and examine the intellectual itineraries of Kermode in Part One and those which produce the interpretations in Part Two – are heterogeneous, and fittingly so in a volume addressed to one who (not without personal cost) has stood for the tolerance of diversity within the academy of literary study. Indeed, this diversity of discourses together with the diversity of objects of attention – whether general questions or specific texts – provide a measure of, and tribute to, the scope and diversity of his interests and influence. To have moved amongst such different discourses, to have addressed such different objects, and with sufficient authority to have commanded the attention of specialists as well as non-specialists, is perhaps what makes the achievement of Kermode so exceptional.

Within the diversity of Kermode's writings there are, of course, patterns and recurrences, as the essays in Part One show. Just so there are recurrences in this volume, some of which indeed echo those in Kermode's own work. Thus Kermode's theorisation of what he calls 'hermeneutic activity' (cited by Fowler) and its determinants is mapped and interrogated in Part One by the philosophical discourse of Bernard Harrison, who argues against the tendency to 'textual solipsism' discernible within that theorisation. In Part Two Dominic Baker-Smith analyses the formal determinants of the hermeneutic complexity of a Renaissance classic, a complexity which modern (and Kermodean) interpretative strategies dispose us to 'see', while Alastair Fowler argues, at least in part on the grounds of hermeneutic complexity, for the value of Conan Doyle's best detective fiction which, he suggests, deserves a place in the canon of serious literature.

Interpretation and the canon, together with the institution, make up the triad of terms which, for Patrick Parrinder, define the scope of the scriptural analogy in Kermode's mature account of literary study, an account which Parrinder situates in relation to recent developments in critical theory, but which he also interrogates through an alternative, 'demystified' account of the practices of the institution.

One of the problematic aspects of Kermode's account for Parrinder (which he suggests is more generally characteristic of much contemporary theory) is the 'redefinition of criticism as interpretation'. But if such a redefinition is articulated in Kermode's theory, other essays suggest that there is nevertheless a critical thrust to his practice. In Richard Poirier's essay there is the specific instance of Kermode's resistance to the critical consensus established by T.S. Eliot with regard to Walter Pater (a figure we meet again in Stokes' essay), whose importance for modernism and for Joyce in particular Poirier, following what he sees as

Kermode's crucial intervention, seeks to demonstrate. From the same point of departure (*Romantic Image*) John Stokes takes a quite different route, which nevertheless also illustrates Kermode's critical edge, plotting within the Kermodian *oeuvre* revisions of texts and authors which constitute an implicit form of self-critique.

A felt presence, and pressure, in Stokes' essay is the question of history and its constraint on hermeneutic activity. Frank Kermode's response to the pressure of this question in his own work – his itinerary as an historical critic – is mapped, historically, and interrogated in Part One by George Hunter, who detects a trajectory from urbane engagement to ironic detachment. Lisa Jardine, in Part Two, acknowledging the intersection of Kermode's itinerary with her own, lays out the co-ordinates of a discourse, which produces a genuinely new historicism and a persuasive historical interpretation of the 'case' of Desdemona's innocence.

Where, if anywhere, fiction ends and history (or nature) begins defines the scope of the conversation between Kermode and Tony Nuttall. Tackling the problem from the other end, as it were, by looking at beginnings, Nuttall attempts to set limits to what is implied in *The Sense of an Ending* about history – its character as a form of fiction – which is, finally, what makes history so problematic for Kermode.

Recurring most insistently throughout the volume, though especially in Part One, are, of course, Kermode's own texts, though they appear as rather different objects in different essays (Stokes' *Sense of an Ending*, for instance, looks rather different from Nuttall's, Harrison's *Genesis of Secrecy* from Parrinder's), and some features of these objects Professor Kermode is unwilling to acknowledge his. This plurality of objects – of 'Kermodes' – inevitably suggests what he himself has emphasised about the literary classic – its plurality of meaning – though this too he might be reluctant to recognise. Indeed, although the blurring of the distinction between literature and criticism/interpretation, which is characteristic of some recent critical theory, might be regarded as a logical implication of his work, he expresses some embarrassment at seeing his texts (and himself) the objects of the kind of attention hitherto reserved for literature. More importantly, and more urgently, he insists on the need to preserve this distinction and the primacy of literature over criticism, appealing to the 'rare experience of poetry', its power 'to stop the heart' as commentary never can. And yet the piece, itself tracing itineraries as well as engaging with the papers of Part One, generates, in spite of its argument, what the rhetoricians used to call 'pathos'; its lucid modesty and occasional melancholy may not stop the heart, but they undoubtedly move.

That there is finally a ground, or gift, which the best of critics share with the best of poets is implicitly proposed by the last essay, written by a critic and scholar who is also a distinguished poet. This gift, which the essay exemplifies, is that of an ear finely tuned to the multifarious forms of language, or, as Hollander's title elegantly suggests, to the forms of fiction the forms of language are. This gift Frank Kermode assuredly possesses.

One
Essays in Criticism

1

Romantic Image Revisited
John Stokes

The date inscribed inside the cover tells me that I bought my paperback copy of *Romantic Image* in 1963 when I was an undergraduate. I do remember that I had been told to read it by one of the scholars acknowledged in its preface, and that I was in the process of writing a tutorial essay for another of them. That meant a lot to me at the time. It still does.

And because I first read it when I did, *Romantic Image*, which was published in 1957, also has for me the aura of a moment just before that, just before I became, in any sense at all, involved in literary criticism. It belongs to a special and inaccessible time, a possibly 'golden age' I just missed, to which I can never quite belong. *Romantic Image*, if you'll permit, is my Brideshead.

I do know something about that previous moment because Professor Kermode has himself written about university life in the fifties, his own life in particular (Kermode 1981). So I know that he had discovered the Warburg Institute and D.J. Gordon, and that these must certainly have encouraged him in the pursuit of 'images'. I recognise too an informed interest in nineteenth-century Symbolism. I see that even in the discussion of art and nature that features in the introduction to *The Tempest* (1954). And a love of Yeats I know is something that he shared with his immediate colleagues first at Liverpool and then at Reading. I would guess that he was not alone in wishing to displace the Leavisian gospel: though he never, so far as I know, wasted much time on particular squabbles. I would perceive the collection of essays called *The Living Milton* published in 1960 as a kind of corrective to Leavis.

Romantic Image relates to all these intellectual strands, but most of all I would see it as an expression of a more general desire to give to literary history rigour and dignity in the face of the ravages of New Criticism on the one hand and the indulgences of *belles-lettres* on the other.

3

After all, *Romantic Image* – though the preface modestly calls it an essay – is not only Kermode's first book, it is a very big book. It purports to tell of the origins of modern poetry – which makes it both innocent and sophisticated at the same time. It is concerned with big ideas – with 'two beliefs' as set out in the first chapter: with the belief 'in the Image as a radiant truth out of space and time, and in the necessary isolation or estrangement of men who can perceive it' (Kermode 1957: 2). These are 'inextricably associated'. Or again, the same idea in a slightly different formulation: 'The Image, for all its concretion, precision, and oneness, is desperately difficult to communicate, and has for that reason alone as much to do with the alienation of the seer as the necessity of his existing in the midst of a hostile society'.

Everything that follows in the book will be claimed as relevant to the Image and the alienation of those who perceive it, and to be a matter of 'tradition' and kinds of 'continuity'. This will include a dissertation on the subject of Romantic joy, closely connected with Romantic misery. That will lead in turn to a discussion of, among many other things, 'Fatal Women', all of whom are related to each other in terms of the Image; and of the alienation of Blake, Wordsworth and Matthew Arnold, and of their supposed descendants, the 'minor' figures of the 'tragic generation' like Lionel Johnson and Arthur Symons. Yeats, of course, will be everywhere, most of all in the central chapters on the images of the dancer and the tree, everywhere in a book which nevertheless ends with a chapter on the modernist poetics of T.E. Hulme; an investigation of Eliot's theory of 'dissociation of sensibility', seen as an offshoot of symbolist literary history; an account of the changing view of John Donne in the nineteenth century; and considerable mention of I. A. Richards and Wallace Stevens. Narrow specialism this is not.

I have re-read *Romantic Image*, I suppose, at least once every two or three years since that first reading for the tutorial essay. It still strikes me as an inescapable book, though a deceptive one, and I always find in it both more and less than I either expect or remember. In Waugh's *Brideshead* the narrator Charles Ryder confidently, all too confidently, remarks to himself on hearing that he is to be stationed at the family home of the Marchmains, 'I had been there before; I knew all about it' (Waugh 1962: 22). He is wrong of course, revisiting is always a process not only of rediscovering, but of disappointed memories. The tradition shakes and the continuities tremble.

In this essay I shall try to revisit *Romantic Image* in the company of its author, as he too, I suspect, has revisited it himself, consciously or unconsciously, over the intervening thirty years. I know that he is on record as having 'not much time' for his book now, though apparently 'it does not trouble' him that people still read it (Kermode 1981). Which in these circumstances is something of a relief. So I shall journey back via the subsequent writing, taking four moments from works produced after *Romantic Image* that seem to me instances of that continual re-reading and re-evaluation as much of oneself as of the text that is surely the true function of historical criticism. Examining virtually the whole of Kermode's oeuvre, I have made a note of what seem to me certain scraps, traces, tell-tale signs of unfinished business.

Which is why I begin not in 1957 but in 1967 and journey back from there. The first in this series of retrospective re-encounters involves a Romantic poet, William Wordsworth, and a poem that has clearly meant a great deal to Kermode, which he has said is to do with the nature of poetic 'isolation or estrangement'. Here then is a passage from the last chapter of *Sense of an Ending*, which was published some ten years after *Romantic Image*. The chapter is called 'Solitary Confinement'. Kermode has been talking about how the changes in scientific thought in the nineteenth century, in particular Darwinism, are part of 'an historical transition', beginning much earlier, towards more temporal ways of thinking and the production of artistic modes that confess their isolation from reality by creating their own order. He then says that Wordsworth is part of this process:

> One sees why Wordsworth dwelt so much upon those practically motionless old men, useless, utterly poor, but somehow identified with the earth they bowed towards, and so as mysterious as poems. Poems move, for him, out of fear into a moment of love; but they must acknowledge the pressure of fact, and so the best of Wordsworth's poems contain a vertiginous estrangement, a sense of what was later called the absurd, but transfigure it with joy. (Kermode 1967: 168–9)

Kermode connects these 'existences', this transfiguring mood, with panic in the face of 'the long meaningless attrition of time';

and he cites as 'one such "existence" ': ' "Resolution and Independence", to my mind both a very great and a very modern
poem'. He rehearses the origins of the poem as they are set out
in William's letters and Dorothy's journal. He notes Dorothy's
unhappiness about the end, and William's difficulty in encompassing the words of the old man. 'For Wordsworth', Kermode
continues,

> the task is to explain the power of this image, a man 'travelling
> alone among the mountains and all lonely places, carrying with
> him his own fortitude and the necessities which an unjust state
> of society has entailed upon him'.

Yet, he goes on,

> . . . the poem says little about such matters, and it is in fact
> not 'about' the leech gatherer at all. It is, as Wordsworth says
> to Sara Hutchinson, about 'a young Poet . . . overwhelmed by
> the thought of the miserable reverses that have befallen the
> happiest of men, viz. Poets'; and about 'an interposition of
> Providence' that gave his young man a degree of resolution
> and independence, the power to contemplate a certain poverty.
> In the poem the old man appears at a dream-like moment
> when the poet's mind and the morning landscape suddenly
> darken. His tedious talk is not attended to, although it is
> reported in the poem, until a movement of the poet's mind
> convinces him that this may be a peculiar grace, a leading from
> above; the old man merges with the pool, and is metamor-
> phosed into the great stone; the poem is never asking you to
> attend directly to the old man, but to its own transfiguration.
> (Kermode 1967: 170 – 1)

This refers to the end of the poem which clearly states (however
aporetically):

> And soon with this he other matter blended,
> Cheerfully uttered, with demeanour kind,
> But stately in the main; and when he ended,
> I could have laughed myself to scorn to find
> In that decrepit Man so firm a mind.

'God,' said I, 'be my help and stay secure;
I'll think of the Leech-gatherer on the lonely moor!'

Kermode, though, thinks that the 'true end':

is the proof that from time to time, as now, we are by our
own spirits deified; peculiar grace is the property not so much
of grave livers, as of poems. Out of the intangible age and
obscurity of the real world proceeds this extraordinary moment,
with its complex perspectives of past and future. The poem
begins with the loss of joy, and proceeds through a confrontation with the mystery of poverty and tedious age – a confrontation without communication, setting the word against the
word.
    The point is not even Wordsworth's continual anguish, that
nature, which was once as plentiful a provider of poems as of
leeches, will also be leaving it to the poet, as it had to the
leech-gatherer, to 'persevere and find them where I may'. It is
true that here is the first great confrontation of metaphorical
with actual poverty, and that this is what produced the dream
and the poem. Hence the extraordinary complexity of the end:
the old man's poverty is unchanged, and he remains motionless on the moor; there is obviously nothing the poet can do
with his except hope to endure it; and all this is said. But the
poem ends in joy, the joy of its own success in giving a true
and original human shape to poverty. (Kermode 1967: 171–2)

What interests me there in particular are the claims that this
is 'the first great confrontation of metaphorical with actual poverty', and that the poem gives 'a true and original human shape
to poverty', because if we return to *Romantic Image* we find an
earlier reading where the emphasis lies far more upon the poet
and his metaphors, hardly at all upon poverty, metaphorical or
actual. Wordsworth, significantly, is first mentioned in the context of the interdependency of suffering and 'joy', as it is manifested in the poetry of Yeats. Wordsworth is produced as corroborative evidence:

Wordsworth's belief that the poet is more highly organised,
more subtle, than the peasant, in fact puts as much distance
between poet and peasant as between peasant and amoeba.

Already the poet is necessarily estranged, and his work may become increasingly unintelligible and offensive to all who cannot share his dream and his persecution, or believe that the grounds of his joy are true . . . What saves the poet here is the symbol-making power; it is not what the Leech Gatherer says, but the fact that Wordsworth could invent him, that saves his joy and his sanity, gives him his victory. (Kermode 1957: 10–11)

This particular balancing of roles – Wordsworth 'invents' the leech gatherer, and is 'saved' – will enable Kermode to say, a few pages on, that: 'Empedocles was Arnold's Leech-Gatherer' (13), and after an analysis of Arnold's poem to say (18) that to read its last words, Callicles' song, as optimistic would be as absurd as 'saying that the point of "Resolution and Independence" is: "I could have laughed myself to scorn to find / In that decrepit man so firm a mind." '

On page 33 the source of this view of Wordsworth's estrangement becomes rather more evident. There we find a lengthy quotation from Yeats' commentary on his own obituary of Major Robert Gregory in which Yeats brings together Gregory's paintings with those of some other artists as sharing 'certain moods with great lyric poetry, with, let us say, "The Leech Gatherer" of Wordsworth', which becomes warrant enough for Kermode to speak, only one page after that, of 'the archetypal Romantic poem of meditation "Resolution and Independence" ' (34). And the whole process culminates on page 48 with a tribute to Wallace Stevens' poem about a jar:

The poem itself reconciles opposites by using the jar as a symbol (like the Leech Gatherer) of what moves in stillness, is dead in life, whose meaning and being are the same.

The image I am at present, in a very general way, discussing, is without simple intellectual content, bearing the same relationship to thought as the dancer bears to the dance. As in the dance, there is no disunity of being; 'the body is the soul'. We might, as I have suggested, use such language of the solitaries of Wordsworth as conveniently as we may of Yeats's dancers and trees. (Kermode 1957: 48)

This must strike us now as a remarkable collapsing of history

– peasants into dancers into jars – in order to forge a continuity. Not that the synoptic purpose of *Romantic Image*, to link the moderns with Romanticism, has of course ever been denied, quite the reverse.

Near the start of *Romantic Image* we read that a key figure in the process was Walter Pater, who carried out major changes to the Romantic, specifically Wordsworthian, notions of 'sensibility':

> Pater's position . . . that the estranged morality of artists is the only genuine kind. Now it is well known that Pater's account of the tension between the wisdom of the Image and a more utilitarian knowledge, between the artist's and the received morality, were gospel to the 'tragic generation'; for all their perversity, for all their inferiority to these great predecessors, that generation transmitted the doctrine to the twentieth century and fed the imagination of its major poet. (Kermode 1957: 22)

That, though, is to blur Pater's difficult account of Romanticism, again in the interests of Kermode's own continuities. Pater wrote quite often about Wordsworth, specifically in an essay of 1874 (later included in *Appreciations* (1889)), but also much more generally by giving to his own prose a *gravitas* borrowed from Wordsworthian speech. And when Pater wrote that 1874 essay he did so with a view to placing the Romantic poet according to the passage of subsequent history. Wordsworth was remarkable in that he could only escape orthodox religion by embracing pantheism, and pantheism works in two ways, naturalising man, but humanising nature. Thus Pater:

> And it was through nature, thus ennobled by a semblance of passion and thought, that he [Wordsworth] approached the spectacle of human life. Human life, indeed, is for him, at first, only an accidental grace on an expressive landscape. When he thought of man, it was of man as in the presence and under the influence of these effective natural objects, and linked to them by many associations. The close connexion of man with natural objects, the habitual association of his thoughts and feelings with a particular spot of earth, has sometimes seemed to degrade those who are subject to its influence, as if it did but reinforce that physical connexion of our nature with the actual lime and clay of the soil, which is always drawing us

nearer our end. But for Wordsworth, these influences tended to the dignity of human nature, because they tended to tranquillize it. By raising nature to the level of human thought he gives it power and expression; he subdues man to the level of nature, and gives him thereby a certain breadth and coolness and solemnity. The leech-gatherer on the moor, the woman 'stepping westward', are for him natural objects, almost in the same sense as the aged thorn, or the lichened rock on the heath. (Pater 1889: 48–9)

Wordsworth then, according to Pater:

sees nature full of sentiment and excitement; he sees men and women as parts of nature, passionate, excited, in strange grouping and connexion with the grandeur and beauty of the natural world: – images, in his words, 'of man suffering, amid awful forms and powers'. (139)

I have quoted at length because this seems to me to be some way from the 'estranged morality of artists' which is, according to *Romantic Image*, Pater's major deduction from Wordsworth. It is clearly not the poet's suffering alone, but 'man's suffering' that interests Pater.

Perhaps then we should look elsewhere for the transitional interpretation – to Arthur Symons for example. Symons also wrote on Wordsworth – in *The Fortnightly Review* in 1902, an essay that was reprinted in *The Romantic Movement in English Poetry* (1909). What Symons found in 'Resolution and Independence' is not entirely different from Pater, though neither is it exactly like Kermode. Symons writes that,

In what seems to me his greatest, as it is certainly his most characteristic poem, 'The Leech-Gatherer', he has gathered up all his qualities, dignity, homeliness, meditation over man and nature, respectful pity for old age and poverty, detailed observation of natural things, together with an imaginative atmosphere which melts, harmonises, the forms of cloud and rock and pool and the voices of wind and man into a single composition. (Symons 1909: 88)

' "Resolution and Independence" ' says Symons, is one of those poems 'in which Wordsworth is most human, and at the same time most himself as a poet'. Poems in which all 'are motionless, or moving imperceptibly, like the old beggar . . .', a natural truth that Wordsworth conveys 'to us as no other poet has ever done, no other poet having had in him so much of the reflective peasant' (91–2). Now, although Symons will go on to respect Wordsworth's power to experience joy through 'sacramental silence' (94), even he makes no mention of the 'estranged morality of artists', but stresses instead Wordsworth at his 'most human', and what the poet has in common with the 'reflective peasant'.

So, although it would be absurd to say that nothing had happened to the Romantic sensibility between Wordsworth, Pater and Symons, the critics whom Kermode had claimed as the most important vehicles for its transmission, the tradition seems to have rather less to do with 'alienation', or with 'the Image' even, than with ways of preserving 'the human'. And that fact is, I would hazard, recognised by the mildly corrective view implied in the re-reading of 'Resolution and Independence' offered in *The Sense of an Ending*, with its admiration for the 'true and original human shape'.

Mention of Arthur Symons and his admiration for 'sacramental silence' takes me to the start of my second backwards foray which is prompted by a remark in Kermode's next major book after *Sense of an Ending*, *The Genesis of Secrecy* (1979):

> If there is one belief (however the facts resist it) that unites us all, from the evangelists to those who argue away inconvenient portions of their texts, and those who spin large plots to accommodate the discrepancies and dissonances into some larger scheme, it is this conviction that somehow, in some occult fashion, if we would only detect it, everything will be found to hang together. (Kermode 1979: 72–3)

Like *Romantic Image*, *The Genesis of Secrecy* is taken up with transmissions of ideas, with continuities and traditions – but these are now modelled on the precedent of biblical exegesis. By the time of *Genesis of Secrecy*, Kermode is much more concerned with 'interpretation' as the desire and perhaps duty of the critic, a desire often fed, as he says, by millenial fears. At the same time he is wanly conscious of interpretation's infinite disappointments.

Romantic Image had no such exegetic model, but it did have

some prophets and preachers, and Arthur Symons, the poet,
critic and journalist of the 1890s and the early years of the century, is among the most important. When Kermode was writing,
Symons, once hailed by Yeats, Eliot and Pound for having
brought an awareness of French symbolist ideas to English poetry
had been dead for twelve years, effectively silent for maybe
thirty, forgotten by almost everyone, except by John Betjeman
who wrote a poem in which he remembered seeing him 'very
old and very grand' (and very lost), in the Café Royal in the
1930s. Symons was most certainly passed over by academic critics
and his rediscovery is one of the unshakeable achievements of
Romantic Image. Kermode gives over a whole chapter to him with
biographical detail, and he credits Symons with having seen:

> more explicitly and more influentially, than any of his
> contemporaries . . . how to synthesise the earlier English tra-
> dition – particularly Blake, on whom he wrote a good, and in
> this connexion revealing, book – with Pater and those European
> Symbolists he knew so well. (Kermode 1957: 107)

Here *Romantic Image* has become the victim of its own insti-
gations. Some thirty years after Kermode's re-discovery of
Symons we have a full-length biography, a bibliography and
some good critical studies – and what all these reveal is that
if Symons did synthesise these traditions he did so gradually,
intermittently, and to a quite considerable degree, antithetically.
The young critic and poet who so greatly admired Pater's
impressionism had, by the nineties, begun in many respects to
distance himself from his master. Pater, Symons came to believe,
was unique (perhaps deluded) in his belief that the process of
knowledge through beauty – the high aesthetic goal – was open
to all. 'Pater', he later wrote,

> seemed to draw up into himself every form of earthly beauty,
> or of the beauty made by men, and many forms of knowledge
> and wisdom, and a sense of human things which was neither
> that of the lover nor of the priest, but partly of both; and his
> work was the giving out of all this again, with a certain labour
> to give it wholly. It is all, the criticism, and the stories, and
> the writing about pictures and places, a confession, the *vraie
> vérité* (as he was fond of saying) about the world in which he

lived. That world he thought was open to all; he was sure that it was the real blue and green earth, and that he caught the tangible moments as they passed. It was a world into which we can only look, not enter, for none of us have his secret. (Symons 1916: 319–20)

This disengagement was to go so far as to enable Symons not so much to mimic Paterianism as to re-write it, in order to make it fit Symon's own concept of the Symbolist line. It would eventually lead Symons to intone in the 'Conclusion' to *The Symbolist Movement* that:

Our only chance, in this world, of a complete happiness, lies in the measure of our success in shutting the eyes of the mind, and deadening its sense of hearing, and dulling the keenness of its apprehension of the unknown. Knowing so much less than nothing, for we are entrapped in smiling and many-coloured appearances, our life may seem to be but a little space of leisure, in which it will be the necessary business of each of us to speculate on what is so rapidly becoming the past and so rapidly becoming the future, that scarcely existing present which is after all our only possession. (Symons 1958: 93)

Symons' injunction, 'to shut the eyes of the mind' – to reduce the fear of death through an overall reduction in sensory perception – is couched as an exact betrayal of Pater's famous command in the Conclusion of *The Renaissance* that 'our one chance lies in expanding' the intervals of our life, getting 'as many pulsations as possible into the given time'. 'Great passions', believes Pater, 'may give us this quickened sense of life, ecstacy and sorrow of love . . .'. Only we must be sure it is passion – that it does yield this 'fruit of a quickened, multiplied consciousness'. This is a kind of wisdom, according to Pater, to be found most of all in 'the love of art for art's sake': 'for art comes professing to you frankly to give nothing but the highest quality to your moments as they pass, and simply for those moments' sake'. (Pater 1980: 190)

Pater's aestheticism is clearly a secular doctrine, whereas Symons's apostasy will enable him to describe Symbolism as:

this revolt against exteriority, against rhetoric, against a materialistic tradition; in this endeavour to disengage the ultimate

essence, the soul, of whatever exists and can be realised by
the consciousness; in this dutiful waiting upon every symbol
by which the soul of things can be made visible; literature,
bowed down by so many burdens, may at last obtain liberty
and its authentic speech. In attaining this liberty, it accepts a
heavier burden; for in speaking to us so intimately, so sol-
emnly, as only religion had hitherto spoken to us, it becomes
itself a kind of religion, with all the duties and responsibilities
of the sacred ritual. (Symons 1958: 5)

To announce, in effect, the new dispensation. Its church finally
was to be modernism.

And it is Symons's spiritual pronouncements that fuel in turn
Kermode's masterly digest of *The Symbolist Movement* in *Romantic
Image* which, in a broad retrospective gesture, links Blake via
Pater via Symons to Yeats and to modernism as a whole – and,
at the same time, insists upon the link between magic and poetry
which is apparent in hermetic systems of belief.

So although it is true that in his *Symbolist Movement* Symons is
doing something like what Kermode in *The Genesis of Secrecy* was
to claim all critics do – acting like a priest, interpreting our
history, and even offering literature as redemption (from nothing
less than death) – it is because Symons does indeed become
that kind of evangelical critic, much concerned with secrets and
salvation and with a human need to find a 'wholeness' beyond
the Paterian immediate, that we must question his testimony, see
it as human in fact, as provisional, driven by other needs. Just
what these needs are then becomes the interest of the critic. John
Goode has argued that the totalising unities of modernism are
produced by the breakdown of utilitarianism in the face of
advanced capitalism. Menaced by monopoly, modern intellectuals
turn to an abstract spirituality which simply reproduces what
threatens them. (Goode 1979: 110 – 11). I have myself suggested
that the specific pressures of modern journalism – the rhythms
of its production, the demand to instruct and entertain according
to a preconceived notion of the market – may have given cause
for the privileged despair of the mystic critic (Stokes 1989).

Here then – in the case of Arthur Symons – we have an
example of Kermode developing in *Romantic Image* a critical prototype: critic as mage, which I think is more of an historical devel-
opment than he will allow – that Kermode will expect to serve

under all circumstances, and who will be canonised in *Genesis of Secrecy*.

The making of criticism, like the making of art, is a material practice, therefore subject to change, yet art is never more material than when it is physical, when it takes place in a theatre, where the continuity of the human body is involved.

My third backtrack is in pursuit of bodies, and it is prompted by another later book, *Forms of Attention* (1985). The first chapter is called 'Botticelli Recovered' and it is to do with the ways in which that painter came to be newly studied and appreciated in the course of the nineteenth century, in particular by Aby Warburg and by Herbert Horne. Horne, though his name does not actually feature in *Romantic Image*, belongs among the 'tragic generation' poets who are discussed there; and Kermode introduces him in a way that takes us directly back to the earlier book.

Horne was always serious about the arts, and very nearly supreme among them was the art of dance. His interest in the Gaiety and in the Alhambra was by no means entirely a matter for lusty hours of leisure. Of course, one object was to pick up the dancing girls; but there is something distinctive about the aesthetics of such activities . . . The dance was associated with the Mass as well as with the poetic image, and from Loïe Fuller and Jane Avril to Nini Patte-en-l'air, dancers were adored; respectable clergymen as well as artists and professors waited for dancing girls in back alleys, since the ritual required it . . . At all events, a quantity of poetry was dedicated to the dance and to dancers; there were many set pieces on Javanese and other exotic dancers, specially by Arthur Symons, and many on Salome. Out of this movement, and after great transformations, came the dances and dancers of Yeats and Eliot. Waiting in that back alley, Horne was doing nothing out of character for a nineties artist . . . (Kermode 1985a: 8–9)

This summary is slightly more candid than the account that we get in *Romantic Image*, but otherwise it covers much the same ground and in a relatively unchanged way. The conviction that the dance-cult united many disparate figures remains the same as in *Romantic Image*, where they occupy the chapter called 'The Dancer', and as in Kermode's long article, written a little later, entitled 'Poet and Dancer before Diaghilev' (Kermode 1971b). In

Forms of Attention Kermode argues that it was the typicality of
Horne as a nineties figure that would allow him to bring a particular focus on Botticelli, a focus not entirely removed from that
of Warburg who:

> too was fascinated by the dancing Salome; for him [Warburg]
> as for Yeats, such a figure represented the survival into mod-
> ernity of images perpetuated in a process of memory that tran-
> scended the individual . . . Warburg's explanations tend to
> have a scientific character, as his training required; Yeats pre-
> ferred magic. (24–5)

Horne is a representative figure who breaks out of one mould
– decadent Paterian – into another – responsible art-historian.
That is as may be; but if Horne's activities were typical, what
were they typical of? Not of Warburg exactly, though there are
very interesting similarities, nor of Yeats, though he too shared
the fascination with dancers.

In *Romantic Image* the main intention is to show how the dancer
– who 'turns in her narrow luminous circle, still but moving,
dead but alive' (59) – is closely associated with other 'images of
the Image', representing 'a higher order of truth, of being as
against becoming, which is dead only in that it cannot change'
(91). The process will culminate in the famous reading of 'Among
School Children' which explains how the image of the human
dancer comes to interweave with that of the tree.

Romantic Image will also tell us over and again that there is a
'pathological' aspect to the interest in dancers, which is not quite
the same as the interest Kermode is pursuing (it is Praz's ground
rather), but which is still relevant. 'The *femme fatale*', for example,
'is, certainly, the pathological aspect of this Image', though 'for
the most part I omit considerations of pathology' (60–1). Nevertheless, there are to be discussions of the dancer in Heine,
'because it is useful to know the emblem can exist in isolation
from its pathological aspect . . .' (67). And Salome too must feature because 'her ancestry in Flaubert, and her function as a
symbol of the pathological aspect of decadence' (68), emerge in
Huysmans' description of her where,

> What Huysmans does is to correlate the pathological and aes-
> thetic aspects of the Dancer motif. Intellectual and physical

isolation are easily represented by diseases which are the consequences of uncontrolled feeling; and when this becomes the
artist's preferred subject he evolves the Herodiade emblem,
representing at once the cruelty of the isolation and the beauty
(distinct from life yet vital) of its product. (Kermode 1957: 70)

This is in contrast to 'The English Herodiades' who 'occasionally
degenerate into mere demonstrations of the dancer's pathological
aspect'. The 'image' of the dancer, then, is related to, but most
certainly not identical with, pathological attitudes.

But pathology, disease, must necessarily imply the possibility,
if not of full-blown health, then certainly of some sort of norm
from which it has diverged. And where is the 'normality' in, say,
'Among School Children' where the 'organic' image of the dancer
is strangely 'inhuman'? Throughout *Romantic Image* Yeats' supposedly natural scenario is accepted with barely a demur: the
dancer – turning, 'in her narrow luminous circle, still but moving,
dead but alive' – *vis-à-vis* the poet – lone yet representative,
questioning, but in a rhetorical way: 'How can we know?'

One might accept the accuracy of that as an account of Yeats'
dance aesthetic, and still query its typicality, and its own pathology. Given his final vatic cries one might wonder if even Yeats
could maintain the aesthetic poise; and of course he could not.
Kermode himself cites 'The Circus Animals' Desertion': 'Those
masterful images because complete / Grew in pure mind, but out
of what began?' and the play, *The Death of Cuchulain*.

But the question of where the 'pathological' might begin or
end, does open all manner of critical questions about the relative
value and use of the dancer as 'Image': queries of a rather different order from those broached in the book, though to a large
extent prompted by its discoveries.

According to Kermode, Yeats' image of the dancer is closely
linked with an ideal both Aristocratic and Romantic which:

applies equally to the beauty of women and to the beauty
of the work of art. Proportion, movement, meaning, are not
intellectual properties, but belong to that reality of the imagination which is a symbolic reality. The beauty of a woman, and
particularly of a woman in movement, is the emblem of the
work of art or Image . . . Women and art were, at this time,
speaking bodies. (57–60)

Now this is a version of Symbolist theory whose patriarchal air
the *imprimatur* of Mallarmé does little or nothing to dispel. There
is a paragraph from Mallarmé's essay *Ballets* that Kermode cited
on a number of occasions during this period. The passage reads
in full as follows:

> A savoir que la danseuse *n'est pas une femme qui danse*, pour
> ces motifs juxtaposés qu'elle *n'est pas une femme*, mais une
> métaphore résumant un des aspects élémentaires de notre
> forme, glaive, coupe, fleur, etc., et *qu'elle ne danse pas*, suggér-
> ant, par le prodige de raccourcis ou d'élans, avec une écriture
> corporelle ce qui'il faudrait des paragraphes en prose dialoguée
> autant que descriptive, pour exprimer, dans la rédaction:
> poeme dégagé de tout appareil du scribe. (Mallarmé 1945: 304)

In *Romantic Image* it is quoted at the bottom of a page (85) in
which the image is described by the feminine pronoun 'she' no
fewer than five times. Not that that in itself, of course, is enough
to challenge Mallarmé's disclaimer. The determining point is that
it is Mallarmé himself who simultaneously inserts and withdraws
the writer from the process of writing, whose freedom is made
possible by, and must be credited to, the 'dancer' who is not a
dancer, the woman who is not a woman: 'poeme dégagé de tout
appareil du scribe'. Writing occupies that ever-shifting female
space. Consequently Mallarmé is a poet and theoretician whom
a contemporary feminist critic such as Julia Kristeva can designate
as an explorer of new ground and, though the issues are conten-
tious, 'Écriture féminine'. Clearly it is no longer sufficient to
explain Symbolist theory by Symbolist theory alone.
    To which one might add the more commonplace observation
that if woman's physicality precedes her transfigurations, indeed
is required for them to take place, then it must be visible in the
result – the dance. The trace of a human 'shape' will still be
seen. Which brings me simultaneously to the end of my third
journey and to the start of my fourth.
    'The writer is always the complex person looking at an Other,
whose complexity is made evident only by that look'. My fourth
and final retrospection is stimulated by *History and Value* (1988)
from which that sentence is taken. It comes in the context of a
discussion of utopian desire between the classes in the thirties,
between lovers both homo and heterosexual – a pastoral dream

of undivided union, for which the hermaphrodite might be the ultimate emblem. As Kermode points out, such partnerships can never be truly equal: 'the writer is always the complex person looking at an Other, whose complexity is made evident only by that look' (32). It is a principle that lies at a curious tangent to Kermode on Yeats' definition of the beauty of the Image in *Romantic Image*: 'independence of intention, beautiful because perceived as beautiful' (57).

What then of those, the dancers and others, who are the 'imagified'? 'Beautiful because perceived as beautiful'? Adored or feared by the 'complex' writers who perceive them, in whose gaze they are held?

It is striking, in fact, how little they seek that gaze. In Wilde's *Salome*, it is true, there is a battle of looks: 'I will not', protests Jokanaan, 'have her look at me' (Wilde 1966: 558). 'The moon', says Herod, thinking of Salome, 'is looking for lovers' (561). 'If thou hadst looked at me thou hadst loved me' says Salome herself to the head of Jokanaan – when it is far, far too late (574). But even this is unusual.

More often the male look is not sought, let alone acknowledged. The dancers in the poems of Arthur Symons turn back and gaze upon themselves:

> Alone apart, one dancer watches
> Her mirrored, morbid grace:
> Before the mirror face to face,
> Alone she watches
> Her morbid, vague, ambiguous grace . . .
> (Beckson 1987: 85)

Here the dancer is unheeding, at the same time proliferating beyond the poet's vision, and therefore uncontainable. Or she joins with others in some alien chorus: 'Dull, shrill, continuous, disquieting . . .' (Beckson 1987: 76).

A portion of Mallarmé's own *Hérodiade* was translated by Symons, who read it in turn to Yeats

> 'The horror of my virginity
> Delights me, and I would envelope me
> In the terror of my tresses, that, by night
> Inviolate reptile, I might feel the white

And glimmering radiance of thy frozen fire,
Thou that art chaste and diest of desire,
White night of ice and of the cruel snow!'
                         (Beckson 1987: 156).

This is as chilly, as strange as the 'Romantic Image' is supposed
to be, but also autonomous, self-sufficient. The complexity of the
spectator finds no resting place here. What, then, if the Other-
ness, the impersonality, the apparent 'deathliness' of the female
dancer is truly another place, privately inhabited, where images
burgeon beyond his gaze? What then would be the comforts of
romantic alienation? For the 'Image' is always the object of a
gaze: leech gatherers, dead faces, dancers, all are the recipients
of a look that they might, or might not be able, or might not
wish to return. Though not all female, it is in the image of
woman that they accumulate: that 'true and original human
shape'.

When then if the paradoxical femaleness of the 'inhuman'
image should be a mark of *excess*, of what Julia Kristeva would
call the semiotic 'chora' whose rhythms lie beneath the text?
What if the Romantic Image should be the 'true and original
human shape' of some original moment of division? In *Forms of
Attention* Kermode will pay attention to the great labour of Aby
Warburg to associate the shape of the 'Nympha', with continual
irruptions of emotion into art, with our deepest memories.

I believe it is with such questions in the very forefront of our
minds that we will very likely re-read *Romantic Image* today. It is
with such questions at the back of his own mind that, I suggest,
its author has continued his own work.

At which final point, I should, I suppose, complain that in the
end all literary history is a kind of temporary fiction, that all
patterns are imposed and that traditions and continuities, when
not merely deceptive, are downright illusory. Strangely, I find
my author has beaten me to it. For in his last chapter, writing
of Eliot's theory of the 'dissociation of sensibility', which he sees
as closely linked to 'image' poetics, Kermode concedes:

When, in fact, the poets and aestheticians of the Image turn
their attention to history, it is in search of some golden age
when the prevalent mode of knowing was not positivist and
anti-imaginative; when the Image, the intuited, creative reality,

was habitually respected; when art was not permanently on the defensive against mechanical and systematic modes of enquiry. (Kermode 1957: 143).

Is this a premonition of things to come in later works? Or an already awakening realisation that what survives of poets is less their belief in their own alienation and in a previous golden age than those 'true and original human shapes' that only masquerade as 'images'?

2

The Sense of a Beginning
A. D. Nuttall

In his sense of an ending is my sense of a beginning. Frank Kermode's Mary Flexner Lectures delivered at Bryn Mawr in 1965 set a wholly new standard. Thereafter we had all either to think or else, in a manner, to declare ourselves enemies of thought. *The Sense of an Ending* exposes the problematic ontology of literary form. It caused my mind to race, even at first reading, between the seemingly antithetical poles of a natural end and a formal ending. At the same time I was obscurely uneasy lest, by some trick of an unperceived conceptual hyposphere, the polarity itself might be resolved into an identity. What if all supposedly natural beginnings and ends are really cultural fictions, read into the world but never, in truth, read off from it? In *La Nausée* Annie says to Roquentin, 'Il n'y a pas d'aventures' (Sartre 1938: 206). There is something heady – even delicious – in the *glissando* of this thought. For a while it feels a little like flying. Nevertheless, even then, I resisted. Every death is a natural termination. Births really are natural beginnings. And so, I thought, are many other things. The foundation of a new university is, very clearly, an ideological act which is translated into natural fact. In 1936 there was no University of Sussex. In 1966 there was one. The precise moment of its inception between those dates may be indistinct, confused and muffled by pre-echoes and corroborative ceremonies, but we are forced to say, nevertheless, that it had begun to exist.

I was willing to grant that religion might be wholly fictitious and that we shape history in accordance with our desires, but in assessing such spectacular feats of cultural fiction I felt myself to be reviewing a tensely contested field, rather than the flat, unbroken surface of a foregone conclusion. Whig History, it seemed to me, while manifestly enforcing a certain fiction, contained a higher quotient of natural fact than, say, Mormonism. Most crucially, I thought that every demonstration of the ways in which we actively shape the world was a demonstration of distortion, and the notion of distortion presupposes a natural Is, a fact or set of facts which is fictively transformed. Indeed, to say that *everything* is fiction and nothing is fact is like saying that everything is left and nothing right (I plagiarise G. K. Chesterton here). 'Is it a fact then', one is tempted to add, 'that there are no facts?'

As the habit of rebellion grew, I found myself doubting where before I had easily acquiesced. It seemed harder and harder to find the truly unconstrained, pure fiction, uncontaminated by nature. I suddenly wished to answer Sartre's Annie, 'Yes, there are, in addition to the adventures we retrospectively construct, certain real adventures'. In 1871 Stanley really did find the emaciated Livingstone in Ujiji. The note of converse excitement, the rebellion of earth against air, bearing the standard of nature some distance into territory conventionally held by fiction, can be sensed in George Orwell's sudden and astonishing concession: 'Revolutionaries keep their mouths shut in the torture chamber, battleships go down with their guns still firing when their decks are awash' (Orwell 1970: II, 193). Usually, I grant such things are either constituted or improved in the telling. But not always.

It is, then, too easy to consider all human discourse as a field of variable fictions. Rather one's thought must be dialectical: no form without matter, no art without nature. Even within the field of manifestly fictive, artful poetry, the dialectic is sustained. The most arbitrary conclusion is in some remote sense the mimesis of a death. Literary beginnings, meanwhile, group themselves with surprising clarity, either as devoutly natural (David Copperfield's 'I Am Born') or as proudly artificial. The Bible (which may or may not be seen as literature) provides most people's example of *the* natural beginning, the Genesis of the world. But Homer in the *Iliad* begins in the middle of the Trojan War and presents a narrative unity which presumably did not pre-exist the poem, the unity of Achilles' wrath. Though Hesiod wrote a *Theogony*, with a 'deep' natural beginning, it remains in general a striking characteristic of Hellenic culture that it should, so to speak, make a point of the non-natural character of its own greatest literary openings. Aristotle praises Homer for his interventionist opening, and scorns the low writer who imagines that unity is to be attained by such means as recounting all the things that happened to Theseus (*Poetics*, 1451a, 16–22). Horace was never so

Greek-minded as when he gave the world the approving phrase, *in medias res*, 'into the midst of things' and disparaged the practice of beginning *ab ovo*, 'from the (natural) egg' (*Ars Poetica*, 146–9).

Virgil's *Aeneid* defers to this powerful assertion of *les lois du texte* against the laws of nature. It begins *in medias res*. Yet there is another side of Virgil (traditionally regarded as in some sense Hebraic) which betrays a nostalgia for the other, natural beginning. The poet inside the poem (the Carthaginian bard Iopas at the end of Book I) sang, as Caedmon sang in the first English verses to come down to us, of the origins of men and beasts, a creation song (*Aeneid*, 1,740 f.). Aeneas himself, caught in the artful literary toils of flashback and prolepsis, strains with a sort of famished desire for something better than this mess of shadows, spectral cities, Greek images – for a Roman home which is also an origin. Again, older critics were less afraid than we are to say: 'Here Aeneas is Virgil, who was turned out of the farm he loved, deracinated from his proper earth.'

After Virgil we find, especially among texts regarded as canonical, beginnings which are dialectically stretched between natural origins and artful intervention. The word *mezzo* in this first line of Dante's *Commedia*: 'Nel mezzo del cammin di nostra vita' owes something to the *medias* of Horace's *in medias res*. (Dante quotes another phrase from the *in medias res* sentence at *Vita Nuova* xxv; on Dante's knowledge of the *Ars Poetica* see Moore 1896: 197–206.) The *Commedia* is commonly regarded as the paradigmatic mediaeval poem, merging the world and the book in an eschatologically structured unity: nature is now the work of a divine author, and the poem's author, Dante, is a pilgrim within his own poem – which is itself the universe. Yet Benvenuto da Imola in the fourteenth century discovered the lineaments of a classical prooemium behind the '*Visio*' opening of the *Commedia* (Benvenuto 1887). The supposed grand fusion of world and book is in fact excitingly incomplete. I have suggested that Dante's *mezzo* echoes Horace's *medias*, but that where the Horatian term connotes authorial intervention Dante's word directs us to the point at which God intervened in his mere fiction of a life, reappropriating it to the major poem, the divine creation (we may remember Auerbach's argument in his essay 'Figura' that in Dante's universe, it is we who are the fictions, the shadows). This huge feat of theological imagination, this turning inside-out of the relation of poetry – God's poetry or making – to a now *posterior* nature –

has, in addition to its power to move us, an almost mathematical elegance. Yet it cannot quite work, and Dante knows this. A gritty, pragmatic knowledge that it is Dante, the Florentine poet, who orchestrates his own erasure cannot be destroyed (just as later, with all the sharpened sense of individual identity which Protestantism could confer, George Herbert was to remain, irremediably the poetic master of his own, repeated, elegant-devout self-effacements, *The Temple*). God for Dante is indeed the volume in which the scattered leaves of the universe are gathered:

> Nel suo profondo vidi che s'interna,
> legato con amore in un volume,
> ciò che per l'universe si squaderna
> (*Paradiso*, xxxiii, 85–7)

It would be wrong to forget, in the exaltation of this vision of unity, the force of the words *si squaderna*, 'are scattered' or 'scatter themselves'. The leaves of the world are for us – that is, in ordinary experience – scattered before the mellowing of time. Through this dispersal room is made for human poetic art – for Dante's art. C. S. Singleton is not wrong when he says the *Commedia* means to mirror God's world (1967: 95), but the glass is flawed, by time, humanity and fallen nature. This transforms the various relations, between the author of the poem and the author of the world, between the poet and the pilgrim, between arrogant fiction and devout transcription, into continuously dynamic, unresolved engagements.

We can see in the openings of the *Aeneid*, the *Commedia*, *Paradise Lost*, an ever-shifting process of imaginative negotiation between natural and formal inception. Virgil plunges *in medias res*, in Greek fashion, by beginning with Aeneas sailing before the wind, with his dispossessed followers. But in the preliminary invocation he obtrudes – in un-Homeric contrast with one another – his own personality and the declaration that the subject of his poem is the *real* beginning of the Latin race, the lords of Alba, the walls of towering Rome. If we accept from Donatus the restoration of four *preceding* lines, we have a syntactically odd 'opening-before-the-opening'; Virgil presents himself as emerging from a forest, leaving behind the flute (of pastoral *Eclogues*) to subdue the farmlands (*Georgics*), thereafter turning, at last, to arms and the man. The effect of this is greatly to strengthen the intuition of personal significance of Virgil's placing *'cano'*, 'I sing', before the Homeric 'Tell, O Muse'. The sentence thus restored is indeed strangely extended, producing a reduplicative effect through the tacking on of relative clauses, first to the poet and then to the hero, who has likewise emerged, embarked upon a journey. Thus in Virgil the beginning of the *poem's* story is matched (and deliberately mismatched) with something Homer could never admit (or even, perhaps, conceive), the beginning of a real organised History, the true story of those then and there listening to the poem. Yet even as this deep engagement with the natural is proudly declared, the poet's sense of his own separate individuality is not healed but is exacerbated, and the grand progression of Roman history is eerily pre-echoed by a sequence which is personal and literary.

Dante's poem is of course thoroughly mediaeval and unequivocally Christian, but even here the negotiation with the other, 'counter-natural' opening is sustained. The poem begins *in medias res*, in the middle of the journey of Dante's own life. Yet, as we have seen, Dante is here in one way the object, the matter of the poetry: we are asked to believe that the intervention is not the poet's but God's. *He* enters *in medias res* and in beginning the poem starts a transformation of Dante himself in which he grows into accord with the real shape of the universe. The ordinary march of events is broken in upon, not by something confessedly less real, an artful fiction, but by something more real, by that which is itself the beginning and end of all things, Alpha and Omega. We are as far as literature will permit, it would seem, from the weakly arbitrary novel-opening: 'La marquise sortit à cinq heures'. As with Virgil, so with Dante, we come to see that the circle is not closed. We are made aware, not only of the real story of the world, but of the real poet: as Virgil speaks of himself as *egressus silvis*, 'emerged from the woods', so Dante finds himself in 'una selva oscura', 'a dark wood'. 'Mezzo' is moreover implicitly structured not only with reference to the real but also with reference to the structure of the poem. Benvenuto da Imola, writing in the fourteenth century, said that the first canto *prohemizatur ad totum opus* (Benvenuto 1887: I, 21). That is to say, it offers a classical prooemium in which the whole work is adumbrated: *mezzo* then implies the three stages both of life and of the *Commedia* itself, vice, penitence and bliss (*Inferno*, *Purgatorio*, *Paradiso*).

The metallic clarity of Benvenuto's allegorical method is alien to us in this age of scotophilia. In fact, however, he is reading with real intelligence. *Mezzo* is indeed stiffened by a sense of symmetry which is fundamentally mediaeval (think of triptychs) and is wholly absent from the Horatian formula.

The narrative of *Paradise Lost* begins with Satan, now cast out from Heaven, staring wildly on the surrounding desolation. It begins *in medias res*. But, as with Virgil but still more radically, the preceding invocation joins the beginning of the poem to the beginning of the Story Of Us All, as we are fallen creatures. As Johnson wrote in his *Life of Milton* more than a hundred years later, 'All mankind will, through all ages, bear the same relation to Adam and Eve, and must partake of that good and evil which extend to themselves' (1905: I, 174–5). The first line, 'Of man's first disobedience, and the fruit', tells of the first, constitutive act of humanity as we know it in ourselves. It is not, indeed, a Creation-of-the-World opening, but we are moving closer to that Hebraic extreme.

I am suggesting that an exclusively formalist account – an account which admits no concept of beginning other than that created by a fictive reading *in* – will never be adequate for these canonical openings, for all their manifestly literary character. Even when we wish to register an appropriation of nature by art, we must notice the temporarily separate identity of that which is ineluctably appropriated. This feature of binary negotiation is continued, into the classic period of the novel. The first three words of *David Copperfield*, the chapter heading, 'I Am Born', exhibit this with extraordinary grace and economy. Dickens uses the convention of the summary present tense in chapterheadings – 'In which our hero is unexpectedly rescued' and the like – to produce, in combination with the self-reference of the first person pronoun, a nuance of absurdity. The result is a kind of fleeting joke which is nevertheless obscurely exciting. Only a book can say, 'I am born' (new-born babies never can). Nevertheless the beginning of the novel is here, with Victorian gusto, triumphantly fused with the natural beginning of birth. The project, we sense, is to be a sustained, richly Philistine defiance of Aristotle; we are indeed to be given 'all the things that happened' to not Theseus – but David. Dickens is, to be sure, too intelligent to proceed without negotiation. It will be said by the Formalist that the wit here confesses what the narrative mode men-

daciously denies, that all is art. This however will not quite
do; where birth is once named, real beginning cannot be quite
forgotten.

The wittiest of all openings is surely that of *Tristram Shandy*.
Here the Horatian opposition between a despised beginning-
from-the-egg and an admired plunge *in medias res* is joyously
exploded. Tristram, the supposed teller of the story, begins
indeed from his own insemination, invoking as he does so, with
crack-brained inverse scholarship, the authority of Horace. But
Sterne simultaneously bewilders the first-time reader, who is pit-
ched *in medias res*, into the middle of an ill-conducted marital
engagement, which is simply unintelligible until we know the
previous history of those concerned.

Here the comedy works not simply by the incongruous juxtaposition of the formal and the natural, but by a sudden wilful
movement (having, I think, real philosophical force) into the
territory of the natural, which can be made to appear *inherently*
opposed to the notion of a beginning. The ploy is to show, first,
that there is something which appears to be a far more radical
beginning than Birth, namely Conception, and *then* to show, in
the same breath, that if you *look* at a conception you will find
that you are not looking at a beginning but merely at a nodal
point in a larger process. Frank Kermode (who was not, as far
as I know, thinking of Sterne at the time) had the same thought:
We die, he says *in mediis rebus* and are born *in medias res* (Kermode
1967: 7). To show the conception of Tristram is to show two
mid-life persons in a relation which is, necessarily, only partly
intelligible. They, not he, will fill the screen, if only because they
are so much bigger! Sterne, as if in response to this very thought,
switches his attention to the microscopic operations of spermato-
zoa, but here too we encounter not a clear inception but rather
a baffled and baffling multiplicity of *process*.

At this point my resistance suddenly became radical. For the
logical tendency of this insight is to abolish all beginnings from
the order of nature, to relegate them firmly to the Indian Reser-
vation of Discourse – with one (empty) concession: the mystic,
inherently un-inspectable Genesis of the Universe may stand as
the sole permissible natural beginning. If a beginning is that
which is unconnected with any previous event, then only the
origin of the world will serve. Even the beginning of the Bible,
seemingly the most absolute of all written openings does not

satisfy the criteria, for this creation was preceded by a Creator. The matter is further complicated by a strange tremor in the Hebrew: *bereshit* perhaps properly invites, as the most literal translation possible, not 'In the beginning God created . . .' (Authorised Version) but 'In a beginning when God created . . .' (though this in its turn is attended by problems which propel the mind back, in the direction of the Authorised Version) (see Josipovici 1988: 53–74). The ghost of that extra 'when', can ever so faintly reinforce our sense of a history before History began, of creation as intervention rather than radical beginning.

To put the matter at its lowest and simplest. A concept which has only one application, and that to something which is intrinsically unavailable, is surely unlikely to figure prominently in language as one of our commoner words. Cosmic origin makes other paradigms of latency, such as the Freudian Unconscious or the *Dieu caché* of the Protestants, look like vividly familiar, friendly faces by contrast. It is possible indeed that the concept is in fact never employed at all (for I set aside Biblical Genesis). Even those physicists who speak of creation allow, I understand, the notion of prior conditions. The truth is that the word is common because the thing is common. The world is full of natural beginnings. If Shakespeare did not exist in 1563 and did exist in 1565, then between 1563 and 1565 Shakespeare began, or, as we say, was born. This is not a social construct. It is true that Shakespeare's birth was preceded by a complex biological process, that he did not arise from nothing and it is further true that we are in a manner 'set' as organisms to read off the point at which Shakespeare, so to speak, crystallises as having especial importance. An ant watching the whole affair would notice something else. The perspectival schemata operated by different organisms or different cultures may on occasion be interrogative rather than constitutive, as I have argued elsewhere. If you are 'set' to read off bicycles, say, from the given field, this need not mean that you are feigning 'bicycles', within a featureless and therefore infinitely indulgent environment; rather, you may be *asking*, 'Bicycle?' and receiving a perfectly clear 'Yes' or 'No' from the world. Once this converse thought is allowed and nature, so often driven off with a pitch-fork, has come running back, it becomes clear that even indistinct natural beginnings can be allowed – the beginning of manned flight, say, or even the beginning of the Reformation.

We are accustomed in the late twentieth century to seeing the apparently natural suddenly appropriated by form: propositions like 'Zola-esque naturalism is really pure convention' are the rule. But the ball *can* roll back. I began by contrasting the opening of the *Iliad*, as fundamentally formalist and fictive, with the natural beginning of the Bible. But if the Trojan War was real history, as the first listeners to Homer may have assumed, it is conceivable that the wrath of Achilles is a real though doubtless indistinct beginning. Alternatively, if the *Iliad* was taken as fiction, it was certainly taken as more or less plausible fiction, in which case the beginning of Achilles' wrath is founded, as plausible hypothesis must be, on real risings-up of anger in real, dangerous persons. In fact I do not suppose that the first listeners to Homer were so foolish as to believe, with the hard credulity of a modern, in the details presented to them. Pre-literate or quasi-pre-literate cultures tend, as it were, not to hope for – not to expect – exactitude, but are instead content with an exciting Limbo of possibles. A kind of wisely passive sophistication may have been destroyed by the Sophists, when they appeared on the scene with harshly binary questions, 'True or false? Yes or no?' Either way, fact or fiction, there turns out to be a more or less firm link with the natural. Thus my strong contrast between a confessedly fictional, interventionist opening (Homer) and a Natural Beginning (Genesis) begins to blur, to transform itself perhaps into a weaker antithesis: between culturally prominent, publicly baptised beginnings, and more fugitive, shyer beginnings, which the individual artist chooses to make prominent.

Kermode's *Sense of an Ending*, indeed, sometimes follows the other, stony track. By this path, all beginnings are merely suppositions or impositions. 'What can be thought must certainly be a fiction'. This shrill apophthegm from Nietzsche stands as an uncontested epigraph, and the infinitely subtle, discriminating Kermodian prose which follows seems, with its use of 'make sense of the world' as a recurring catch-phrase, to be gently urging what is at last the same desolating view. The famous paradigm of sense-making is our ability to 'hear' a merely serial 'tick-tick-tick-tick' as the symmetrically organised 'tick-tock, ticktock'. Even as we think we are hearing, we are in fact composing. Some people in response to this passage pointed out (what is true) that older clocks make two distinct sounds in repeated sequence – that is, they actually do 'go tick-tock, tick-tock'. Meanwhile, however, it is equally true that people can do the thing of which Kermode speaks, they can hear 'tick-tick-tick-tick' as 'tick-tock, tick-tock'. The basic counter-argument was always, therefore, to point out that Kermode's demonstration, where it succeeded, depended on a prior ability to determine what sound the clock was really making (otherwise this remarkable self-deceiving dexterity of mind could never have been exposed to view). And that means that there is such a thing as an unconditioned apprehension of reality.

But *The Sense of an Ending* does not acquiesce in this false simplicity. The dialectic is sustained. It may be that Professor Kermode thinks, fairly modestly, that historical 'periods' at least, are purely imposed shapes, read *into* the past. I imagine that for most historians 'periods' are excitingly indistinct natural beginnings, rich material for dispute precisely because their credentials are in doubt. If it were easily admitted on all hands that there are no natural credentials at all – that there is no cognitive sense in saying, for example, that classical civilisation was succeeded by a different order – then of course the argument tails off into silence. Kermode suggests near the beginning of *The Sense of an Ending* that the notion of an epoch is 'something entirely in our own hands' (7), but later (101) observes, with all the energy and engagement of one who still believes in such things, that we live in a technological age. Here he uses – without the apologetic inverted commas which have become *de rigueur* – the phrase 'in fact'.

Within a few pages he is commending W. B. Yeats' 'regard for the reality which will not be reduced' (106) and suggesting that the contempt for reality (including ethical reality) which we find in the early Modernists is a 'treason of the clerks' (109). Indeed in this lecture, 'the Modern Apocalypse', he ascribes to Eliot – by no means derisively – a critical position which is almost the opposite of the one from which he began. Instead of saying, 'That which is preceded by anything at all is no true beginning', he forces us to attend to a more complex proposition: anything which is importantly new – as distinct from the trivial posturing of the *avant-garde* – must emerge from a context: 'Nothing on its own can be new' (120). It is a mistake, then, blankly to oppose genesis and metamorphosis Here below the level of the moon, every genesis involves a transformation, but there are real begin-

nings because in this way things which did not exist before came
into being.

If what I have suggested is true, we are left with an enigma.
Homer is the grand puzzle. Why did he, at the start of European
poetry, enter obliquely with the seemingly non-natural opening?
Everyone else followed the advice of the King of Hearts: 'Begin
at the beginning' – that is, the known, public beginnings. We
have creation myths, the lives and exploits of heroes, battles
and wars serially expounded, chronicles. 'Carles li reis, nostre
empereur magne / Set anz tres plein ad ested in Espagne', and
away we go. But for Homer, Virgil (who is indeed scarcely
imaginable without Homer) might have written annals, like
Ennius. The problem seems insuperable. Perhaps we can nevertheless advance our understanding if we narrow the enquiry, for
a moment, to a technical question of language. There is a difficulty, long familiar to commentators, about the meaning of *ex
hou*, 'from when' in line 6 of *Iliad*, Book I:

> Sing, goddess, of the wrath of Peleus' son, Achilles, the
> accursed wrath which laid ten thousand wars upon the Achae-
> ans and cast down many strong ghosts of heroes into the house
> of Hades and gave their bodies to be the spoil of dogs and all
> the birds, and the purpose of Zeus was accomplished, [*ex hou*]
> from when Atrides, King of men and godlike Achilles first fell
> out in strife.

The question is whether *ex hou* is to be taken with *aeide*, 'Sing',
in line 1, or with *eteleieto*, 'was accomplished' in line 5. By the
first interpretation the general sense is, 'Begin your song, Muse,
at that point in the saga where . . .'. By the second interpretation,
ex hou is firmly located within a story already begun: 'Sing, goddess, of the wrath which ruined all – and how Zeus's purpose
began to be accomplished [*ex hou*] when those heroes first
quarrelled . . .'.

I should say first that the second interpretation may well be
the right one. *Ex hou* is a very long way in the sentence from
aeide, 'Sing', and it can be argued strongly that the most natural
presumption is to take it with the nearest preceding verb, 'was
accomplished'. But we cannot be certain. It remains possible that,
instead, a reflexive reference to the *poet's* memorial feat was
marked and made conventionally clear by, say, a pause and a

loud stroke upon the lyre, when Homer sang. Auerbach taught us that there is no latency in Homer, that, despite the technique of flashback and anticipation, the surface presented is so to speak at a uniform distance from the eye. Yet if *ex hou* means 'from the point in the saga at which' there is a huge latent poem, a poem behind the poem we possess. The bard's performance (memorial feat, inspiration) entails his temporary immersion in a huge, ever-flowing Iliad. The Middle Ages continue instinctively to understand this, for they have a name for the poem behind the poem: the Matter of Troy. For Homer the division is not between poetic invention and objective reality. Almost certainly he never saw the pre-existing poem of Troy in a book. Rather, it lived in the throats and memories of singers, and, to a lesser degree, in the memories and responses of their listeners. The poem and the history were therefore in a manner one thing. The poem lies outside the ego of the particular bard who is in some ways an executant rather than a maker. It follows that the divinity who is to inspire the process is a divinity of *song*, a Muse, and not one of the usual Olympians. One senses that Horace's *in medias res* might have been *in medium poema*, but for the fact that Augustan Romans, with their books in their hands, could see that the *poem* began with the first line on the page. Note that we are not dealing here with a poetic ambiguity. *Ex hou* means one or the other of the above; not both.

Look now at a sophisticated post-Virgilian, Ovid. The *Metamorphoses*, so many centuries after Homer, has a beginning of primitive elemental naturalism; it narrates the genesis of form from chaos:

> In nova fert animus mutatas dicere formas
> Corpora; di coeptis (nam vos mutastis et illas)
> Adspirate meis primaque ab origine mundi
> Ad mea perpetuum deducite tempora carmen!
> Ante mare et terras et quod tegit omnia caelum
> Unus erat toto naturae vultus in orbe
> Quem dixere chaos. . . .

[My spirit moves me to tell of forms changed into new bodies; gods (for it was you who changed those forms) breathe kindly on the work I have begun and draw out the thread of my perpetual song from the origin of the world to my own times.

Before sea, or lands, or sky covering all, nature in all her round
had but one face, and this they have called Chaos. . . .]

For all its primordial weight, however, this is manifestly the
work of a late-born poet, not primitive but primitivist. The poet
betrays the initiating role of his own separate, individual psyche
in the fourth word, *animus*. The poem is brought into being not
by a poetry-god, a Muse, but by Ovid's own mind. When gods
are addressed, they are the Olympians who act upon the world
– upon that world towards whose origin the poet gestures with
what might be called ontological nostalgia. We saw in Virgil an
un-Homeric reduplicative effect, in the opening sentence (as
given by Donatus), doubling the poet and the hero. In Ovid the
deep, Mosaic note of 'In the beginning' is counterpointed from
the first by a lighter, more capricious music, which translators
cannot catch. *In nova fert animus*, the first four words, naturally
suggest a wholly literary meaning: 'My spirit moves me to treat
a new subject', but then, as the inflected sentence gradually
unfolds, a different grammar is asserted, and we realise that we
must take *in nova* with *mutatas* rather than with *fert*, we must
think, within the narrative, of forms changed into new bodies
rather than, extra-poetically, of a spirit propelled into new subject-matter.

All this suggests that Homer is able to perform his feat of
intervention partly because he is exempt from the anxiety of
individual consciousness. He is not making up a poem, in antithesis to the known sequence of reality. He is entering a pre-
existent saga, guided and inspired by a goddess who is herself
saga. In Ovid, conversely, we may glimpse the beginning of
consciously false cosmological thinking. There is a marvellous
passage in *The Sense of an Ending* (38) in which Kermode describes
the Third Reich as having a cosmology which it always knew, in
a manner, to be false: the most disquieting example extant of
what philosophers call 'making it true'. Ovid's phrase, *carmen
perpetuum*, 'perpetual song', similarly combines sophisticated dou-
bleness with nostalgia. The phrase itself is knowingly literary –
almost an arrogant joke, for it echoes the *aeisma diènekes* of Callimachus (1949–53: I, fr. 1, 1). Callimachus notoriously thought a
great book was a great bore and coined the phrase, 'continued
song' as a pejorative description. Within his grand opening, Ovid
is therefore impudently contradicting his Hellenistic teacher.

Although Troy and Rome enter Ovid's poem in Book XII, I do not agree with Brooks Otis' suggestion that the reader will feel in the *Metamorphoses* 'a definitely historical structure: a temporal movement from the Creation to the present reign of Augustus' (1970: 47). The labyrinthine interwoven narrative of the *Metamorphoses* contrasts strongly with the teleological majesty of the *Aeneid*. Nevertheless we may hear, in Ovid's phrase, an allusion to the now distant, ever flowing river of saga, whether this be the matter of Troy, or the vast body of god-stories. Remember the question Nisus asked:

> Dine hunc ardorem mentibus addunt,
> Euryale, an sua cuique deus fit dira cupido?
> *(Aeneid, IX, 184–5)*

[Do the gods put this spirit in our hearts, or does each man's fierce desire become a god for him?]

To be sure, Virgil is echoing Homer. 'I do not know', says Medon of Telemachus, 'whether some god set him on, or whether his own spirit stirred him to go to Pylos' (*Odyssey*, IV. 712). But Medon is putting two mutually exclusive alternatives; one or the other of these things must, he supposes, have actually happened. In the words of Nisus, on the other hand, we sense that the poet is flirting with the notion that these may be alternative descriptions of the same phenomenon. Between Homer and Virgil lie Heraclitus, *ēthos anthrōpō daimōn*, 'Character is a man's destiny-god' (fr. 119) and Menander, '*Ho nous gar hēmōn estin en hekastō theos*, 'Our mind is, in each person, a god.' (1921: Gnom. mon. 434, fr. 762k; 1880–88: III, 214; this phrase was quoted by Plutarch: *Moralia* 999e). Thus the suggestion grows that these are not coexistent states of affairs but rather rival languages, with the implication that 'god-language' could be replaced by psychological language. In which case the Muse herself might die, replaced by the *animus* or spirit of the individual poet. In Virgil the *ego* is already growing strong but the Muse is still (though belatedly) invoked. In Ovid *animus* is the confessed origin of a poem which terminates, likewise, in the personality of the poet; *vivam*, 'I shall live' is the last word of the *Metamorphoses*. (See Galinsky 1975: 44). The gods invoked are the gods of a nostalgically viewed cosmology, something other than the poet and the poem.

I have moved somewhat from my original anthithesis. The difference between a natural and a formal beginning becomes, as we close with the mystery of the Homeric intervention, less important than the growing distance between the poet and the matter of his poem. The Muse is, by this process, slowly starved. In the centuries which followed we may watch the Muse becoming as *mythos* was for Ovid, in her turn the matter of nostalgia, or else the object of a systematically defeated quest. In Milton the separate individuality of the author reaches a crisis, out of which the poet *strains towards* the divine guarantor of the first blind poet. There is a sense of terrible need: 'Something other than I must sing this song.' The first fourteen lines of *Lycidas* tell of a voyage made in a strange darkness, in which seasons are confused, Spring with Autumn, unripeness with brown myrtle and frail, scattering leaves. Virgil's already sharply personal *cano*, 'I sing', is transposed into an elaborately deployed future: 'I – come – to – sing – again – soon – yet – before – due – time.' The poem must find its own voice before the sisters of the sacred well can touch their lyres. Nor are they the sources of the poem in any stronger sense than Milton is, or Edward King, or Orpheus, or that eeriest of 'doubles', the genius of the shore. We are in a world in which poets will seek nourishment from ghost-muses, dead versions of the poets' themselves (as in Gray's *Elegy*, say), from prompting friends, urging them to write, from unseen readers who are, again with conscious falseness, depicted as semblable and *frère* to the poet writing. Otherwise, as with Wordsworth's *The Prelude*, the poem will begin at last to flow with the remembered sound of water, not Arethuse but the stream behind his father's house.

Here as the Muse dislimns in secondary images of herself, my own discourse tails off. My thoughts *si squaderna* in questions: who or what was the Muse? Are poems and novels now inertly free to begin *in any way at all*? Why did Homer (as his sole contribution to the Iliad, for everything after the first paragraph is from the Muse) *tell* the Muse where to begin, instead of being told by her? And, still over-arching all the other questions, how did Homer ever come to do what he did?

Note

Some of the material from this essay will appear in the author's forth-coming *Openings* (Oxford University Press).

3

Secrets and Surfaces
Bernard Harrison

I

'Both art and life,' says Nietzsche, directing a 'critical backward glance' at the youthful Schopenhauerianism of *The Birth of Tragedy*, 'depend wholly on the laws of optics, on perspective and illusion; both, to be blunt, depend on the necessity of error.' (Nietzsche 1956: 10) As often with Nietzsche, it is unclear whether the implications of this thought are joyful or depressing ones. Does it redeem art by showing it to proceed on the same principles as life, or damn life by showing it to be the same kind of painted sham as art? For the late Nietzsche 'life' is too privileged a category for there to be much doubt which way the argument will go: put the same point in the hands of Frank Kermode and doubts, as chilly as they are no doubt salutary, come seeping in.

The main line of argument in *The Genesis of Secrecy* is easily grasped. Literary criticism, in so far as its methods involve pursuing, by means of paraphrase and explanatory gloss, the true meaning of the text ('the recovery of the real right original thing' – Kermode 1979: 125) shares with a long tradition of biblical hermeneutics the idea that texts have both a 'carnal' and a 'spiritual' meaning; the former accessible to any outsider who can read the language in which the text is writen, the latter accessible only to insiders, who have through membership of a privileged hermeneutic community acquired knowledge of the secret relationships and correspondences constituting the true and authentic sense lying beneath, or behind, the surface of the text. Kermode has both epistemological and moral objections to this way of construing the enterprise of interpretation. The epistemological ones I shall get to in a moment. The moral ones often, I suspect, get passed over by readers of the book, and are worth more than a passing glance. In ascending order of seriousness they are, first, that the pursuit of spiritual sense comes at times,

38

and perhaps always, perilously close to the kind of divination that proceeds by sticking a pin into a copy of Virgil or the Bible. Second, and more seriously, the effect if not always the conscious aim of making the distinction between the carnal and the spiritual central to the practice of interpretation is to establish 'the superiority of latent over manifest sense' (Kermode 1979: 2): to exclude outsiders and to reserve to an authoritative institution the practice of hermeneutical divination. Third, and more seriously still, the hermeneutic privilege thus established 'may determine matters of life and death' (20). Thus Matthew's fiction that 'the Jews, after Pilate washed his hands, voluntarily took upon themselves the blood-guilt of the Crucifixion' (*loc. cit.*) helped to determine the subsequent course of European anti-semitism.

Fourthly, finally and most seriously of all, there is the forgetfulness of the distinction between truth and meaning which is central to the hermeneutics of secrecy, and which is the chief source of the recurrent tendency of hermeneutics to breed nightmares. The moral centre of Kermode's lectures seems to me to lie here, in their espousal (119) of Spinoza's dictum that in exegesis 'we are at work not on the truth of passages but on their meaning'. This is something most of us would pay lip-service to. Whatever biblical exegesis may yield, most of us would be happy to concede, it cannot yield us knowledge of the Jews' having accepted the blood-guilt of the Crucifixion. But at the same time most of us continue to hope, or to talk as if we continued to hope, that the authors we most admire have 'something to say to us': some insight, some truth or other about 'life' to communicate, which a proper, a just reading would excavate and put on show. Kermode wants to rid us of these last vestiges of the notion that exegesis has anything to do with truth. At the same time he is conscious of the loss that this involves. 'All modern interpretation that is not merely an attempt at 're-cognition' involves some attempt to divorce meaning and truth' (122). But to the extent that it succeeds in this aim structuralist and post-structuralist criticism takes on the aspect of the doorkeeper in Kafka's Parable of the Law which recurs as a *leitmotiv* of *The Genesis of Secrecy*. The door closes, shutting out the radiance beyond; and to prevent or delay its closing it is all too likely that we shall abandon the painful attempt to separate questions of truth from questions of meaning and 'slip back into the old comfortable fictions of transparency, the single sense, the truth'. (123)

I have dwelt at some length on the moral aspects of Kermode's argument partly as a way of measuring the distance we have travelled from the seemingly febrile Zarathustrian cheerfulness with which Nietzsche, in a late phase, greeted the thought that transparency and the single sense are unattainable, that all is 'perspective and illusion'. *The Genesis of Secrecy* is not a cheerful book. But it is a serious one, and its un-Nietzschean preference for truth over illusion is not one that can easily be laughed off. Nevertheless, I think the gloom can be mitigated a little. I want to suggest that it is possible to preserve something of what Kermode calls the 'radiance' of the text while also preserving a decént respect for Spinoza's dictum that in exegesis what is at stake is meaning, not truth. I want to suggest that it is possible to remain wholly upon the surface of the text, making no attempt to penetrate by judicious paraphrase to a hidden meaning beneath or behind that surface, but yet find on that surface more than an enigmatic shimmer of words and rhetorical devices.

II

Kermode's thesis is that the hermeneutics of secrecy is founded upon an illusion, or rather upon a whole string of them, and pursues a non-existent goal. Texts have no secrets, at least of the kind that interpretation strives to unlock (studies which confine themselves to questions of 'meaning', such as philology, linguistics or structural analysis being, of course, another matter). Kermode's arguments for this thesis seem to me to fall into three groups:

(1) Arguments which endeavour to show that any text admits of an irreducible plurality of interpretations;
(2) Arguments which endeavour to show that the elaboration of narrative is responsive to purely formal (or 'internal' or 'literary') considerations rather than to the faithful representation of reality;
(3) Arguments which endeavour to show that latent or spiritual sense is a product of interpretation.

Taken separately as types of argument against the hermeneutics of secrecy, (1)-(3) do not all seem to have the same degree of force. Arguments of type (1) seem particularly weak. It is hard to see why any determined champion of the hermeneutics of secrecy should be much disturbed by the thought that latent sense may be irreducibly plural. Texts are produced by persons, and persons, being themselves irreducibly plural, often do mean more by what they say than they appear to mean, and often more than they take themselves to have said or meant. Arguments of type (2) seem a bit stronger, but not all that strong. Much depends here on what one might have in mind by speaking of a text as 'transparent' (something we shall come back to in a moment). If a transparent narrative is one which faithfully records an occurrence, then obviously its transparency is threatened the moment it begins to be subject to processes of literary elaboration designed to make it a more interesting story, or a more telling one from the point of view of some set of moral or institutional demands external to that of mere fidelity to the events recounted. Kermode deploys this point persuasively in Lecture V ('What Precisely Are the Facts?') when he observes that 'Mark is not a simple chronicle, such as, in the days when its priority was being first established, people hoped it might be, but a history with a literary structure.' But although the point sustains Kermode's immediately following comment, 'To speak so is to speak as one does of a fiction,' (Kermode 1979: 116) it does not altogether sustain the conclusion which that comment seems to invite, that the presence of any trace of literary elaboration in a text is sufficient to write off its claim to historicity, or more generally to transparency, *in any sense whatsoever of those terms*. There might, that is, be weaker senses of 'transparency' which allow a text to be in very large measure a literary construction while yet allowing it some bearing upon extra-textual reality.

This is precisely what is excluded by arguments of type (3), which I shall call arguments for textual solipsism. These arguments seem to me much stronger than those of types (1) and (2). Not only are they sufficient in themselves, if they can be made to stick, to demonstrate the futility and delusiveness of the hermeneutics of secrecy; they also add greatly to the force of Kermode's other two types of argument. The thesis of textual solipsism is that all latent, 'spiritual' meaning is the product of interpretation. The project of the hermeneutics of secrecy is thus rendered futile because interpretation *per se* is futile, its pretended discoveries no more than the gross, alien-seeming shadows cast by its own processes, and by the patterns of institutional expectation and assumption which motivate and direct those processes, upon the passive and inscrutable surface of words which is all that a text ultimately offers to our excited and self-deluded scrutiny. Both the argument for the irreducible plurality of latent sense and the argument from literary elaboration are probably best seen, therefore, as ways of elaborating and filling-out the argument for textual solipsism. 'No doubt,' says Kermode of the Parable of the Samaritan, 'the parable has a carnal sense which does not vary materially; its spiritual sense is not so constant' (Kermode 1979: 36). But his account of the diversity of spiritual senses which Augustine and the Fathers drew from it is meant, I take it, precisely to bring into question whether this diversity is really being discovered in what is, after all, no more than 'a simple exemplary tale' (35), or distilled out of the very processes of interpretation, with their accompanying and directing institutional imperatives and assumptions, to which Augustine *et al* subjected it. As we read Kermode at this point, our cheerful willingness to grasp the nettle of semantic plurality in the manner I suggested a moment ago subsides within us. Similarly, the argument from literary elaboration gains in force if we take Kermode's point (101: 'texts are from the beginning and sometimes indeterminately studded with interpretations'; 20: 'spiritual senses . . . may in their turn be treated as if they were carnal'; and *passim*) that the literary elaboration of texts passes with no clear methodological break into their interpretation and *vice-versa*.

Kermode offers in addition to these detailed studies of hermeneutic practice a quite general and knock-down argument for textual solipsism, which is that it follows as a simple consequence of the latitude texts necessarily leave to interpreters. We may not be able to make just any interpretation square with a text (an important caveat, to which I shall return) but we can make enough square with it to make the choice between them depend upon supplementary principles of interpretation which are themselves determined, often below the level of consciousness, by history and cultural situation. Our 'acts of divination . . . *determine* undetected latent sense' (Kermode 1979: 4; my italics). They exercise this determining role because divinatory paraphrase is in essence the art of connecting up parts and aspects of the text to reveal an occult pattern of coherence. And 'All such operations require the interpreter to practise a grandiose neglect of portions of the text' (20); so that 'every time you read *A la Recherche du*

temps perdu it can be a new novel, says Roland Barthes, because
you skip different parts each time' (54). The movement of possible
senses must be brought to a halt, Kermode suggests, because
bringing it to a halt (this, I shall argue, is questionable) 'is our
only means of reading until revolutionary new concepts of writing prevail' (71). But the only thing that can bring it to a halt is
the constraint of some fore-understanding (Kermode's way of
rendering into English the German *Vorverstandnis*) which will of
necessity be 'ideological and institutional' in character.

It is Kermode's awareness of the solipsistic implications of the
thesis that latent sense is the product of interpretation, I think,
which gives *The Genesis of Secrecy* its pervasive atmosphere of
sadness, defeat and loss. For if we accept Kermode's argument,
after all, all those insights and glimpses of insight which make
reading narrative fiction exciting to us become merely glimpses
of our own interpretative practices and fore-understandings. The
window which narrative fiction appears to open upon a world
of wonders which is also our world becomes a blank sheet of
opaque glass offering back nothing but a distorted image of the
observer's own eye. Metaphors of screens and opaque glasses
have long been familiar to us, of course, as part of the standard
rhetoric of philosophical idealism. (Do you really take me,
demands Philonous of Hylas, to be defending principles 'that
lead us to think all the visible beauty of the creation a false
imaginary glare?' (Berkeley 1910: The Second Dialogue, 244) –
and one senses that the anxiety which reverberates in the extraordinary energy of the concluding phrase, triply buttressed as it
is with predicates of sensory and cognitive obstruction, is not
only that of Hylas.) So one would expect to find such images
cropping up in *The Genesis of Secrecy*. And on page 125 we duly
find Kermode speaking of 'our readiness to submit the show of
things to the desires of our minds; of the structures of explanation
which come between us and the text or the facts like some wall of
wavy glass'. The same metaphor recurs in Kermode's distinction
between 'transparent' and 'opaque' texts; and in the door which,
in Kafka's parable of the Law, becomes not a means of access to
an Elsewhere, of escape from the airless room of the self and its
obscurely conditioned fore-understandings, but one more wall
closing off the – in any case fictive – radiance beyond.

We have in fact to deal in this book with two Kermodes. There
is the sceptical, Lockean Kermode, out to teach us the plain and

unexceptionable truth that a story is a story, and not a message in code; and to debunk the Baconianism, the obsession with ciphers, occult meanings, covert identities such as those of the Man in the Macintosh in *Ulysses* or the young man in the sindon in Mark, Dark Ladies of all kinds, which feeds off the contrary view. And then there is the Kermode who has discovered, like Locke's philosophical heirs, that an empiricism begun in mirth and gladness all too easily ends first in idealism and then in solipsism; but who like them sees no honest way of repudiating these further steps. In the remainder of this essay I shall do my best to set an obstacle or two in the path of this literary version of the familiar philosophical slide from robust empiricism (where that involves among other things respect for the distinction between asking what 'p' means and asking whether p is true) to blank misgivings about the possibility of egress from the closed world of the self.

III

Setting opacity aside for a moment, what would the transparency of a fully transparent text consist in? Kermode defines the terms 'transparent' and 'opaque' only contextually, no doubt because he does not think them particularly problematic; but the contextual clues are sufficient to yield an answer. Lecture V opens with the sentence:

> If so many causes act in concert to ensure that texts are from the beginning and sometimes indeterminately studded with interpretations; and if the texts in their very nature demand further interpretation and yet resist it, what should we expect when the document in question denies its opacity by claiming to be a transparent account of the recognisable world?

Transparency, it seems, consists in what philosophical discussions of the nature of truth call correspondence: a match, in other words, between a true sentence and a fact; in this case between a true narrative sentence and what it asserts to have taken place. The trouble with transparency in this sense is that, as anti-foundationalist philosophers, such as W. V. Quine, or Paul Feyerabend, or Thomas Kuhn, or Richard Rorty, have fairly plausibly argued (Kermode employs some related arguments him-

self), it is simply not available for any discourse sufficiently elaborated to be interesting. Observation is always and irremediably
theory-laden. What we recognise and record as a fact is always
relative to the current state of scientific and commonsense construal of how things *in general* stand in the world: is already
saturated, as Kermode would have it, with fore-understandings.

Taking this anti-foundationalist line, however, only commits
one to denying guaranteed correctness or finality, in the sense
of incorrigibility, to any of our descriptions of Reality. Anti-foundationalism, that is, while it no doubt is incompatible with some
forms of philosophical Realism, certainly does not, and cannot,
commit us to the view that reality is a 'linguistic construction' in
the sense of being made *in principle inaccessible* by the theory-
ladenness of our concepts and descriptive schemes – 'shut off
from us behind an opaque screen of words', or something of the
sort – because to assert *that* would be precisely to assert that
whatever concepts or styles of description we happen to dispose
of at any given moment, say the present one, are in principle
incorrigible: to assert, that is, exactly what anti-foundationalism
denies. To hold that all our descriptions are theory-laden is to
hold that no scheme of descriptive concepts occupies a place in
our language guaranteed by its simply corresponding to reality.
But the assertion of the existence of a gap of that kind between
reality and our ways of describing it would be vacuous, unless
there were a real possibility of the displacement of such a scheme
coming about because of the discovery of relevant natural possibilities exceeding the capacity of that scheme to handle, or to
handle fruitfully or naturally. The answer to someone who says,
'But couldn't we have a pair of competing conceptual schemes
of equivalent capacity to handle all observable differences in a
given area, so that choosing between them would be a matter of
purely social or institutional agreement?' is the Wittgensteinian:
'In such a case, since *ex hypothesi* there could be no difference in
use, and so no detectable difference in meaning, between the
two sets of terms, what would be the force of the hypothesis
that we dispose of two sets of terms belonging to two different
conceptual schemes?'

Anti-foundationalism plausibly and consistently construed,
then, presupposes some more or less Popperian picture of disconfirmation as constituting the interface between Reality and our
never-finally-adequate attempts to describe it. The thought which

I now wish to pursue is that that picture may have some bearing on the problems which Kermode raises concerning the interpretation of narrative fiction.

The obvious objection which such a proposal invites, of course, is that encounters with narrative fictions cannot reveal defects in our fore-understandings of how things stand in the world, in the way that, say, encounters with awkward experimental data can, because narrative fictions are (no prizes for guessing) fictions. But this objection is not as strong as it looks. The web of fore-understandings from within which each of us confronts the world is not just made up of beliefs, which only experiment or observation could reveal to be mistaken, about specific, discrete matters of fact. Much more importantly, it is made up of preconceptions about the limits of natural possibility. Such fore-understandings tell us that Reality divides up into contrasted types of fact which conjointly, as we confidently suppose, exhaust the possibilities of nature or human life. Let us call these *structural fore-understandings*. Such fore-understandings can, certainly, come under pressure from direct experience, as when we come across an apparently undeniable case of Lamarckian inheritance, or meet a man whose acts and personality cannot be satisfactorily classified according to any of the short list of stereotypes we customarily apply to persons of his class, nation or race. But structural fore-understandings can also find themselves under threat from an argument, from a mathematical model; or for that matter from a fiction. For all that need be shown, to put such a preconception under stress, is that commonplace facts about nature or human life can be reordered or transformed, by appeal to principles which we already know to operate in relevant cases, in such a way as to generate a possibility incapable of being brought easily under any of the alternative descriptive rubrics which the structural fore-understanding in question asserts to be conjointly exhaustive of natural possibility.

It is, in fact, because mere fictions can pose substantial challenges to our structural fore-understandings[1] that scandal has always been a main motive of interpretation. Kermode on page 82 notes this principle in operation:

An unfamiliar foreign expression, or the interpretation of a difficult part of the Law, or a story which, in the course of time, had come to seem ambiguous or even indecent, such as

Sarah's sojourn in the harem of the Pharaoh, might prompt midrash. . . . How did it happen that Joseph married the daughter of Potiphar, an Egyptian? An Alexandrian romance maintains that the daughter was first converted; a rabbinical explanation has it that she was really the daughter of Dinah, reared by the wife of Pharaoh, but a born Jew. Thus discrepancies, or indecencies, are eliminated by the invention of romantic narrative.

The issues raised here, it seems to me, go deeper. Our structural fore-understandings make us what we are: Marxists or Methodists, for instance, mechanists or vitalists. We cannot surrender them without undergoing the pains of insecurity, loss and amputation, that personal change entails. We want knowledge, of course, since knowledge not only satisfies curiosity but is, in both the engineer's and the Foucaultian's senses, power. But we hope very much that our knowledge, as it advances, will compose itself submissively into an orderly array of facts of the types sanctioned by our most cherished structural fore-understandings, not only posing no threat to their integrity but showing how well-chosen they were in the first place, and that no mockers or hecklers will intervene to force upon our attention facts, or possible facts, of which we can gain nothing by taking cognisance.

Much serious narrative fiction has, I would suggest, as one of the more important of its many functions, that of thwarting this modest and entirely understandable hope. It adds insult to injury, in a way, that not one of the torrent of sentences of which it consists expresses a single factual, empirical truth. It makes no attempt to sweeten the bitter pill of its contumacy with any admixture of useful knowledge. It confines itself, as Aristotle taught us, to sketching possibilities;[2] but possibilities which, while they may seem sometimes merely fantastic, are even in those cases often too fully and sharply realised, too much in accordance with what we know very well to be the case when we come, or are forced, to think about it, to be easily kept from threatening our structural fore-understandings. Hence the venom which great narrative fictions often attract before interpretation has revealed ways of allowing them modest and discreet entrance into the canon whose gates they rudely assault. And hence also the rage to interpret itself. We interpret often enough, as Kermode suggests, because we are scandalised. But that in itself must mean:

because we are very far from taking fictional narratives to be mere stories, pipe-dreams without power to challenge our sense of how life itself is organised into structures of possibilities. Being scandalised we trust we have misheard or misread: that, to use one of Kermode's most telling examples, when Jesus says that the true sense of parables is concealed from the wicked *in order* that (*hina*) they might not turn and be saved he must mean not *hina* but *hoti* ('because'). Being conscious of the presence of a power to disturb we wish to appropriate that power to the support of the very fore-understandings it appears to challenge, by equipping the text with some wholly benign sense. We hope, to use Kermode's chillingly felicitous phrase (54), to 'process the text into coherence'. Thus hoping, we become Insiders.

I agree with Kermode, for his reasons among others, that the Insider's enterprise is doomed to failure. My concern is with what ways of reading remain for the rest of us, for Those Outside to whom *The Genesis of Secrecy* is after all dedicated. Certainly we should accept Spinoza's principle that in exegesis 'we are at work not on the truth of passages but on their meaning'. But should we also accept the two further premises which Kermode in effect adds to Spinoza's principle; namely, (1) that to 'work on the meaning of a text' in any sense other than a purely structural or philological one is necessarily to attempt to make it cohere in the interests of some paraphrase, and (2) that many paraphrases, at best distinct from one another and at worst in conflict, can be grounded in any text? Premises (1) and (2), taken together with Spinoza's principle, yield textual solipsism: the thesis that undiscovered latent sense is the product of interpretation; or, to spell it out more dismally still, that no cognitive gains may be expected to accrue from reading narrative fiction save those of disillusion with such reading; that while the theoretical reflections which break the spell of reading may have some bearing upon real life, nothing that we do or think while under that spell can have. If we accept Spinoza's principle plus (1) and (2) then, it seems, we must choose between the rather drab options which Kermode offers us. We must embrace disappointment as our lot, allowing the door to close finally upon the fictive radiance of the text, and betake ourselves either to structuralist hermeneutics of the type practised by Jean Starobinski, which Kermode admires in Lecture VI for its austere taking-to-heart of Spinoza's dictum, combining it, perhaps, with some form of reductive criticism of the Marxist or the Foucaultian variety; or else to the celebration of incoherence and fortuitousness, as offering a release from slavery to 'codes implanted in our minds by the arbitrary fiat of a culture or an institution', which Kermode fastidiously refrains from endorsing on page 54 ('There are current at present much bolder opinions than this one . . .').

Is there no other option? I think there is one.[3] The instructed Outsider should reject what I have called Kermode's second premise, for the excellent reason that it is false. The meaning of a text need not be sought by endeavouring to 'process it into coherence' with some explanatory paraphrase or other. On the contrary, it may equally well be sought by investigating the points at which, and attempting to understand the reasons why, a text resists specific attempts at paraphrase. Textual solipsists will want to argue, of course, that 'the meaning of a text' cannot be sought in this way either. Their position is that the whole notion of 'the meaning of a text' is defective, and should be discarded, because meaning, or latent sense, is a product of interpretation. But Kermode's arguments for textual solipsism, because they work by raising doubts about whether constraints internal to the text can determine a unique paraphrase, can only work against an opponent who is committed to the Insider's strategy of trying to discover a latent sense capable of being expressed as a paraphrase or 'reading'. They can have no force, that is, against an Outsider who has discarded what I have called Kermode's second premise. In order to block *that* move the textual solipsist needs to shift his ground and argue for a far stronger and hence less plausible claim. He needs to argue that the Outsider's project of investigating the points at which texts resist specific attempts at explanatory paraphrase is as inevitably doomed to failure as the Insider's, although for different reasons, because there just are no such points: that all the constraints upon interpretation emanate from sources 'external to the text' in the sense of being freely variable from interpreter to interpreter; from 'culturally-imposed codes', 'institutional requirements', 'fore-understandings' and the like.

Kermode appears at times to flirt with a position as radical as this. It is certainly strongly hinted at by his suggestion (143) that we 'know' (my inverted commas) that we cannot read the gospel of Mark 'as a work of irony or a confidence trick' only because 'We have acquired fore-understandings which exclude such readings'. And it seems overt in his later remark that narratives 'may be narratives only because of our impudent intervention, and susceptible of interpretation only by our hermeneutic tricks' (Kermode 1979: 145). But elsewhere in the text the externality of the constraints upon interpretation is not so strongly insisted upon. Thus on page 13 we find Kermode making room for what I suppose is the basic hunch I am defending here, by granting that 'texts interpret, or deceive, their interpreters, who should know they do so, and make allowances for it'. And on page 36, dealing with what Augustine and the Fathers made of the parable of the Samaritan, we find, 'No doubt the parable has a carnal sense which does not vary materially; its spiritual sense is not so constant.' To admit that carnal senses do not vary materially is to admit that there are some constraints upon interpretation which are not variable from interpreter to interpreter; constraints to which an interpreter does not force the text to submit at the behest of a 'hermeneutic community' or his own 'fore-understandings', but rather constraints to which he himself must submit, in common with every other would-be interpreter, as the price of finding himself confronted with a *text*, rather than a string of enigmatic marks. Of course these constraints too are founded in *social conventions*, and recent critics do sometimes write as if they thought that the mere fact that natural languages are *conventional* systems of communication were sufficient in itself to establish the textual solipsist's contention that all constraints upon interpretation are external to the text in the sense of being freely variable from interpreter to interpreter. However, a moment's thought is sufficient to show that this cannot be right. A system of constraints upon interpretation (however conventional in character) which was not, at some level, invariant from interpreter to interpreter would simply not serve to constitute a natural language (there would be no way of ensuring that any sentence of the language would express the same proposition to different speakers, for instance). All talk of 'language', or 'texts', or 'interpretation' in such a context, indeed, would be nugatory, because it would be vacuous.

Kermode is clearly right, therefore, to grant the community and the invariance of the carnal: the contrary view is incoherent. The question is, though, at what level, exactly, does the carnal end and the spiritual begin? Is it just *the meanings of the* (English or Greek) *words* that is carnal, that defeats all attempts by pious Insiders to meddle with them (as Kermode thinks is the case with all attempts to change *hina* to *hoti* at Mark 4: 11–12)? Or does the autonomy of the text, its power to send our impertinent suggestions packing, extend to higher levels of textual organisation than that? The answer, I think, is pretty clearly going to be a matter of degree and of arguing out the pros and cons for particular cases and levels of discourse. My own feeling is that while emblem, metonymy, symbol, upon which quite a lot of Kermode's argument in Lectures I and III focuses and depends, shade off into the spiritual, the structure of narrative and things like the relationship between plot, action and character (despite the very interesting and telling things which Kermode has to say about this, which would open up another chapter of argument) remain rather solidly carnal. But if anything at all in narrative is impervious to our 'hermeneutic tricks', then it remains permanently possible that our hermeneutic endeavours and the fore-understandings which motivate and direct them may find themselves running into a brick wall. Such an experience, while painful and in one way negative, may not, as Sir Karl Popper has argued in other contexts, be entirely devoid of cognitive gains. My suggestion, in short, is that in literature as in science we escape from the limpid darkness of solipsism not at the point at which the triumphal chariots of theory rumble to final victory over the phenomena or the text, but rather precisely at the point of failure, of confusion, of silence and falling short.

IV

By way of conclusion I shall offer a necessarily brief and sketchy example of how a resolutely Outsiderish approach to reading narrative might develop in an actual case. The text I shall choose is a notoriously scandalous one, *The Taming of the Shrew*. The *Shrew* is nowadays considered a difficult play to come to grips with, because on the face of it it tramples upon our century's new-found moral belief in the equality of the sexes. Katherina's final speech in particular, in which as we tend to see it she knuckles under, strikes many people as profoundly shocking. It would be nice, therefore, if we could simply dismiss the play as propaganda for an outmoded and wrong conception of relationships between the sexes; if we could get it out of our minds and finish with it by exposing the power-relations it serves and propagates. Unfortunately the play will not altogether play ball with this vision of what it is about. For a start Petruchio does not take the obvious step of simply beating Katherina into silence and submission. Instead he chooses to behave like a lunatic: in effect to outmatch her at her own game of revolt against the ordered structures of society which she sees, rightly, as demanding (at least the appearance of) silence and submission of her. Certainly his strategy disorients her, removing from life the least scrap of rational structure and Renaissance decorum which she might use as a basis for a revolt of her own, but beyond making her hungry, tired, uncomfortable and infuriated he does not physically harm her. Secondly, the obedience in which he schools her serves her ends as well as his. Petruchio's yoke is easy: all he demands of her is that she fall in trustingly and unquestioningly with his nonsense. Having finally paid that modest price she finds herself delivered from the oppression of her family, presiding at a feast instead of kept in confinement as something approaching a madwoman, and herself beating her superior sister Bianca at Bianca's own chosen social game of being the good, socially acceptable daughter. She has, it might almost seem, been led by Petruchio (whom we are beginning to be tempted to see as the practitioner of a crazy kind of therapy) back into life, from a fatally self-destructive strategy of living to one in which she has a real chance of formulating and achieving some goals of her own.

A perfectly possible reaction to this, of course, would be to say: All right, *The Taming of the Shrew* is a *cunning and subtle* defence of a Renaissance view of male supremacy. But even if one admits its subtlety it is still *false to life*: in real life a fortune-hunter of the kind Petruchio advertises himself to be, having gotten hold of Katherina's dowry, *would* simply have beaten her into submission, and the story would have ended much sooner. So saying we take a stand precisely upon the question of what options exhaust the possibilities of 'real life': either a strict equality between the sexes, as our theory-laden self-image, not our ambiguous and constantly shifting practice, defines that, or else male domination founded upon brutality. The whole trouble is that the play persuasively elaborates a further possibility which questions and undermines the putative exhaustiveness of those very options, which is why we dislike the play, feel uncomfortable with it, and fear it.

All this is very summary, no doubt. But suppose an exceptionally generous opponent were to find it persuasive, and were to say by way of conceding: All right; I grant that *The Taming of the Shrew* is not merely a subtle but a convincing defence of a Renaissance conception of how relationships between the sexes should be ordered. Would this be any truer? Wouldn't, that is, any imaginable defender of anything one could plausibly represent as 'a Renaissance conception of' the proper subordination of wives to husbands see just as much scandal in the play, see in it just as much of an attempt to question self-evident proprieties and decencies, as feminists do today?[4] The 'good daughter', the model of Renaissance feminine propriety, is surely Bianca. But equally surely the message of the sub-plot and the wager scene is the familiar comic one that the conventional proprieties she represents are hollow: Bianca is obedient neither to her father nor to her husband. Then again Petruchio is a poor paradigm of that Adamic paternal authority which according to Filmer invests the King and should reign also in the household. He does not behave with the distance, the sure and authoritative wielding of a divinely and legally constituted right, which that conception of paternal authority entails. Instead he enters into a duel of riot and misrule with Katherina: a duel conducted on her ground, played out according to strategies she has determined, his frenzies following and matching hers fit for fit. As he says, this is how a falconer tames a hawk; but as we know from T. H. White's personal account of that process, it is a painful one for the falconer as well as for the falcon. He must sit up all night if need be with his bird, for if he sleeps he has lost her. There is love and self-denial in it as well as mastery: it is as if the magistrate, instead of merely sitting in judgment upon the criminal and sentencing him to a whipping or the wheel, were to go alone into his cell and wrestle with him.

Finally, what emerges from the duel between them is less like the humility and submission proper to the wife of *bien-pensant* Renaissance theory than a collusive and unholy alliance of one enemy of conventional decorum with another. Katherina's ringing defence of meekness and submissiveness in woman is not faltering enough by half, is altogether too flamboyant, in fact, for its sentiments not to give rise to some suspicion of conscious parody; especially when one remembers that the thicker she lays it on the more she triumphs over a sister at whose hands she has doubtless endured much, and even more so when one recalls

the immediate grounds she has for appropriating these conventional sentiments as a convenient means of expressing self-
approval of a type wholly foreign to their overt content: after all,
as a direct result of her new-found willingness to engage in
parodically operatic flights of submission the Katherina-Petruchio
gang has just taken the table, as it were, for twenty crowns and
Bianca's reputation, not to mention the further twenty thousand
which has just been added to the original wager by the marvelling
Baptista. Has Katherina seen the light she preaches, or has she
just decided that Petruchio's apparent nonsense and clowning,
daft and excessive as it may seem to more conventional souls,
may be trusted in general to conceal some sound calculation
which will not leave her own interests out of account? And how
far does that thought itself have the seeds of love and trust as
well as calculation in it? Are they not, after all, two of a kind?
In any event the magical zone from within which Katherina and
Petruchio confront their dumbfounded fellow-feasters does seem
to have something that one might want to call radiance about it:
the radiance of an Elsewhere very remote from those conventional moral pieties about submission and paternal rule in whose
breakdown into recrimination, loss and disorder the other characters stand at this point enmeshed.

The possibilities which the play explores, that is, can equally
well be seen as undermining a paternalist conception of how the
world divides up exhaustively into possibilities – either the copy-
book proprieties of paternal rule or else shrewish incivility and
domestic disorder – which complements and confronts the feminist construal of the possible options I mentioned earlier. Of course
the second half of what I have just said about the play might be
taken as a way of 'recuperating' it, as people say, for feminism,
just as the first half might be taken as a way of recuperating it
for paternalism. The point is, though, that a feminism or a
paternalism capable of accepting these as recuperations would
have had to have moved a little from earlier and cruder stances.

My thought is, in effect, that the text – the carnal text – stays
where it is, unmoving, while readers turn it about, or turn about
it, each trying to subdue it to his or her way of looking at things,
and each finding in it a meaning which is 'new', and specific to
that particular reader, only in the sense that it expresses the
commerce of the unmoving carnal text with the special set of
fore-understandings which he or she has addressed to it. This,

as Gabriel Josipovici pointed out to me, is rather reminiscent of a verse in the *Pirkhe Avot (Sayings of the Fathers)* 5: 25: 'Turn it and turn it again, for everything is in it.' But this again suggests a different understanding from Kermode's of the point of *midrash* in general: not to impose closure on the text in the interests of the particular type of coherence required by some set of institutional requirements, but to leave it, precisely, stonily and carnally open in order to leave it its power to astonish and confute: to see what it will illuminate next. I have a suspicion that some deep division between Jewish and (at least some kinds of) Christian religious sensibility may lie at the root of these two ways of looking at the business of interpretation.[5]

This brings me to my conclusion, and for one last time to Nietzsche's enthusiasm for 'perspective and illusion'. In my role as self-appointed Outsider I have been content to remain brooding upon the surface of Shakespeare's text. In accordance with Keats' excellent advice to avoid irritable grasping after fact and certainty, I have foregone any attempt to grope beneath that surface for a paraphrasable 'meaning' or 'message'. All I have done is to examine in some detail (though for reasons of space not all that much) some of the obstacles which the text, as it presents itself on the most superficial level to any callow Outsider with a seat in the pit but without a hermeneutic key to bless himself with, sets in the path of attempts to equip it with a 'message', either a paternalist or a feminist one. And I have tried to show that such a purely negative, purely on-the-surface enterprise, besides giving the play, and ourselves, room to breathe, permits us to enter into a relationship with the play which allows it to criticise us, to elicit from us some saving modesty before it; some sense that the fore-understandings in terms of which we endeavour to shape it to our liking might themselves come to appear defective under a light – a radiance if you like – which it has power to shed upon them. Such knowledge as narrative fictions can grant us, knowledge of the incapacity of our fore-understandings to exhaust, as they claim to do, the possibilities of things, may not as I said earlier feel much like knowledge, but is knowledge all the same.

Now for a parting glance at Nietzsche. Half the time Nietzsche talks as if he has dispensed with the notion of truth; it is a 'mobile army of metaphors', and so on. The other half he displays a touching faith in the continued availability of the familiar con-

cept of truth as correspondence between what is asserted and
what is the case. The reason, I think, is this. Nietzsche wants to
say that no human theory, or vision of how things stand in
general, comes with a transcendent guarantee. The cheerfulness,
in such contrast to Kermode's prevailing mood of disappointment, with which Nietzsche embraces 'the necessity of error'
comes of course from that thought: no transcendent reality con-
strains us; we are free, we can create. But Nietzsche also wants
to say that the construction of any habitable human order
involves *work*, and work of a more than merely practical and
physical kind: that the exercise of the Will to Power is not *effortless*
because arbitrary, in the way it would be if the choice of a set
of values and social arrangements were simply insulated in principle from all contact with reality. There is a kind of sadness,
from which the eighteenth century suffered a good deal, which
comes from too strong a conviction that the world is transparent
to reductive reason; that nothing can stop the spade of theory
from exposing the roots of both human and natural reality. And
there is another, contrary kind, which comes from the suspicion,
nourished by philosophical scepticism and relativism, that we can
make *just anything we like* of reality, that as creators of the human
order we operate in a vacuum. One of the enduring merits of
Nietzsche, as in related ways of Keats and Blake, is that he offers,
patchily but on the whole effectively, defences against both these
ways of depressing art and ourselves. One of the worrying things
about a good deal of current critical theory is that it seems at
times anxious to reanimate both of them at once. But then, one of
the things that gives such philosophical bugbears their perennial
power is that they can easily appear to be entailed by very much
more interesting and substantial lines of thought from which, in
fact, they do not necessarily follow at all.[6]

Notes

1. It is perhaps worth emphasising that the fore-understandings I
   have in mind are, as will appear, fore-understandings concerning
   natural – that is, extratextual – possibility; not merely *formal* expectations concerning the conventions governing genre, topos and
   other formal features of the text. The challenges posed by literary
   texts to such fore-understandings also do not, as I see it, amount
   merely to disconfirmations of such purely formal, text-based expec-

tations. I am not, that is, just talking about the phenomenon of *ostranenie* as that is usually understood; though at the same time I think there is good evidence that some Russian Formalists, Shklovskii for instance, actually *meant* by the term something closer to what I am talking about here than to the purely formal processes of disconfirmation to which it is generally taken to refer. (See, for instance, Steiner 1984: 49)

2. Here my argument parallels that of my friend and ex-colleague A. D. Nuttall in *A New Mimesis* (1983: 55 *et seq*).

3. I think for that matter that there is another way of reading Kafka's parable (as there more or less has to be on Kermode's principles). In my *midrash* the doorkeeper's authority represents the authority of our structural fore-understandings. When he says, 'this door was meant for you, and now I am closing it for ever' what he means is 'this door was meant for you, and you might have passed through it had you not, by clinging to your fore-understandings, raised up doorkeepers to bar your way'.

4. Catherine Belsey explores this possibility in 'Disrupting Sexual Difference: meaning and gender in the comedies', in Drakakis (1985).

5. I find myself confirmed in this thought by an article by Rabbi Dr Jonathan Sacks, Principal of Jews College, London (1989: 30): 'Rabbinic Judaism is a protest against privileged hierarchies of knowledge. It had no place for the prophet's revelation that silences argument by its self-authentication. . . . The culture of argument had to defend itself against a succession of over-authoritarian establishments. One religious head of the community, Rabban Gamliel, was deposed for his refusal to let a contrary opinion be heard. . . . A leading theme of rabbinic thought is that Torah is acquired only through dialogue, between teacher and disciple and between colleagues. Dialogue constantly discloses new interpretations. "It is impossible for there to be a house of study without new discoveries." Through argument Judaism is renewed.'

6. This essay will appear in the author's forthcoming *Narrative and Reality: Literature and the Limits of Theory*.

4

'Secular Surrogates': Frank Kermode and the Idea of the Critic

Patrick Parrinder

There are those who argue that the history of criticism is a history of error; but if we stay within the tradition, rather than seek to overthrow it, we shall have to say rather that it is a history of accommodations, of attempts to earn the privilege of access to that kingdom of the larger existence which is in our time the secular surrogate of another Kingdom whose horizon is no longer within our range.

Frank Kermode, 'Prologue' to *Essays on Fiction: 1971–82*
(Kermode 1983a: 31–2)

Less than a year after the 1916 Easter Rising, Ezra Pound committed himself to the rather breathtaking pronouncement that 'If more people had read *The Portrait* and certain stories in Joyce's *Dubliners* there might have been less recent trouble in Ireland. A clear diagnosis is never without its value' (Pound 1917, Read 1968: 90). I will start with the observation that, if more people had read the sequence of Frank Kermode's works beginning with *The Classic* (1975), the recent controversies over literary theory might have been more productive. At the theoretical level, *The Classic* and its successors offer a clear and helpful diagnosis of the assumptions and underlying ambience of present-day literary criticism: what disturbs me, however, is that for much of the time Kermode appears to be perfectly content with what he sees. So towards the end of this essay I shall perhaps stir up a little trouble myself, and will ask whether Kermode's idea of the critic *is* in fact an idea of the critic, or of something else. But let me begin by affirming his value as a diagnostician.

A surrogate, from the Latin *surrogare*, was traditionally a deputy – specifically, the deputy appointed by a bishop. The qualities that literary texts and the institutions of literary study may be felt to 'share with the sacred' (Kermode *Forms of Attention* 1985a: 62) have been a consistent theme of Kermode's writing in the last fifteen years, if not earlier. He has invoked the scriptural analogy for literary works as a means of reconciling, on the one hand, his powerful urge to be understood as the exponent of a distinctively modern sensibility and, on the other, his conservative attachment to historical and institutional continuities. For Kermode, modern literature and literary commentary are privileged both as a basis of intellectual power (it is taken for granted by Kermode and his fellow-editor in *The Literary Guide to the Bible*, for example, that a modern reading of the Bible would necessarily be a literary reading), and as a site and source of spiritual virtue. Kermode's understanding of the good has been articulated with specific reference to literary study (see for example *Forms of Attention* 1985a: 91–2), and the endings of several of his books have the form of a benediction. At the same time, the image of virtue which the contemplation of literature affords is, he admits, only a shadow; for if in our modern secular societies literature and its institutions turn out to possess some degree of mythic or magical aura, this must be as a result of surrogacy rather than direct incarnation. Literature deputises, we may say, for the sacred reality which in secular society is no longer accessible to us.

If this notion of literary surrogacy is to be more than the idiosyncratic statement of a personal faith or vision on Kermode's part, it will be necessary to show that metaphysical premises of the same order as those that he invokes are implicit in other representative versions of literary theory today. The way to do this, I believe, is to examine the idea of *interpretation*, as it is developed both in Kermode's own writing and in a broad spectrum of contemporary theory. Interpretation is one of a triad of terms – the others being the *canon* and the *literary institution* – which define the scope of the Kermodean scriptural analogy. As a general rule, whenever he outlines the purpose and function of criticism he tacitly redefines criticism as interpretation. The purpose of criticism, he wrote in 1983, is 'briefly, illumination' (Kermode 1983a: 5); illumination rather than judgment or appreciation. *The Sense of an Ending* begins with the statement that 'It is not expected of critics as it is of poets that they should help us to make sense of our lives; they are bound only to attempt the

lesser feat of making sense of the ways we try to make sense of
our lives' (1967: 3). Whether or not that is genuinely a 'lesser
feat' (to a structuralist it would presumably be the primary feat)
it is unquestionably a task of interpretation. In *The Classic* again,
it is interpretation, not criticism, which is the 'instrument' of the
'renovations of the classic, in one epoch after another' (1983b: 7).
The special force that Kermode gives to interpretation is further
evident at the beginning of *The Genesis of Secrecy*, where he speaks
of the division of readers into insiders and outsiders, the former
privileged to have access to the hidden and latent senses of the
text, the latter condemned to make do with the manifest 'and
pay a supreme penalty for doing so' (1979: xii, 3). The fact that
he has frequently voiced a sense of obligation towards, and even
of allegiance to, the outsiders must be weighed against Kermode's
habit of writing as an inveterate insider (or would-be insider) –
as one for whom the drama and pathos of life itself can be
expressed in epistemological terms, so that the hermeneutic task
and the likelihood of hermeneutic failure come to stand as the
horizons of moral experience. 'Hot for secrets, our only conversation may be with guardians who know less and see less than
we can; and our sole hope and pleasure is in the perception of
a momentary radiance, before the door of disappointment is finally shut on us' (1979: 145), writes Kermode in his most parabolic
style at the end of *The Genesis of Secrecy*.

In this moment of visionary pessimism, Kermode produces a
reductive and Kafkaesque vision of the world as will and
interpretation; but elsewhere, in more sanguine and more professional moods, he endorses the modern ideal of 'symptomatic
reading' as the key to all texts (and to all mythologies). What he
calls 'Our era of interpretation' began with that epitome of successful hermeneutics – the dramatic solution of a mystery which
had baffled all previous researchers – Freud's *Interpretation of
Dreams* (Kermode 1983a: 30). The idea that modern interpretation
necessarily privileges the symptomatic and latent over the
intended and manifest is central to the argument in *The Classic*;
far from insisting on the need for painstaking historical research
to recover the original meaning of the classic work, as Schleierma-
cher and E. D. Hirsch had done, Kermode viewed the classic as
a 'more or less open text from which new readings may be
generated' (1983b: 75–6). The modern reading of the classic was
characterised by 'plurality of interpretations' and 'extreme variety

of response' (118–19), and the texts felt to be more hospitable to variety of response were the ones most likely to be granted classic status. Kermode's permissive and pluralist approach to interpretation involves the rejection both of traditional philological criteria (such as would permit a firm distinction to be made between 'reading' and 'misreading' the text) and of the singular master-codes associated with Marxist and Freudian symptomatic reading. The classic, or any text, offers no specially privileged set of symptoms, nor is there any one correct way of understanding those symptoms. It is in *The Classic* that Kermode emerges as an ideologist of the modern institution of literary study, which opens its doors indiscriminately to Marxist, Freudian, Lacanian, New-Critical, structuralist, feminist, deconstructionist, and all other systems of interpretation. His attachment is not to any particular interpretative system but to the notions of the canon of 'classic' (or plurally interpretable) texts and of the professional practice of interpretation.

The redefinition of criticism as interpretation seems to me to be characteristic of contemporary literary theory as a whole, though some individual theorists would naturally dispute this point. Kermode knows both that the horizon of most contemporary literary study is one of interpretation (not criticism), and that the *'illusion of the single right reading is possible no longer'* (1983a: 102). Where symptomatic interpretation does serve the illusion of a single right reading (as for example in many versions of Freudian interpretation), it is relatively easy to show that the interpretative procedure is based on an implicit metaphysical premise rivalling but also paralleling the premise of Kermode's own theory. In other words, such methods necessarily approach the text as the surrogate of some more profound reality which only the skilled interpreter can tease out of it. For Freud and Marx, texts, like dreams, neurotic symptoms and political ideologies, only *seem* to be intelligible at the level of manifest content: 'Actually, they have no meaning without interpretation. To understand *is* to interpret.' (Sontag 1967: 7; see also Olsen 1987: 202). And once the prior reality or textual 'unconscious' has been brought to light, the process of interpretation is complete and no further activity of judgment or appreciation is needed.

There are, however, various contemporary positions which reject, or claim to reject, the horizon of interpretation while continuing to privilege the latent (or, as they might prefer to say,

the structural) features of texts. The argument seems to me to
polarise around what Kermode calls the chimera of the single
right reading. Since such a reading may, as in Empson and the
New Critics, encompass a number of alternative readings,[1] and
since most declared opponents of singular reading tend to back
their own readings, the choice between the principles of singular
and plural interpretation is not a straightforward one. The deconstructionists have done most to repudiate the notion of singular
reading, and have done so in the knowledge that as a consequence any form of meaning may be imperilled, or as they would
say, deferred. According to Derrida the 'reassemblage of the
totality of the text into the truth of its meaning' annuls the 'open
and productive displacement of the textual chain' (Derrida 1980;
Krupnick 1987: 10). Paul de Man has similarly argued that 'a
deconstruction always has as its target to reveal the existence of
hidden articulations and fragmentations within assured monadic
totalities' (de Man 1979; Olsen 1987: 206). I would argue that the
effect of deconstructionist rhetorical analyses is certainly one of
bringing to light an 'unconscious', in the sense of a field of
repressed contradictions which subverts and disrupts the manifest pretensions of the discourse. Derridean deconstruction apparently denies any metaphysical Presence in the text only to discover behind it, as it were in surrogate form, the anarchic 'secrets
in the heart of reason' (Handelman 1987: 120), the suppressed
aporias and contradictions on which the whole of Western
thought is said to be based.

Two other prominent modern opponents of interpretation have
been Roland Barthes and Susan Sontag. In fact, it would be
possible to read some of Kermode's later writing as a covert
polemic directed at these two. In 'The Death of the Author'
Barthes sought to unleash an 'anti-theological activity' of reading
and writing by abolishing the figures of the Author, the Critic,
and, of course, of Interpretation. 'Everything is to be disen-
tangled, nothing deciphered . . . the space of writing is to be
ranged over, not pierced; writing ceaselessly posits meaning
ceaselessly to evaporate it, carrying out a systematic exemption
of meaning' (Barthes 1977: 147). The apparent theoretical consequence (as we see in Barthes's later work) is to abandon reading
for meaning in favour of reading for pleasure. Similarly, Susan
Sontag argued in her essay 'Against Interpretation' that criticism
of modern art should revert to the tasks of formal analysis and

surface description, to a recovery of the sensory immediacy of the works concerned; what was needed was not a hermeneutics of art but an erotics. 'Against Interpretation' was written in response to what Sontag saw as a 'flight from interpretation', a retreat from interpretable content in avant-garde painting, poetry and cinema. First published in 1964, this manifesto could have been taken as an expression of the traditional conflict between the producers and the appraisers of contemporary art; but it also turned the tables on interpretation, unmasking it as an ideology or historically-situated technique rather than as a universal project of human understanding:

> interpretation is not (as most people assume) an absolute value, a gesture of mind situated in some timeless realm of capabilities. Interpretation must itself be evaluated, within a historical view of human consciousness. In some cultural contexts, interpretation is a liberating act. It is a means of revising, of transvaluing, of escaping the dead past. In other cultural contexts, it is reactionary, impertinent, cowardly, stifling. . . . Today is such a time, when the project of interpretation is largely reactionary, stifling. . . . In a culture whose already classical dilemma is the hypertrophy of the intellect at the expense of energy and sensual capability, interpretation is the revenge of the intellect upon art. (Sontag 1967: 7)

Whether Sontag's 'erotics of art' could lead to a genuinely non-interpretative criticism of literature cannot be at issue here; but she is one of very few contemporary critics who openly privileges evaluation over interpretation. I suggest, however, that we may regard Frank Kermode's writing of the 1970s and early 1980s as a kind of cumulative manifesto *for* interpretation – one which recuperates and validates interpretation not only by conceding its necessary plurality, but by removing it from the sphere of cultural politics which Sontag invokes by her references to a cultural context. Interpretation, for Kermode, is simply not subject to periodic transvaluation in the way that Sontag suggests. Instead, it is one of humanity's most stable and long-term projects.

For Kermode the project of interpretation presupposes a canon of texts, although in his first book on this theme, *The Classic*, he does not call it that. At this stage he was preoccupied with the relationship between the ancient and modern classics, and not with the scriptural analogy for literary study. His archetypal ancient classic is the *Aeneid*, a work which Kermode tries to hold in balance with such 'modern classics' as *The House of the Seven Gables* and *Wuthering Heights*. Virgil gave birth to an 'imperial classic', the 'voice of a metropolitan whole of which we are but provincial parts' (1983b: 18); what can this possibly have in common with such de-centred, ambiguous, and manifestly 'provincial' masterpieces as those of Hawthorne and Emily Brontë? The expression of feelings of awe in front of the imperial classics is, of course, far less characteristic of present-day literary academics than of the Victorian and Edwardian 'Men of Letters' (of whom Kermode has lately written with considerable affection). Arnold Bennett, in his book *Literary Taste* published at the turn of the century, instructed the would-be student of literature that 'If you differ with a classic, it is you who are wrong, and not the book' (Bennett nd: 33). What Kermode rather remarkably manages to do is to reconcile this point of view with its opposite: the post-structuralist position that we all differ, and we all differently differ, with the classics. His argument, crudely summarised, is that the classic text is one that we repeatedly (though differently) come back to, valuing it precisely on account of the 'surplus of signifier' or scope for plurality of interpretations which it uniquely affords. If the *Aeneid* is to remain a classic for modern readers, it must be found to be as open to reinterpretation as *The House of the Seven Gables* or *Wuthering Heights;* otherwise it would become a mere historical document, or monument in the history of taste. *The Classic* ends with what I take to be a statement of faith that the old 'imperial classics' will not be found wanting in terms of the possession of 'surplus of signifier'; but he says nothing of the educational considerations likely to be paramount in any discussion of whether the *Aeneid* will (or even, dare I say it, whether it should) continue to attract a significant readership.

In his next book, *The Genesis of Secrecy*, and in a crucial essay on 'Institutional Control of Interpretation' (1979; in 1983a: 168–84) Kermode introduced the triad of *canon, interpretation* and *literary institution* which forms the basis of his mature account of the nature of literary study. *The Genesis of Secrecy* is devoted to a literary interpretation of St Mark's gospel, and in it Kermode speaks of interpreters as forming a 'guild' (1979: 2), and of readers as being divided into clerisy and laity. In 'Institutional Control of Interpretation', the parallels between the literary and scriptural canons and between the activities of literary study and of the traditional Christian and Rabbinical interpretation of texts are made manifest. The Church, Kermode writes, is the 'most exemplary' of institutions with a primary duty to interpret texts and to nominate a certain body of texts as deserving or requiring exegesis (1983a: 171–2). Literature – the modern surrogate institution – 'like its senior, though much less effectively, . . . controls the choice of canonical texts, limits their interpretation, and attends to the training of those who will inherit the presumption of institutional competence' (1983a: 176). In his later work, *Forms of Attention*, Kermode explores the process by which an individual work comes to be incorporated into the canon, and the effects which flow from this. Survival outside the canon is a haphazard and arbitrary process; once inside it, survival is guaranteed by the medium of commentary. Furnished with 'the kinds of reading they require if they are to keep their immediacy at any moment', the works in the canon enjoy both permanent value and perpetual modernity. Interpretation, charged both with preserving the canon and demonstrating the indispensability of the institution it serves, takes on a peculiar intensity:

> [Canonical works] are inexhaustibly full of senses only partly available to any previous reading, and the cumulative influence of tradition upon new readings is fitful and partial. Every verse is occultly linked, in ways to be researched, with all the others; the text is a world system. And since the canonical work is fixed in time but applicable to all time, it has figural qualities not to be detected, save at an appropriate moment in the future. Interpretations may be regarded not as modern increments but rather as discoveries of original meanings hitherto hidden; so that, together with the written text, these interpretations constitute a total object of which the text is but a part or version: an Oral Torah, or Oral Tradition, preserved by an apostolic institution, equal in authority to and coeval with the written. (Kermode 1985a: 75)

That, then, is the mirror in which Kermode asks us to recognise the contemporary institution of literary interpretation and criticism; and in many ways I do recognise it. The devoutness and intensity of modern exegesis, the revelatory style in which its

results are presented, and the institution's obsessive and monotonous return to a core of texts which might seem scarcely in
need of further elucidation – these are all features which invite
the scriptural analogy. The attempts of deconstructionists and
other self-styled opponents of canonicity to install their own not
particularly innovative canons, and the reverence they demand
and elicit towards these canons, provide us with further evidence.
But the scriptural analogy is only an analogy: and, in some
respects, a mystifying one.

   The fact is that today's interpreters of literary texts are not
the lineal descendants of some 'apostolic institution', or self-
perpetuating body of devotees, stretching back across the Christian era to the birth of Judaism. Instead they are, almost without
exception, teachers, functionaries within the modern educational
system. Western education has, in general, a very different myth
of origin from the one that Kermode invokes. Already in the
nineteenth century Matthew Arnold set culture on a Hebraic-
Hellenic base: not only was modern education deeply influenced
by the clerks and priests, but it also privileged science and philosophy over theology, and found a place for reasoned debate as
well as for priestly indoctrination. The institution to which most
modern literary interpreters profess allegiance is nowadays
known as the 'academy' (not as the seminary). It could be that
a more inclusive myth, taking account perhaps of what we owe
to the Arabs as well as to the Jews, Greeks and Romans, is now
needed. Yet the ritual invocation of myths of origin, whether
Kermode's or any other, can easily serve as an obstacle to clear
thinking about literary study and the humanities in general. As
the historian Keith Thomas has recently written, 'Virtually all the
reasons which originally led to the introduction of the humanities
into the curriculum have become obsolete. The nature of the
subjects themselves has radically changed and so have the persons who teach them and those to whom they are taught'
(Thomas 1988: 19). It is this new class of educators, and not
Kermode's priestly acolytes, who are responsible for literary
interpretation today; and interpretation itself is not a timeless rite
but the preferred form of research in a branch of the modern
humanities.

   Keith Thomas goes on to pose the question whether the
humanities are now regarded as a field of hermetic learning, or
as 'an essential training for the active life outside the universities'

(16). In this regard it is worth recalling that Freud and Marx, the scientific and scholarly precursors of our modern interpretative systems, were supremely attuned to the life of praxis, the one as a doctor and the other as a political revolutionary. Their literary successors are not so attuned, and Kermode as an apologist for modern interpretation seems to glory in the absence of any 'active' dimension: interpretation is apparently an end in itself. 'The institution with which we have to deal is the professional community which interprets secular literature and teaches others to do so', he writes in 'Institutional Control of Interpretation' (1983a: 168). Like a Church, this institution is 'much concerned with questions of canon, and wont . . . to distinguish sharply between initiate and uninitiate readings'; and it displays 'the necessary conservatism of a learned institution' (1983a: 171–2). The main difference between the Church and the literary academy is that the latter is much less successful in imposing its authority, though since 'we are waiting for [institutional] consensus to re-form' (1979: 137), there is some hope that this difference may be eliminated in the near future.

Now what I note in these essays of Kermode's is the absence of any reference to the teaching function of the 'literary institution' – the only teaching that he mentions is what is necessary to perpetuate the institution's own membership. The ideal of preparing pupils for life outside the universities – though this, it may be argued, is what most of today's literary interpreters are or ought to be doing during a large proportion of their professional lives – is no longer mentioned. I certainly do not think that Kermode has abandoned this ideal. In a recent interview, for example, he told Imre Salusinszky that 'Fond as I was of Paul de Man, one thing that I differed from him very violently about was the notion that the study of literature should be confined to very small groups of people' (Salusinszky 1987: 109 (Interview with Frank Kermode); see also Kermode 1985b). That expresses a consistent sentiment on Kermode's part, but I have looked for a theoretical defence of the need for widespread (not to mention universal) literary education in his writings, and I have not found it. A Church does not merely concern itself with the training of theologians and seminarists, but Kermode's literary institution sounds as if it has little or nothing – except for the wry concession that we are all, in an ultimate sense, outsiders – to offer to the uninitiated. Certainly a defence of the continuance of literary education outside the elite universities could be, and to some extent ought to be, mounted from Kermode's standpoint of secular surrogacy and the scriptural analogy, or what (echoing Derrida) he has called our 'desire for a realm'; but in practice the defence of this aspect of literary education has been left in the hands of more manifestly secular critics.

I would even suppose that Kermode may have a bit of a conscience about this. For example, he has sometimes written about the 'sacred' texts of the modern literary institution in airily cynical fashion. Here he is on Joyce's *Ulysses:* 'The institution controlling literary interpretation thinks well of the book; and I, as a reasonably docile member of it, endorse its valuation; . . . [it] offers certain opportunities to interpreters – opportunities which, fortunately for one's younger colleagues, have every appearance of being inexhaustible' (1979: 49). It's nice to know that there are jobs for the boys and girls, but shouldn't Kermode pay more attention to the unprecedented social and economic forces which could be held responsible for today's demand for plurality of interpretations? Priests, monks and rabbis were not faced with the demand to 'Publish or perish'. But having said that, one must add that Kermode's praise of the literary institution coincides with certain twinges of radical unease on his part about the inward-looking nature of its current membership. Writing of Botticelli in *Forms of Attention*, he observes that the ability of a work to become part of the canon depends not only on its intrinsic qualities but on chance and on the partisanship of what Arnold Bennett referred to as the 'passionate few'.[2] In 'The Decline of the Man of Letters' he laments the passing of the Victorian and Edwardian 'bookmen', those passionate insiders who conscientiously sought to purvey literary education to a wide public. And in *History and Value* he challenges canonical valuations and revives at least one distinctly non-canonical work, Stephen Haggard's novel *Nya*. *History and Value* proclaims Auden's 'Spain 1937' (which the author eventually excluded from his own canon) as 'our best political poem except for Marvell's' (1988: 78), and reviews the proletarian literature of the 1930s as a kind of love story, a romance both spiritual and (at times) very physical between sections of the intellectual bourgeoisie and the proletariat. *History and Value* itself is a kind of literary love-story, a confession of a secret taste for uncanonised books, and it could not be further removed from his cold acknowledgment of the canonical status of *Ulysses*. At the conclusion he reminds us that 'there is no magic by which immanent value ensures survival' (1988: 145), but *History and Value* pays scrupulous attention to some aesthetically and politically unfashionable texts, thereby implying a certain faith in what Matthew Arnold might have called the 'natural magic' attaching to their immanent value. Here Kermode has joined the passionate few, and has thrown aside the caution of the trained and institutionally-controlled interpreter.

In his earlier book *Continuities* Kermode contrasted the criticism of Northrop Frye and R. P. Blackmur, writing of Blackmur that he was 'essentially a very unsystematic critic and believed, dangerously but correctly, that criticism is mostly anarchic, though dependent on a difficult art of submission and then on the critic's having a mind with useful and interesting contents' (1968: 118). It is this note that I find missing in his writing of the seventies and early eighties, though that is not to say that he will not rediscover it. But this raises the question, which we can no longer avoid, of the function of criticism and the idea of the critic. Is there a position not reducible to interpretation which the contemporary critic could still occupy? Is such a position to be found in Kermode's later theoretical writings? After reading him, we are likely to accept that the concept of literature requires a canon, and that the scriptural analogy conveys some important truths about the implicit assumptions of present-day literary study. But should we not go further than this? Kermode's conservative myth of origin affirms the continuity of an institution deriving from the hermeneutic traditions surrounding the Judaic and Christian scriptures: but this is clearly a case of willed affiliation, not of natural filiation, to use Edward W. Said's terms (Said 1984: 14–22). It misrepresents the scriptural past (in which the penalty for plurality of interpretation was often a disturbingly physical one) and it also misrepresents the literary present in which interpretation is kept going by the needs of an educational system to which most interpretation appears, in itself, either hostile or indifferent. Moreover, writing itself is sold short by a paranoid hermeneutic (characteristic of contemporary literary theory) in which writers and critics can no longer be credited with responsibility for their discourses. Writing as canon-and-interpretation becomes a sort of perpetual-motion machine, with the individual 'scribe' and 'interpreter' providing both the energy to drive and the corn to feed the relentless mill-wheel of scripture and commentary.

There are strands in Kermode's theoretical work which seem to me to point towards the following proposition: it matters not what is taught, but how it is taught. It is not the works in the canon which count (since immanent value does not ensure survival), but the forms of attention we bring to them. Such a position is relativist, and postmodernist, but taken seriously it would tend to make education impossible. And indeed I am far from thinking that he really holds it. On some grounds one might suspect him of going to the opposite extreme, which is Northrop Frye's contention that the Bible ought to be the central text in literary education; but this too would be mistaken. Kermode's sometimes eerily detached pursuit of the scriptural analogy has perhaps had the unintended result of obscuring what he really thinks on these points. Edward Said, in *The World, the Text, and the Critic*, has cited Kermode as part of an influential trend towards 'religious criticism', and Said has labelled his own approach as 'secular criticism' (Said 1984: 1–30, 291). Not only is there a suspicion of posturing in that,[3] but Kermode himself would deny that he is a religious critic. What I should like to do is to confront his view of institutional control with another voice, a voice which might be considered both absolutely central and utterly apocryphal in terms of the canon of contemporary literary studies: the voice of a critic who began his long career by attending to the forms of attention, and ended with a remarkably challenging account of what ought to be taught.

In his book *Beyond*, which he published in 1974 at the age of eighty-one, I. A. Richards comments as follows on the variety of interpretations which surrounds canonical works:

The history of most great books shows them as having very often been praised for what may seem almost unimaginably wrong reasons. Mistakings, wrenchings, and distortions to an extraordinary degree seem to have been strangely frequent. How far this is a true picture, or how far it is an appearance produced through conditions in our contemporary scholarship, deserves to be pondered. Despite all this, the masters, on the whole, seem to have remained with a remarkable constancy in high favor. (Richards 1974: 39)

Though the tone is different, this is surely compatible with Kermode's account, as is Richards' further suggestion that conflict of interpretations, the 'vibrant interplay between rival interpretants – perhaps incompatible or even in seemingly mortal opposition' (118) could be a cause of the continuing vitality of canonical texts. But when Richards writes of interpretations in mortal opposition to one another, and of books praised for almost unimaginably wrong reasons, he is not posing as a disinterested observer or spokesman for institutional continuity: he tackles these matters with a missionary fervour. *Beyond* uses the scriptural analogy to establish 'how deeply cultures are shaped by their sacred books' (Richards 1977: 88); but for Richards the shaping must now be seen as a mis-shaping, and the books and their interpretations may well be the wrong ones. *Beyond* analyses the *Iliad*, Plato's *Republic*, the Book of Job and the *Divine Comedy* – representing our culture's Hellenic and Hebraic scriptures. The tradition of commentary on the Book of Job and on Dante, according to Richards, is indeed a history of error, since the dominant interpretations of either book were at pains to conceal the glorification of divine vengeance, the resort to violence rather than to instruction, that the texts enshrine. Hence Job and the *Divine Comedy* (and one could think of other scriptural books, or of whole traditions of interpretation such as the orientalism surveyed by Said) are 'extraordinarily corruptive' (Richards 1974: 177) in the lessons that they teach. They should now be replaced by a different canon, and by other scriptures: Richards aims to promote Blake's *Jerusalem* and Shelley's *Prometheus Unbound* in the place of Job and the *Divine Comedy*, or at least alongside them. Quoting the line 'Giving, receiving, and forgiving each other's trespasses' from Blake's poem, he concludes that 'This last line, well understood, could be our Key to Paradise' (1974: 200–1).

This is breathtaking stuff – but should we call Richards' interpretation an act of 'secular criticism'? I want to suggest that what qualifies criticism as criticism is not that it is secular (or religious) but that it is in some degree iconoclastic. It assails what it takes to be false values in the name of true values. Admittedly, the aggressive element in criticism, the inherent violence of some of its language, is something of an embarrassment to the reader of *Beyond* – after all, Richards' aim was to show how a change in our sacred books could contribute to survival and the avoidance of a nuclear holocaust. Kermode's Broad Church of literary interpretation avoids these traps, but at the cost of neutralising and perhaps neutering the critical act, since the members of his corps of interpreters no longer have any clear message to convey to the people outside. I. A. Richards, naive and misguided as many have thought him, took the task of education very seriously indeed; so much so that between *Interpretation in Teaching* (1936) and *Beyond* the majority of his writings had little or no connection with literary studies. It may be because he had made himself so thoroughly an outsider that in *Beyond* he was able, as very few other contemporary critics have done, to question the educative function of central texts in the literary canon.

We return here to our questions of the purpose of the canon and of criticism itself. I suppose there was once a time when the study of English literature was chiefly of use to its practitioners; then it became a source of moral education and an agreeably civilised form of expertise. Later the idea of the 'modern classic' led to the constitution of English literature as a subject for study, and much was heard of its currents, lines and traditions, though not as yet of the word 'canon'. And even now, when all is either inside or outside the canon, if one wishes to demystify the canon one has only to redefine it in terms of what in educational parlance is called the subject – in other words, one has to focus on the relationship of canon and syllabus. In searching for models of the relationship between canon and syllabus, I find myself looking at mathematical metaphors; the canon is the syllabus raised to a higher power of abstraction, or the canon is the area described by the curve of the syllabus. The merit of thus rejoining the notions of canon and syllabus is to remind ourselves that the contents of the canon, the considerations surrounding what is taught, possess both ideological and strictly practical significance; and the institutions upholding the canon also take on a more material, and less mystical, shape. The difficult polarity of criticism and teaching – the one engaged in cultural definition through acts of innovation and iconoclasm, the other bearing responsibility for the ceaseless accommodations (to use Kermode's term) involved in cultural reproduction – might then be recommended, or revived, as a way of conceiving the purpose of literary study. For if criticism prefers to reduce itself to interpretation and to stop asking what is taught and why it is taught, then unfortunately these questions do not lapse or pass into irrelevance; somebody else, perhaps somebody far more sinister, is always pronouncing on them.

Notes

1. Kermode, who greatly admires Empson, has cited him as an ancestor of deconstruction (1983a: 7).
2. Bennett n.d., *Literary Taste*: 19. Kermode cites Bennett as the sort of writer undervalued by the modern literary institution in *Forms of Attention* and in the prologue to *Essays on Fiction*. He has cited *Literary Taste* in 'The Decline of the Man of Letters'.
3. There is also a considerable history behind it, leading for example to the criticism of R. P. Blackmur, who appears (in rather different ways) to be a seminal figure for both Kermode and Said. Blackmur's 1948 essay 'A Burden for Critics' is perhaps the first serious treatment of the scriptural analogy by a modern academic literary critic. Blackmur claims in this essay to 'speak from a secular point of view', but his readers have often seen things differently. Richard Foster finds a 'quasi-religious commitment to art as the mode of virtual salvation' in Blackmur's later essays, while Said (in a generally adulatory study) refers to his 'bourgeois humanism in a churchyard'. At this point ironies multiply. See Blackmur, 1955: 207; Foster 1962: 97; Said 1987: 102.

5

The History of Styles as a Style of History

George Hunter

In the third lecture of *Forms of Attention* Frank Kermode calls himself 'a historian of sorts'; the context of that typically circumscribed admission offers still further circumscription: occasion for this sort of historian is provided by those 'systems and theories' that never made it into history, and so exist as a kind of flotsam, disconnected from what Kermode himself calls 'the nature of the case' (Kermode 1985a: 88). The remark and its context point, I take it, to the possibility and also to the difficulty of my subject. I take heart, however, by believing that when I refer to Kermode as a 'historian of styles' I am at least pointing to one of the ways in which he is 'a historian of sorts'. That leaves open the further and defining question: What sort of historian is a 'historian of styles'? There is, of course, an obvious answer to this question, though it is one I wish to set aside. Styles are often attached to history as names for cultural epochs: epithets such as Gothic, Baroque, neo-classical, *Jugendstil*, etc. present chronology as a series of stylistic 'fixes' on the world, a series of interpretations of its meaning, derived from responses to dated cultural monuments that can be wedded together to generate 'periods'. By now there is a splendid academic inheritance deriving from the legitimacy of these kinship associations; but doubts have inevitably risen about this prominent family's early history. How do historians know the relationship of cultural monuments to the events of their time? Critical judgments are made in the present, and are inevitably conducted through the perspectives of the present, often through a narrowly personal or cliquish perspective in the present, by processes that cannot be falsified, by an interrogation of malleable witnesses, required to speak in the language of modern sensibility. *We* interrogate the past, looking for confirmation of present assumptions (the more unconsciously the more powerfully). We search for the past we need; though I do not deny the possibility that a genuine amateur (or lover) may sometimes find what changes his assumptions, there is not much space in the modern professional world for such amateurism.

When I am speaking of *style* I am thinking of it therefore less as a period marker and more as the formal quality in an individual work which defines its unique power for readers and viewers, a power which recurs, but which is also protean, and which turns up also in other works in various and changing forms. For to think of *style* as simply a period quality with an objective historical status is to abstract it from the gaze of the viewer who finds its radiance and so creates the unity that binds its protean expressions.[1]

As I have noted, the usual compromise between style and history sets out their relationship not so much in terms of chronology as of 'periods' – static situations that hold together elements not necessarily congruent, which then, at a given signal, seem to fly apart, but only to re-form eventually (and mysteriously) in a new configuration (or 'style'). To think this way is, inevitably, to subordinate particular responses to general structures. Wölfflin remarks that 'To *explain* a style cannot mean anything but to fit its expressive character into the general history of the period, to prove that its forms do not say anything in their language that is not also said by the other organs of its age' (Wölfflin 1888: 58; quoted in Gombrich 1969: 25).

The idea of explaining textual responses by the history of events has become generally suspect in the later twentieth century; but this suspicion is by no means new. It has never been plausible[2] to see the styles of the past as a developing sequence. The power of individual authors is too obviously a personal gift to allow judgment of value to be subordinated to the story of sequential events. There is in this a clear pressure towards atomism; yet as long as the Idea of Progress ruled the historical imagination as the motor and explanation of historical change, so long was it possible to construct a meaningful and satisfying diagramme: the works of culture could then be used effectively to supply a supportive though differentiating counterpoint to the main tune. Since the basis of our response to the art of the past is the discovery of analogical selves inside the remoteness of its styles, this immediacy could be used to show how the perceptiveness of the modern was potentially present in the imagination of

the past. Culture thus became a part of 'the story of liberty',
documenting the aspirations of minds that were basically like our
own, of persons who were struggling forward to realise that
identification in social and political institutions. But when 'the
story of liberty' ceased to supply the motto theme for history,
the indeterminacy of culture was revealed as mere indeterminacy.
'Style' became anything that anyone chose to say, a page in the
Sunday supplement, a mode of talk in which groups of people
describe their world. All things thus being equalised, there is no
easy way nowadays for cultural historians to answer the political
charge that the culture of the past (and usually of the present)
is always a reinforcement of unjust societies, and that positive
responsiveness to it is therefore a wrong, an effete and anti-social
activity.[3]

A 'historian of styles' cannot persuade, it has come to be
assumed, without drawing on a specifically approved system of
social justice to support his perceptions. Writing or painting can
only be historicised (and so justified) as a social activity, like any
other mode of production, so that systems for the explanation of
works of art in the past can be found most relevantly in sociology.
'It is only at the level of literary *functions* (production, communication, consumption) that such a history [of literature] can be
written' Roland Barthes tells us in 1963, '. . . literary history is
possible only if it becomes sociological, if it is concerned with
activities and institutions, not with individuals'.[4] Historical culture thus recovers its backbone again, but at the cost of removing
the element that gives great literature and art its apparently
unmediated grip: its power to evoke direct response to what
Kermode calls 'the object of our attention' (1985a: 88), seen in
that light as if free of the social circumstances of its production
or the method by which it was marketed, whether *that* elicits our
praise (donation to a progressive cause) or abhorrence (dedication
to an aristocrat). But if response must be directed to the social
circumstances of 'cultural production' then the identification of
self must be found in a relation to such circumstances. The culture of the past becomes a set of documents that define modern
men not as the inheritors of the secret imagination of the past
but the guilty heirs of the social inequalities that are 'inscribed'
on its art forms. The counterpoint between culture and history
which was sustained by 'the story of liberty' having collapsed
into a homophony, the monuments of the past can only be

characterised by the power-hunger, racism, misogyny, colonial-
ism, religious bigotry incorporated in its culture. It becomes the
duty of the scholar to uncover (demystify) these, and of the
teacher to inculcate the moral.

As a historian of styles, Frank Kermode has thus lived through
a set of cultural changes which have redefined the terms within
which such actively must operate. As one activity involved in
the cultural life of the age, it is remarkable how uncommitted,
though not unaffected, he has managed to remain amid the
struggles of these modernisms. It would be fascinating to explore
the extent to which cultural journalism has protected him from
the inbred sillinesses of the academy. Certainly the need to write
with clarity for a miscellaneous audience, and the (related)
requirement to address specific topics in measurable space, are
disciplines that could have a salutary effect in many places. But
this is not my topic.

Frank Kermode began his writing career as a straight academic,
drawing on the assumptions and values that were current in the
scholarly culture of that time (the early fifties). The relationship
between his earliest work and the subsequent critical climate can
be nicely illustrated from responses to his edition of *The Tempest*
(1954). Kermode's treatment of the play shows its age by its
organisation in terms of 'themes'. But these themes are not the
usual pieces of arbitrary pattern-making; they are derived from
and buttressed by the documented intellectual assumptions of
Shakespeare's age. The contrast between art and nature is the-
matic here, not so that we can judge Shakespeare right (or wrong)
in preferring one to the other, but to present a 'paradox' that is
central to Renaissance thinking, specifically in its thinking about
magic and about the New World. The historical material is thus
held in focus in a contemporary intellectual framework which
controls and presents human values less as a datum than as a
problem for our consideration, made accessible to us by our
generic understanding of 'a play of an established kind' (Kermode
1954: xxiv) – a pastoral tragicomedy, a 'romance', an analogue to
the masque. In its concern with magic and art, and the problems
they pose for human understanding, Kermode's approach here
belongs clearly to the milieu he was currently associated with:
the Warburgian milieu of Donald Gordon, Frances Yates, Perkin
Walker, Joe Trapp

The post-Foucaultian 'new historicists' can, of course, only think of these methods as elitist mystification. To such critics *The Tempest* does not point us to mental constructions but to their social causes, so that the edition becomes chiefly notable for its failure to connect the play to 'colonialist discourse' – contemporary justifications of white rule over coloured races – in its lack of sympathy for Caliban as the type of the subjugated native animalised and worked to death in New Spain, or for Sycorax as the abandoned pregnant woman, its reluctance to condemn Prospero as the exploiting white expropriator.[5] It is not clear how modern egalitarian assumptions (noted above) allow us to deal with such reversals. Is this only a matter of a modernist pot calling a modern kettle black? I would argue not: it is true that Kermode's presentation of Prospero as a Renaissance magus/prince be-nimbused by both art and nature, fits in with certain fifties interests, just as Greenblatt and Francis Barker reflect the eighties; but the differences between these positions go beyond merely temporal separation. Kermode's Prospero remains within the parameters of a system of meanings available to Shakespeare's contemporaries, and appreciation of it modifies received modernities, so that we have space to enjoy the teasing dialectic; but Greenblatt's dissolution of Harriot's opportunist piety into a modern antithesis – either opportunism or piety – simply appropriates the mentality of the past in order to assert the value system of the present.

I should like to consider this ur-Kermode in a less fraught context. In 1952 he published in *Essays in Criticism* (its second issue) an essay on Marvell's 'Garden' – work clearly associated with the pastoral anthology published in the same year. Written with overpowering elegance and urbane severity, the essay validates pastoral as a style of understanding, an art of disengagement and playful seriousness, though trampled down by heavy-footed academics who seek to render its allusions into propositions.[6] This is a world contained by unformulated customs, not by axioms. We meet Marvell in a richly varied late-Renaissance company: Lipsius, Montaigne, Stanley, Randolph, Carew, Cowley, Lovelace, Mildmay Fane, Fairfax, Katherine Phillips, Hawkins, Tasso, Guarini, Spenser, Saint-Amant, Théophile de Viau, as well as their classical mentors. Marvell himself is present, as it were, as the guest of honour at a literary *fête champêtre*. And as at a reception as well conducted as such a guest-list would require, we are not supposed to question any of these guests for too long (or too seriously); they serve as a defining crowd, a cloud of historical witnesses, creating the atmosphere within which we feel we understand what it would be like to be part of this scene.

I use the image of a social occasion deliberately, for in such an essay the author is presented to the reader very much as a host-impresario who defines his occasion by inclusion and exclusion. Professor Milton Klonsky, for example, though capable of 'astonishing feats', is ignorant of the rules by which literary relations are conducted. Our host is urbane, dry-witted, learned but not pedantic, light in touch, considerate but not pressing; he provides us with the comforting possibility that we are not excluded, that we too may be poised and learned, alert to every allusion and half-quotation, that, in short, 'we' are the kind of readers we would like to be.

This essay illustrates very well what I mean by a 'historian of styles'. The coherence of the past 'period' is allowed, but so is its considerable diversity. The guests at Marvell's garden party belong together as 'period' figures. But they have not been assembled as a kind of fund-raising claque to support a new theory about the past; they have come together for this one occasion only. But this relaxed mode of conversation is now usually regarded as 'elitist' or 'mandarin'. It certainly has connections with a neo-classical assumption that there is a continuity of civilised discourse which stretches from the Renaissance to the present in an unbroken line, even if it ends up in a quasi-*Dunciad* world of literary criticism. It is this continuity indeed that gives such discourse its claim to cross the epistemic breaks and to provide access to the world of Marvell. But it does so by drawing on the Horatian techniques of indirection, velleity, and unstated assumption – the very characteristics that have been labelled *Bad Faith* in Paris. The demand that debate should consist of alternating statements of opposed total systems would (if it was feasible) put an end to all such conversational elegances. That it has not stopped Frank Kermode from being an allusive and elegant writer is obvious enough. But I have a sense that, since the time of these early writings, Kermode has shown a reduced confidence in his power to interrogate the texts of the past in the unjustified terms of the conversational mode, and has preferred to investigate the *theory* that it is possible to read the styles of the past without withering the immediacy of literature in the aridity of its positioning. The knowledge that the past talked another language and that translations out of its dialect are always treasonable has led him to what look (from a fifties point of view) like a series of rearguard actions, representing his (and our) engagements with the past in minimalist terms, as self-confessed fictions rather than apparent truths, as reflecting the necessity to make it up, to 'make sense' of it.

The role of *Romantic Image* in this progress is interesting, though tangential to my brief. The modernism of Hulme, Pound, Eliot, their proclamation of a 'make it new' aesthetic, is revealed in this book as a mere fiction, covering their true continuity with the French symbolists, so that their 'classicism' emerges as only another version of romanticism. When it was published, it seemed as if this might be a description of a special case; but Kermode has established in the series of books that followed – *The Sense of an Ending, The Classic, The Genesis of Secrecy, Forms of Attention* – that the modernists' way with *their* past is a model of the mode in which we all survive the past, by inventing fictions, either to separate things joined or to join things separated, in either case to explain a present that needs a history to justify its character. The argument can be seen as part of a widespread suspicion of historical 'facts', which has led to an increasing dependence on culture to describe the past. The interpretability, the openness or patience, of works of art makes them easy to co-opt in this enterprise, and it has increasingly been the role of literary criticism to supply material, often carelessly torn from original contexts, to serve current systemic explanations. But Kermode has not chosen to move from the indeterminacy of 'fictions' to the rigidity of 'systems'; his literary criticism remains sensitive to claims of the reader who expects explanation to enhance response. Clearly he would like to find a way of linking the aesthetic and the intellectual, the reader and the theorist, the journal and the academy, define a means of controlling the limits of permissible interpretation, as the genre card controlled admission to Marvell's garden party. He has not done so. He remarks at the end of *The Genesis of Secrecy*: 'at present we are waiting for [institutional] consensus to reform' (*re-form* I suppose). I wonder what kind of 'wait' this is. It sounds like waiting for Godot; and perhaps, like waiting for Godot, it simply defines an unchanging human situation.

My role is to talk about *Forms of Attention*, and it is high time that I turn such form of attention as I possess to that task. It is a book that seems to me to be so radically misrepresented by Lentriccia's introduction that I wonder if I am really in touch with it at all. But I can only deal with it as I read it. In these terms, it appears naturally in the sequence initiated by *The Sense of an Ending*, a sequence of books investigating the power of fictions to impose themselves upon us as necessities. The first lecture or chapter deals with Botticelli, rescued into canonicity by Herbert Horne and Aby Warburg. It asks the question: how did Botticelli, now universally admired as a 'great' painter, apparently canonical beyond cavil, come to occupy this niche? As we have learned from other Kermode books, such historical situations do not emerge from intrinsic quality; it cannot be assumed that Botticelli's 'greatness' is simply a fact. As the chapter tells the story (with novelistic sharpness), the judgment emerged from an indirect, even arbitrary, exemplarily human, process, not because of understanding or foresight – had these been present it might never have happened – but by what we may call 'a sense of style', by a kind of blind-man's-buff, by bumping into things in the dark, making a guess at what they could be, identifying them in terms of something else already seen, holding them close to one's self so that perception modifies them as they modify perception (Kermode 1985a: 30). In chronological terms we are shown how Horne brought the dedication and continuity of scholarship to bear on his taste, thus 'converting opinion into knowledge'.[7]

These are, I take it, the key words in this book, and I have to confess that I find them very mysterious. Perhaps I do so only because I am reading it against the grain, as I am certainly reading it in separation from Mr Lentriccia. I ask how 'opinion' is converted into 'knowledge', and I do not find a satisfactory answer. Of course one can say that Horne acquired knowledge by his work in the archives, as a result of which he was able to purify the Botticelli canon and exclude suppositious works – works that had been instrumental in supporting early opinions about him. But what are we talking about when we talk about his 'opinions'? Are we dealing with opinions about Botticelli's life, his associations, his sources, his technical methods, or with the opinion that he was a great and exciting stylist? If it is the former, then, clearly, there is no problem. But the issue being discussed is only worth discussing if it is the latter. It was an opinion that Botticelli was worth spending a life on that drove Horne to acquire knowledge.[8] No doubt the knowledge modified the opinion, but even then it was still the opinion that directed the knowledge. It seems as if the taste for Botticelli, the opinion that he was a great painter, did not arise from knowledge in the second instance any more than from ignorance in the first one. And the knowledge will not give Botticelli permanence if the opinion veers away from him. So the 'conversion' does not substitute knowledge for opinion but only attaches one to the other in the manner of consubstantiation rather than transubstantiation.

Let me pass on, for the moment, to the second figure in Kermode's first chapter, Aby Warburg, who reached his conclusions from a very different beginning. Horne started (like Berenson) from Paterian aesthetic reverie.[9] Warburg started from the advice of his *kunstgeschichtliche* mentors that he should attend to the 'construction of theories intended to have great explanatory power' (19) – especially those that have the power to justify modern culture by construing its representative artefacts as mementoes (tamed and civilised mementoes) of Dionysiac energies in the primitive past. By this method the aesthetic appeal of the *Primavera* or the *Birth of Venus* can be stabilised inside a system of scholarly explanation (with an Institute to institutionalise it); a version of history is invoked to suggest the continuity of our basic responses. This looks like knowledge; and no-one entering the Warburg Institute today can doubt that he is entering a temple dedicated to knowledge. But what is the relation of this *knowledge* to that *opinion*? Warburg was not content, as it seems Horne was, to keep Opinion and Knowledge in separate compartments. He hoped to be able to explain the power of ancient objects to reappear in the radiance of opinion by labouring at a system of historical psychology. But this formula for converting opinion into knowledge is no more satisfactory than Horne's vagueness. Gombrich's splendid *Intellectual Biography* of Warburg (1970) makes it clear how far his immense scholarship was driven by neurosis; but even beyond that one can point to a form of anxiety shared by many late-nineteenth-century scholars, most particularly in Germany.[10] But I must leave such speculations before I drown in waters too deep for me; and yet I believe that there is a moral to be drawn. Opinion, as the expression of taste (or of passionate attachment), is conditioned, if not created, by group attitudes operating on individual temperaments; in certain temperaments it expresses itself by laborious scholarship which can, for a while, claim the permanence of 'knowledge'. But such knowledge is powerless to halt the flux of time; so that the materials of scholarship and the institutions to protect them have to be reassembled again and again if they are to recapture the radiant energy of the classic instances. And this indeed is Kermode's central point about the function of criticism.[11] But in these terms the metamorphosis of opinion into knowledge is a mere epiphenomenon.

The second lecture of *Forms of Attention* deals with *Hamlet*, a text chosen not so that a similar story can be told about it, but rather because it provides a story of contrasting method. Botticelli vanished from view (or at least from appreciation) and appreciators needed a new perspective to make him visible again. *Hamlet* has never sunk below the level of the canonical; so here there can be no story of rescue, only a manipulation of perspectives to maintain a constant level of vitality and valuation. To display this manipulation, the chapter engages in a demonstration exercise in modernist 'reading' which is, presumably, parallel to the kind of activity Horne and Warburg engaged in (allowing for difference of context, of course). The reading is given a historical justification: it is a reaction to earlier (character-based) approaches; it substitutes the old periphery (language) for the old centre (character), concentrating attention on syntax and rhetoric (though not, *pace* Lentriccia, in the manner of Paul de Man).[12] In this way *Hamlet* is shown as a text whose appeal lies in its rhetorical details and in its resistance to mimetic articulation, a text suitable for those whose taste is founded on Joyce's *Ulysses* and the *nouveau roman*, held together by internal symmetries and a crossword-puzzle structure that allows one to reassemble them (if one so chooses), a text suitable for teaching in the graduate schools of the eighties, which may, indeed, be thought (on a 'worst case' interpretation) to comprise its main public.

Kermode calls this 'a new and not manifestly absurd way' of talking about *Hamlet*. One must agree. But two difficulties seem to be present. One concerns the degree of commitment (or opinion) with which the matter is put forward. The other concerns the extent to which the *Hamlet* case can be considered parallel to the Botticelli one. There is no reason why a good critic should be a committed proselytiser, and indeed every reason why he should not be: the stance of ironic disengagement which Kermode has preserved for most of his career has allowed him to bring his acute responsiveness to a great variety of texts and to thread his way among the fanaticisms of the modern art world

without succumbing to its sillinesses. And the same detached
tone seems to be manifested in this essay on *Hamlet*. Not only
does he refer to it as 'not manifestly absurd', as an example of
'the way critics nowadays often talk'; he also presents it as 'a kind
of scherzo, not quite a joke but a self-consciously extravagant and
fallible exercise in one kind of modern interpretation' (61; xiii) So
this is not the Kermode *Hamlet* to replace Lionel Knights' *Hamlet*,
or Bradley's or Dr Johnson's. It is something more like a ventri-
loquial exercise in the 'something different to say' that is appropriate to the interpretative community available in 1985.

How can one define this validating readership or community?
Pondering the issue, the idea that comes into my mind is that
of an MLA (Modern Language Association) culture – that of a
wholly professional caste of readers (26,000 at my last count),
whose interest is not in what texts say but in the positioning of
critical viewpoints, and in the arguments that X is thus able to
raise against the methodology of Y. In the third lecture of *Forms
of Attention* Kermode speaks of the Synagogue and the Church
as institutions concerned to define permissible interpretations and
so control the culture that depended on them (75–8), defining
their limitations on opinion as 'knowledge'. Can one conceive of
the MLA as an institution of the same kind? Professor Stanley
Fish has recently indicated that literary academics should think
of the MLA as the world, since it is impossible (he tells us) to
write any criticism that does not fit into a previously defined
space in the totalising system, the professional map.[13] This is
the community that the ironically distanced author of Kermode's
lecture on hendiadys in *Hamlet* seems to be addressing, a community fascinated by method yet cut off not only from the larger
focus that allows books a general readership but from what Kermode calls 'the object that interpretation exists to preserve', in
this case the play of *Hamlet*.

The presentation of an argument that would allow Botticelli to
reappear over the artistic horizon was conducted in terms which
have some resemblance to this, but also radical differences. Horne
and Warburg wrote their monographs for a professional audience;
but their work reinforced the set of 'opinions' that were already
established among 'persons of modern sensibility' (6); they provided the registrations of 'knowledge', and modified, but did not
deny, the shared taste that provided its origin. I do not think
that 'MLA culture' operates in this way; its interest is to exclude

rather than confirm the attitudes of 'mere readers' (though, of course, Kermode would prefer to include them – which may be one reason why he distances his essay from his authorship).

Kermode recurrently describes the relation of criticism in the present to literature in the past as a 'conversation'; but the MLA rhetoric he uses in his 'exercise' is designed to falsify, rather than augment. The model of centre and periphery he sets up, usually aligned with the favourite 'dominance and marginalisation and subversion' system, draws on a vocabulary that seems designed to stimulate the idea of criticism as armed struggle rather than civil conversation – an exciting analogy for those locked inside the graduate school but trivial and pretentious to those outside it. The mimetic function of whole plays, our sense that characters use words to express themselves and their situations, are matters that a modern conversation might well wish to modify; certainly the language the characters use has a density and self-consciousness (whether Shakespeare was conscious of it or not) entirely appropriate to rhetorical analysis (so brilliantly demonstrated here). But can one return by this route to the public world of readers and spectators? Kermode speaks of trying to 'foreground the utterance' to see 'what it tells us about the whole' (48). So far as I can tell he never reaches that point; and I do not know how, using that rhetoric, it would be possible to do so. If one cannot, then the Shakespeare that is locked inside the graduate school must shrink to that dimension; *The Phoenix and the Turtle* becomes his greatest achievement. But I am not disposed to think that the door can be locked quite so tightly. Nor do I suppose that there is no other world, no other 'persons of modern sensibility' out there.

The problem of critical hermeticism should be particularly obvious in the case of Shakespeare. Neither Fish nor Kermode *scherzoso* talk about the conditions of literature inside actual theatres. *Forms of Attention* gives a quick survey of the different ways attention has been focussed on Shakespeare in different ages, but does not note that most of these changes were achieved in the theatre rather than the study, by 'persons of modern sensibility' whose carriage of their bodies, modes of speaking, dressing, and interacting with one another gave the plays (even without textual alterations) the 'perpetual modernity' (62) that Kermode understands as the condition of the classic. It seems possible to say, even today, that the theatre (plus film and television, of course) remains the place where 'persons of modern sensibility' (such as Jonathan Miller, Peter Brook, Kosintsev, Fassbinder, even Brecht) possess most power to mediate between the ancient text and the diffused modernity of a heterogeneous public. Certainly the theatre is the place that most obviously relates today's 'persons of modern sensibility' to the stage-door Johnnies of the Botticelli rescue team (8–9).

This is not to say that the theatre is not as much in the grip of fashion as is the MLA. But the theatre has one great advantage over the academy in that its presentations are so clearly fashionable and therefore ephemeral; their power is thus relieved from any pretension to truth-claims; this is a world of 'opinion' that raises no expectation that it can ever become 'knowledge'. And that indeed may be the final justification of a *scherzando* mode – a mode by which literary criticism disencumbers itself of pretension to truth-claims and aspires to the condition of theatre. It is a consummation we should sigh for. But it requires not only a new devotion to the public language in academic critics, but also a drastic revaluation of the glittering institutions we belong to, which, on this argument, can only raise their pinnacles of 'knowledge' by building their sub-structures on the shifting sands of opinion.

Historians of style can only operate by continually reinventing the past their sense of style creates for them. But if we are to *use* the pastness thus created, and communicate it to a public, we must allow sufficient distance between that past and our own present so that perspective, dialogue, 'conversation' become possible. It is here, it seems to me, that 'knowledge' is relevant, for only knowledge can provide the stable framework of agreed norms that permits cultural conversation to take place. This does not protect knowledge from irrelevance when people no longer want to talk in these terms. But knowledge can probably extend the lifetime of opinion by providing a basis for widely shared talk – and what we can go on talking about we have an interest in still believing. Perhaps this is the 'conversion' that Kermode is talking about; perhaps not. These words are so slippery that they turn in your hand when you try to lean on them. But it would be nice to end by discovering that 'conversation' has led me to conversion.

Notes

1. What I mean by attention to style in its historical context is power-fully illustrated in Kermode's own reading of Auden in Chapter 4 of *History and Value* (1988). The historical circumstances of Auden's *Spain*, for example, are incorporated inside the reading, but Auden's style or rhetoric is not made merely symptomatic of thirties out-looks. The matter of the poem shares much with the circumambient scene, but what is moving in Kermode's response is the discovery not of its representativeness but of a stylistic power that reaches out from the past to the present, making its statement uniquely present as well as historical.

2. The power of Burckhardt's great *The Civilisation of the Renaissance in Italy*, for example, first published in 1860, could hardly be sustained without its resolutely achronological presentation.

3. Kermode has recently discussed these issues in *History and Value*.

4. Barthes 1963: 'C'est donc au niveau des *fonctions* littéraires (pro-duction, communication, consommation) que l'histoire peut seule-ment se placer, et non au niveau des individus qui les ont exercées . . . l'histoire littéraire n'est possible que si elle se fait sociologique, si elle s'intéresse aux activités et aux institutions, non aux individus.' (156) The translation used is that of Richard Howard, New York, Octagon Books, 1977: 161.

5. See, for example, Stephen Greenblatt, 'Invisible bullets: Renaissance authority and its subversion', Paul Brown, ' "This thing of darkness I acknowledge mine" ', both in Dollimore and Sinfield 1985; Francis Barker and Peter Hulme, 'Nymphs and Reapers heavily vanish', in Drakakis 1985.

6. The self-reflexivity present in this does not require underlining.

7. Bernard Berenson's epigrammatic version is 'In the beginning was the guess' (1927: ix).

8. It seems clear that this is what Kermode has in mind; in the Preface he speaks of 'the high *opinion* of a work or of an artist' (my italics) as the basis of the activity he is describing.

9. Berenson moved in a very similar direction: 'To Pater's heightened awareness, then, Berenson added Morelli's detachment and the process by which he claimed to enter into the spirit of a work of art became, in practice, a careful scrutiny of it.' (Brown 1979: 39) And for Berenson also the justification of his system (and its lan-guage) was that it allowed him to look carefully (with Paterian spirituality) at pictures.

10. I refer to the fascination with the Dionysiac erotic energies in the primitive past as a mode of compensation for the perceived emascu-lating constrictions of modern brain-work. When Warburg visited America in 1895 he confessed that among his impulses was the desire 'mich etwas mannhafter zu betätigen als es mir bisher ver-gönnt war' (Gombrich 1970: 88). I stress the Germanness of this because I suspect that the semantic distinction between Kultur and Zivilization must have made the difference seem more 'natural'.

Gombrich, in *In Search of Cultural History* (1969: 2) refers the distinction to 'the lowmindedness of German propaganda during the First World War'; but the fact that the distinction could be reanimated in the official language of the Nazis as soon as they seized power, suggests to me that it had been alive all the time.

11. On page 83 Kermode discusses the provisionality of systems but underplays, it seems to me, the commitment to system that is necessary before opinion could ever be converted into knowledge.

12. Kermode tells us (1985a: 48) that 'the central rhetorical device of *Hamlet* is doubling'. Centrality is not, I suppose, a deManian possibility.

13. See *The Times Literary Supplement* for 10 December 1982: 'any reason one could come up with for doing literary criticism would be a professional reason, in the sense that it could only have occurred to someone already thinking within the assumed goals, purposes, and authorized strategies of the profession. . . . To be convinced that you have something true or relevant or illuminating to say is *ipso facto* to have espied a professional opportunity'. Professor Fish has returned to these views on a number of occasions, most recently in Fish 1988: 739–48. See also Crewe 1986.

6

The Men on the Dump: A Response
Frank Kermode

For obvious reasons I've never been asked to write anything of this kind before, and in addition to a natural embarrassment at being required to go on at some length about my work I feel rather awkwardly and perhaps unnecessarily (though such retrospects seem almost obligatory at seventy) a need, not so much to defend that work, as to excuse or explain – to hint at some sort of narrative – to say how, in professional terms, one came about; how, in short, I happened to be or to become the person who wrote the books and papers to which members of the present company have so generously given their attention. I don't mean to inflict autobiography, of course; the point is that as the books under discussion disappear one by one down the corridor of time there is no reason whatever to speak of them as belonging to the same family (always assuming, as some contributors to this volume obviously have assumed, that they need to be spoken of at all) except that they happen to have been written by me, the product of an education and a temperament that alike belong to an increasingly obscure past. Nostalgia has nothing to do with it; the point is to explain opportunities and limitations relevant to the matter in hand yet not fully understood, though still of some transient interest, to younger persons, a class that from a septuagenarian perspective grows rapidly larger.

Although we have it on other authority that books are not absolutely dead things, we have it on the authority of our own experience that they are habitually moribund things. They slip, in the normal course of events, into a past, and are irretrievable unless, by some act of will or of chance, they are seized by some younger hand than their author's, held in a legible position, read as if they mattered now, even attacked because, whether then or now, they were not exactly what the age demanded.

For nothing could be more absurd than an assumption that books, even 'great' books, to say nothing of little critical books, have in themselves the power to survive, to shrug off neglect; unless it is the opinion that any importance they may have had in their time could persist unchanged into a later epoch. The survival of books, which always entails a measure of transformation, is the achievement of readers, of modern readers. That is why opinions held by aging writers of the books they wrote a long time ago are rarely in accord with what is later said about them, and rarely of very much interest to those later readers; and why the writers in their turn are unlikely to resist with much passion the strictures, or even to be warmed by the plaudits, of those later readers – even of those who, over the interval of years, have kept the books alive or at any rate half-alive, by their decisions and revisions, their approvals and disapprovals.

I hope those *prolegomena* will be a sufficient excuse for the approach I feel obliged to take in these remarks. When I was starting out, rather belatedly, in the fifties, there seems to have been a notion in the air – doubtless given the relatively subdued expression now associated with that period – that what was needed was much new thinking about literature and criticism as well as about everything else; for the war which delayed my debut, such as it was, also constituted one of those chronological breaks, or *coupures* as they are now called, after which it seems necessary to get things going, however parsimoniously, on a new footing. We are now so firmly agreed that the really serious *coupure* didn't occur until the sixties that we have forgotten this earlier one, which was admittedly rather different and less noisy.

In our own chief area of interest we had inherited a way of thinking about the history of literature, especially our own literature, which owed most to Eliot, though much also to the earlier Leavis; we had learned from Richards and Empson, and later from the American New Critics, to give the texts of poems a new kind of attention, and we had even thought quite a bit about theoretical defences of such procedures. We had acquired, long before the French, a dismissive contempt for what they were to call 'Lansonisme', though the courses we had to teach were still, *mutatis mutandis*, pretty Lansonist.

On the whole, then, we were or wanted to be enterprising, to break away from the old institutional consensus, and even to get rid of some of the barriers between different subjects in the humanities. We had before us the striking if uneasy example of Pound, with his wide literary horizons – Provençal, Chinese, Italian – and his political and economic pretensions. We had models for blending criticism with anthropology, psychoanalysis, Marxist historicism, philosophies of various kinds, and – rather potently for a while – theology. We still gave an unquestioned priority to the task of knowing about, and teaching, literature, which admittedly makes us different from our revolutionary successors. Nevertheless, we survivors might agree with John Ellis (1989) that a good deal of what is now calling itself an absolutely new departure in criticism depends for some of its *éclat* on its assiduous ignorance of much that went before. Of course there were many possible conjunctions, confrontations, contradictions that we didn't perceive or feel obliged to take into account, far too many such by the standards of today. On the other hand it did not occur to us to put the whole idea of literature into question – to deny that there was anything that should be so distinguished, or to claim that the distinction was conferred upon it by acts of arbitrary and selfish power – and I think that was right. While it must be thought one of the benefits of the modern obsession with literary theory that it attends to so much that is not, in the old and still familiar sense, literature, it is a worry to some old heads that there are many zealots who see it as an inevitable consequence of this redirection of attention that literature, in that sense, should be done away with.

Everybody, however original, starts somewhere, but in those days, as now, even the journeymen felt it impossible simply to mark time; everybody experienced an urgent need to move on. There were various possible routes – new ways of doing history, as well as new ways of attending to texts. It is surely from an ignorance extraordinary in historians that militant New Historicists can claim to have broken the mould of a universally stuffy, unexamined practice of history, till now protected by 'institutional guardians' and anti-intellectual specialists (Veeser 1989: ix). For there were in those days very serious debates about history, and the philosophy and history of history, and the history of literature; and new ways of doing history, not at all stuffy or institutionally coercive or specialised in the wrong sense, were emerging, for example at the Warburg Institute. And the practice of intensive and ingenious reading, raised to a new level of exhaustiveness, now considered a deconstructionist novelty, was, as I

have said, well established. But inevitably these new ways were
all in some sense continuous with the older ways.

That is why my own first critical book was in some ways
forward-looking, but in others devoted to a critique of what
seemed too definite, too programmed, about the inheritance, an
inheritance to which it was much more indebted than it allowed.
Romantic Image now looks to me like prentice work, subdued to
what it worked in, but its moment being unexpectedly opportune
it must have seemed, at any rate in the eyes of those who were
in a position similar to the author's, fresher and newer than it
really was.

With a little modification, the same might be said of *The Sense
of an Ending*. Both of these books are properly to be thought of
as essays (I remember Graham Hough grumbling that the first
essay was followed, not as one might expect after a ten-year gap,
by a real book, but by just another essay, and at the time I felt
rueful about this, though my view now is that we could do with
more essays and many fewer large books). Anyway, essays is
what they incontrovertibly were: brief, speculative in character,
taking risks, some of which I knew about and took deliberately,
others that I was too ignorant to recognise. It is all too possible
that my books, not merely these earlier ones but all the others
as well, which certainly ought to have progressed beyond the
prize-song stage, contain serious muddles, which it was only to
be expected that keener analytical intellects than my own, when
doing me the courtesy of attending to them closely, as Messrs.
Stokes, Nuttall, Harrison, Parrinder and Hunter have done in
this volume, would be sure to spot.

The cheerful aspect of all this is that they often see connections,
often make sense, where I myself would be unable to do either.
It is after all not amazing that the same man should write a
sequence of books that show some common characteristics, only
that he may be the last to perceive this to be the case, imagining,
as part of the slightly absurd complex of desire and interest that
makes him want to write something more, that the something
more can be something completely new. It is other people who
perceive in us the substance that prevails.

Reading these papers was a bit like having one's palm read:
continuities are noted, lifelines, a character however flawed or
unstable, a presiding critical personality dominated, it is plausibly
though to me rather surprisingly suggested, by a kind of sadness,

a repeated acceptance of disappointment; possessing, no doubt, even worse defects than these, as when the shrewd George Hunter, who has known me and my work for a very long time, catches me in what may be a characteristic attitude of refusing to say whether or not I am being wholly serious. These disqualities are apparent to the practised eye, fixed and constant under the maze of criss-crossed lines, the contradictions manifest or latent, the momentary ironies, the little squiggles of fun and the pose of *Tüchtigkeit*.

However, I feel a fairly urgent need to say that I remain quite cheerful about all this, as I do about being muddled on many other subjects that are, on a loftier and more general view, important beyond all this fiddle. Later on I shall offer occasional polite resistance to some of the criticisms proposed, or do appropriate penance when I can't. But I shall have to do so without pretending that the matter strikes me as a very serious one. I have in my head an image of these scholars standing on a dust heap or dump, among the worn-out tyres and junked basinettes, the detritus of obsolete critical ideas, some perhaps capable of salvage, most degenerating into simple rubbish. I emphatically do not subscribe to the current view that writing criticism is really just the same activity as writing poems, but I do believe that just as a great many poems – an extreme view might say, all poems – become obsolete (unless, I would want to add, constantly rewritten by their readers) so all criticism has its season, in which it lives, if it lives at all, by a dazzle or minor radiance that cannot be expected to last. The best it can aspire to is a shadow of the condition Wallace Stevens thought a poem might achieve, a sort of August moment, a moment of illusory fixity, having the 'Joy of such permanence, right ignorance/Of change still possible' – a sort, as he might have said but actually didn't, of momentary utmost.

Stevens called another of his poems, this time one that might be described as ugly but honourable, 'The Man on the Dump'. It is about the huge discard of poetic metaphors, the dump into which used poems have to go, and about the spring-like moment of new poems, to be discarded in their turn, but in their moment representing or embodying things as they are in themselves:

> the moon comes up as the moon
> (All its images are in the dump) and you see

As a man (not like an image of a man),
You see the moon rise in the empty sky.

This is the season when, for a moment, 'the the' is seen to be
the truth, the simple, the definite, clear of all distraction, without
the evasions and intricacies of metaphor; but in the end, which
will come soon, unendurable to humanity in that desperately
pure form.

This poem often comes to my mind, though on Stevens' argument it is itself destined for some super-dump; and it did so,
with a complicated motivation, when I began to think about these
essays. In Stevens there is, after all, that moment between one
dump and the next when a good poem has still its naked radiance, when the person observing it doesn't 'feel a malady', when
'the poem refreshes life so that we share,/For a moment the first
idea . . .'.

Incidentally this tells me we ought perhaps to manage, or have
managed, our criticism without so much talk of image and symbol
and metaphor, directing attention rather to the essence of the
matter by talking about the poetry or the poem, something we
should all know more and say more about, namely the rare
experience of poetry. We were taught, when young, to sneer at
Housman who could not shave when a line of verse made his
beard bristle, and we were even suspicious of Valéry's *données*,
though liking the qualifying notion that all the work of the poem
still remained to be done when this gift had been received. Yet
in the end we should admit that these things really do occur; in
the real world there are poems that can stop the heart, and poets
who are the recipients of givens or gifts. Not all poems or all
poets possess or need these powers, but since they exist, and
potently, they must be taken into account; and when they fail to
do so critics, even if self-deceived, are guilty of fraud, expressing
ignorance as knowledge.

I was recently reading the previously unpublished work of
Philip Larkin in Anthony Thwaites' edition. When I got to the
end of the poem entitled 'Unfinished Poem' (I don't know who
called it this, for it's not the kind of edition that gives one precise
information; the title seems inappropriate, though I daresay
Larkin might have seen the poem as needing a touch here and
there) my hair did stir if not stand, my voice disappeared into
the last line, and tears stood in my eyes. All this comes from the

shock of encountering the true, in the only sense that the word can be used of a poem – 'the the'. Moreover I know I shall probably never again be able to read that last line aloud; it has created in me what might be thought of as a recursive Housmanian reaction, though I prefer to think of it as a recognition that a poem can be a *the* in the Stevens sense, a part of the real world, a truth. I am not prepared to believe that this 'text' of Larkin's is distinguishable from an advertisement or a white paper or a newspaper report only because a small community of readers wants to 'privilege' one kind of discourse over others. It seems absurd to have to keep on saying so, but there is a valid experience of poetry, a response appropriate to the world as humanly apprehended – proved on the pulses is a usual though worn way of talking about it. Perhaps we need a new poetic of a different sort from any of the current versions of 'the science of literature', which offer so many ways of talking about poems or at any rate texts, but in such a manner as often to make it appear preferable not to do so. It is ominous that there should be a continuing and clamorous practice of criticism, of poetics, when it is not apparent that there is anything distinctly understood as a poem to be practised on.

Stevens had the courage to make poetry of his persuasion that the poem doesn't survive, indeed that 'the plum survives its poems', and he thought of poems as new, lovely and transient gestures, acts 'of the mind in finding/What will suffice', producing 'sudden rightnesses', as of 'a man skating, a woman dancing, a woman combing'. But the poem could not be perpetually sudden, and it is true that as age comes on only a few poems by a few poets can for any one of us stay sudden or, to be more accurate, remind us of that primal rightness. As for criticism, it rarely brings tears to the eyes, and never stays sudden, is indeed never to be thought of as having a very intimate relation with 'the the'. Most of it is like the statue of the general in Stevens: perhaps honoured in its time, but rubbish in the end.

I am now thinking of John Stokes' patient comments on my indiscretions and inconsistencies all those years ago, when, like the people I was criticising, I was rearranging literary history to suit my own programme or my own feelings. I think also of his modest complaints at my seeming rejection of the human person, the self-absorption that was possibly more my own than Wordsworth's in the presence of the leech gatherer. With some reservations I accept his strictures, maintaining on the best available authority, myself, that this is for me one of the world's great poems, and that it is about the poverty of poets, and then about the poverty of a world that cannot sustain them, as it could barely sustain the leech gatherer when over-fishing, or some ecological change, reduced the supply of leeches. And I suppose that one reason why Stevens has meant and means so much to me is because, in his Hölderlinish mood, he too had an apprehension of poverty as the human condition so general that particular cases, even when he tries, in *Owl's Clover*, to think about them in the context of the economic depression, simply become representatives of a poverty more universal, especially apparent to and felt by poets, and the more tragic because set against a world they know to be capable of freshness and plenitude. All the same I do see, as Stokes gently hinted I should, that to speak in this way is to risk being accused of what Auden had in mind when he spoke of 'our metaphysical distress,/Our kindness to ten persons'. Stevens said that poverty was 'older than the oldest speech of Rome', and he still meant 'metaphysical' poverty, in so far as that can be considered on its own. It is easy and even wicked to sublimate the real thing into such abstractions, as if the poverty of, say, Bangladesh were merely another image of a radical poverty, a poverty inherent in existence, the sort we know under various guises from Beckett or Sartre, or Heidegger or Stevens, and momentarily mitigated by various angelic visitations. I leave this problem, only adding that when the poets speak of their poverty they cannot help meaning the leech gatherer's as well as their own, they are men speaking to and for men, major men for minor men perhaps; they mean something they have felt with and for us in the world.

So the first lesson from my Stevens text is this: that there is a necessary angelic force but also a necessary poverty in poetry and poets, that the word 'necessary' means what it says, and that the people I was talking about in *Romantic Image* – people who thought that to be an artist was to be 'estranged' or, as I perhaps unfortunately put it, 'alienated' – had a genuine apprehension of all this, however outmoded their way of expressing or enacting it.

In all I have subsequently written about interpretation and value – the central problem, I think, of modern literary theory – I believe I have at least remembered that apprehension (though

I am naturally sorry Professor Parrinder feels that later preoccupations have made me a bit duller than I was originally). The
images in which I once talked about the 'image' belong, no doubt,
on the dump. *A fortiori*, if the beauty of the gestures of poetry
is such that at any rate in our time it depends upon their ephem-
erality, then those of literary criticism, so often, whether by
choice or incapacity, lacking that momentary grace, will hit the
dump at least as quickly. As indeed the metaphors of ordinary
language must; as all language does, all life indeed; for, to cite
the bold Stevens one more time, 'the theory of poetry is the
theory of life'.

No, I need him once more, in order to repeat that 'there is a
substance in us that prevails'. This is the conditioned reflex I
shall always have to that unspeakable line of Larkin's – in which
the ultimate poverty dissolves and the sudden angel appears. It
is a memory of the poem as the cry of its occasion – its human
occasion. And so much, at any rate, one carries forward, whether
as reader or writer. Yet it is true that nothing must or can be
said in the same way, which is why I see Dr Stokes' investigations
of my book as a patient, humane stirring in a rubbish dump. It
is also why – for reasons different from those of Paul de Man,
who liked to say roughly the same thing – I take it that the
progress of criticism, if it can be called a progress at all, is
describable, with only a little exaggeration, as a progress of error,
and preferably the error of the unexpected, inapt, beautiful gesture; rather that sort of error than the spuriously exact lucu-
brations of the practitioner who simply lacks appetite for poetry
anyway, whose beard has never bristled.

It is unsettling to know that one's certainties are likely – certain
one obviously can't say – to be mistakes, and that may be why
George Hunter finds a certain duplicity in my essay on *Hamlet*.
I can only say that I was wholly involved in that piece, I thought
it true as far as it went and as far as I could judge, and it was
no doubt a rather base feeling that as a professional I should not
indulge myself or risk too much, accompanied by, and in conflict
with, an obscure conviction that in some ways potential error is
more useful than palpable fact to the conversation of criticism,
that led me into a mode of protective irony, if that is the right
way to qualify my tone. The musical analogy – the idea that I
had a precedent for the shape of my book in the musical schemes
of sonata form, scherzo and passacaglia, occurred to me only

when I was writing the preface, but although it may sound like
another move in an unserious game it isn't an altogether bad
idea; criticism is after all one of the arts, and if the arts aspire to
the condition of music, criticism might well, after its fashion, do
likewise; indeed our world would be a livelier place if the great
many people who nowadays practise it would do so with the
presumption that it might at best be a kind of music, having, to
be as bold as possible, Mozart in mind, which is to say wit,
ingenuity, depth of feeling, unexpectedness, structure, a sense
of the power of human beings to be complicated and happy.

Before I leave *Romantic Image* altogether I want to add that like
John Stokes it was educated at Reading. It issued from a literary
community as no other book of mine has – I mean a closer, more
active community, to whom it was not artificial to talk, with
varying degrees of seriousness but almost incessantly, about the
books or the paintings or even the criticism that were at the same
moment engaging the attention of everybody. The leader, D. J.
Gordon, for all his ultimately self-destructive failings, was a
powerful example, a pioneering Renaissance scholar who for
reasons only partly explicable in terms of his own personality
has not had his proper tribute. He combined with an intense
specialism an extraordinarily wide reading in other fields, and to
read, even if you read most of the night, uses up the time other
people spend in more obviously productive ways; but such was
his curiosity, his sheer skill in the handling of books, that he
always seemed to know as much or more about the ideas you
were fondly brooding over than you did, as if he had already
seen them hatched somewhere else or could imagine them in an
adult state. As it happened, his interest in the sort of thing I was
talking about in *Romantic Image* originally derived in great part
from mine, but he saw it differently, gave it an iconological
dimension, developed it quite independently, and, though never
writing a book about it, organised at least two superb exhibitions,
one of Yeats and one of Beardsley – to many, alas, virtually
inaccessible – of greater value though of less permanence than a
book might have been. And there were others, as one now sees
no less important though less obviously glamorous, who made
up the indispensable little salon – people with whom one spoke
almost daily – in the early days Ian Calder, a bow-tied encyclo-
paedia who knew everything about John Dee and, it sometimes
seemed, about everything else as well, and John Wain, who was

somewhat ironical about it all, but made his contributions with brilliant reluctance; and Ian Fletcher, a late joiner, now, like Gordon and Calder dead, who fed into one's thinking about late Romanticism a mass of curious and relevant information one could have found nowhere else. Anyway, *Romantic Image* is very much of that moment, a moment when I presume to think it must have been as great a privilege to read English at Reading as it was to teach it, and to benefit by a spontaneous collaboration the like of which I haven't known since, and which is probably unattainable under modern conditions.

The truly important thing was the focussed but informal talk. It is odd to think that most efforts to achieve relaxed talk, the unguarded exchange of uncensored speculations, as they are made in universities today, founder; nobody keenly wants to take part unless there is some prior acceptance of an ideological programme, there is no sense of what may be found out by the interplay of widely disparate interests; or the possible participants see far too much of each other in the wrong context of cost-cutting administration, or are out of necessity engrossed in their own promotion-fostering research. Just for a few years at Reading I lived in – Stevens again, I'm afraid – a radiant and productive atmosphere. I made mistakes, and I wrote things that are quite rightly thought biased or inaccurate, but I regret none of that, for, as I have suggested, the life of intelligent poetry and criticism is a life of error twinned with truth – like twins, they quarrel and are interdependent – and to have experienced it, if only for a year or two, is to have been presented, all undeserving, with a gift that only scandalous neglect or extravagance could entirely waste. Or perhaps one might think of it rather as a programme, never to be completed, and certainly enough, as John Stokes perceived, for an ordinary lifetime.

No doubt I should now, having said something about those earlier years, go on to explain where I now 'stand', but to do so would be to expose me as what Terry Eagleton once called me, a bourgeois liberal humanist, for that, with qualifications he might dismiss as insignificant, is what in fact I am, as the generalities and complaints already here dispensed will in any case have made obvious. I wasn't always a bourgeois liberal humanist, if I had been born one I might perhaps have got myself educated better and earlier, and even been taught to think in a respectably philosophical way. When I consider Anthony Nuttall's and

Bernard Harrison's contributions to this volume I become aware
that there is a real and, for me, lamentable difference between
their intellectual equipment and mine. They seem to know how
to think. I merely invite in such notions as occur to me as I brood
over ideas more clear and distinct, such as theirs.

Some of these chance occurrences have seemed plausible
enough, like the tick of plot, but at the Warwick conference
I learned, twenty-four years too late, that some clocks really
do say tick-tock, in this respect resembling one that belongs to
Dr Batchelor of Oxford. But I have decided to consider the
Batchelor clock as, in its day, a piece of wit: if everybody insists
that clocks say, or used to say, tick-tock – quartz has now done
away with that figure of the sense of an ending – even though
it could be ascertained that they really did nothing of the kind,
then somebody might make a clock, a joke clock, that actually
did what people merely persuaded themselves all clocks did. In
this way I can dismiss any genuinely tick-tocking clock as a
curiosity without intellectual importance, and dispose of the claim
that it demonstrates 'an unconditioned apprehension of reality'
– after all somebody who had never seen or heard a clock might
think the sound came from an unusual type of cricket – and get
on to thinking how quartz came in about the same time as the
nouveau roman.

In my oral reply at the end of the Warwick conference I said
something impromptu in reply to Nuttall's point about birth
being a beginning in reality, and the establishment of a university
in Sussex as an instance of the same. It is indeed difficult to
refute, and I little thought I should ever have to attempt it.
However, an individual birth gets its importance from existing
conventional human arrangements; it can be a matter for joy or
sorrow, it certainly makes a difference to the persons concerned;
they didn't have a baby and then they did; they buy champagne
and arrange a christening, the state requires them to register the
birth, in some cases they at once negotiate with certain schools,
they prepare for the ritual fussing of grandparents and aunts.
But there is surely a sense in which all this behaviour can be
called arbitrary or even fictive; a different sort of narrative could
be constructed, and is, in other forms of society. A quantity of
DNA is being transmitted, and for one reason or another we
make about this event the fuss of our choice. Indeed I once
heard Francis Crick propose, with apparently no idea of being

outrageous, though the audience was outraged, that no child should be deemed to have been born until, after two days, it had passed certain genetic tests. We do quite a lot of deeming, which is why we speak of legal fictions. Of course the child would have to be born in the ordinary, or what Nuttall calls the natural way, before deeming could begin, but my point never was that there are no natural occurrences; it is that we habitually equip these occurrences with humanly fictive formulations. A building comes completely into being before it is 'topped out' but architects want the ceremony, even when, as in Ibsen, it entails some risk to life and limb.

It is not a fact that there are no facts, indeed it is because there are so many that we need our fictions. Nature scatters, *si squaderna*; it is we who do the binding, with loving fictions, *in un volume*. Of course difficulties arise when one goes on with such thoughts, as Nuttall would be among the first to point out. How, for instance, to deal with his remark about Mormonism? It seems of no less practical use because of its absurdity, yet it is absurd, we suppose, less because of its lack of conformity with fact or nature than because of its own structural preposterousness and its lack of what is now called reality effect. This seems, for the moment, to dispose of the issue of 'natural and formal inceptions'. Like Nuttall's Muse, Nature dislimns, or we dislimn her, into secondary images of herself.

Professor Harrison has my thanks for undertaking to show that it might have been possible in *The Genesis of Secrecy* to allow for a 'radiance' that is not necessarily delusive and can be accessible without recourse to secrecy. He gives more technical expression to some of Nuttall's doubts, and I think he is right about 'transparency' in the 'weaker sense' he proposes; though 'transparency' might itself be called the product of a hermeneutic activity, in a form of it so common, made by practice so easy, that it has, by severe persons, been accorded separate and inferior status, as when Stephen Heath, in his book on the *nouveau roman*, distinguishes between reading and recognition, the passive acknowledgement of familiar codes, or, as Harrison suggests, the provision of material that encourages our confidence in 'correspondence'. Others similarly distinguish ordinary from 'symptomatic' reading. The reduction of textual scandal or noise is easier in the more 'transparent' cases, for the text is purposely designed to simplify the business of processing it into coherence. It must of course be allowed that there is no impassable barrier between carnal and spiritual, everybody is reading though some are reading differently and much more, interesting themselves in what, to exclude the others, is harder, more obscure, more subtly inviting of their learned interpretative skills, and, in the French as well as the English sense, more deceptive.

If I understand Harrison's Outsider's Option, it is not very different from what I have just been saying; it is true, in short, that the 'carnal' varies only a little among people who can read the text at all, and that getting through to the 'spiritual' sense may be regarded by the outsider as a negative achievement at best. He will be satisfied with the exercise of 'turning it about' to find a meaning which, without being 'symptomatic' or 'spiritual' is specific to himself; and however 'stonily and carnally open' it may be, such an encounter with it may be a means by which, without itself varying or revealing 'secrets', it changes its reader.

Since I am said to be both somewhat depressed and on occasion somewhat depressing on such subjects I had better say that I endorse this opinion, while resisting any implication that the change will necessarily be in the more obvious and simple interests of the person so changed. Finally, though I rather like Harrison's interpretation of the doorkeeper parable, I doubt if it is enough to put the blame on the suppliant for not treating the doorkeeper as a delusion engendered by his own consciousness of irrational structures of authority. It seems to me he couldn't conceivably have got in until the moment when it was actually impossible for him to do so. However, to juxtapose these two views is doubtless to illustrate a difference, if not of fore-understanding, then of temperament, between my critic and me.

Professor Parrinder is, like the other contributors, generous, and I owe him a few comments. First, I do believe there can be wrong readings of texts, and for that reason greatly enjoyed Richard Levin's book *New Readings vs. Old Plays* (1979). I remember I. A. Richards, in his dreadfully belated Clark Lectures, jumping up and down and crying havoc on what he called 'omnipossibilism'; and I felt quite at one with him as he did so. But as W. K. Wimsatt once remarked, it isn't easy to define the authority by which one pronounces a reading wrong; we all do it without bothering about the legitimacy of our authority when we tell students that 'she' is not a pronoun, and not the subject of the sentence, in 'And yet by heaven, I swear my love is fair/As any she belied with false compare'. However, as I may have remarked elsewhere, we might not be so quick with the blue pencil if this 'misreading' occurred in *Seven Types of Ambiguity*. It is partly at least a question of the relative rank of the author you're commenting on.

However, the point at which I feel Parrinder's challenge most acutely is in the matter of teaching – teaching not merely one's institutional successors, but people who intend to go out and do quite other things. My eyes fixed on the graduate schools, I may not have said enough, or been explicit enough, about this, but I have said something. I can see, I think, that the entire operation of high-powered academic literary criticism is ultimately dependent on the preservation of a class of readers, who nowadays, if at all 'serious', have usually been through our classrooms, though they almost certainly do not read our books. That is why, like Lionel Trilling, I regard it as essential to 'keep the road open' – to maintain, somehow, a style of talking about literature (in classrooms and in literary journalism as well) which will preserve the reading public, and – quite simply – literature (which we must presume to recognise) from destruction. I regard this as by far the most important single element in the task of university teachers of literature; it is nothing less than the preservation of what we give that name. In their own time they can read what they like and deconstruct or neo-historicise what they like, but in the classroom they should be on their honour to make people know books well enough to understand what it is to love them. If they fail in that, either because they despise the humbleness of the task or because they don't themselves love literature, they are failures and frauds. I hope I make myself clear. I had better add that this is not what I was talking about when I discussed the necessary continuities of the institution, the need to have more people a bit like oneself to carry it on; that is the graduate school, and in the practices of the graduate schools there is much that I could with some eloquence argue against. I will not do so now, wishing the gravamen of this long paragraph to remain as it was; a warm, though not indignant, refutation of the idea that I do not give a damn about the most important part of the job.

I will, however, admit that it was the part of our job that I always felt less good at; a natural incapacity, against which I struggled conscientiously for years, and not, I hope, without success, and certainly never with any loss of my sense of its historic importance. And this reminds me to say that I absolutely detest being called 'post-modernist', though I understand the spirit in which the label was stuck on. Moreover I am willing to recognise Edward Said as a 'secular' critic but not at the expense of being called a 'religious' critic myself; that is simply a misunderstanding (even Derrida can claim that he is misunderstood, though his principles should prevent his saying so; mine don't). Parrinder has seen certain things correctly, alas, but as a whole the portrait seems awry, in the opinion of the sitter, who may sometimes be moved but remains always *incroyant*.

I should repeat, finally, that unlike the authors of these splendid but embarrassing papers, I am not what it would be proper to call a thinking person. I have after all had plenty of time to observe the difference between myself and truly thinking persons. I am one of those who, in the right mood, drift along with the tide of their own thought, occasionally diverted by some book or writer encountered by chance or by professional need. Paul Ricoeur, an incomparably more disciplined and systematic thinker, recently remarked in a Preface to some of his writings, introduced by Professor Mudge, that he thought it most agreeable to have been shown what in fact he had been doing, although it didn't feel a bit like that when he was actually doing it (Ricoeur 1981: 41). I understand that; you feel as if you're moving on from one thing to another, as the spirit lists, and it is other people who can see the continuities and patterns, the substance that prevails, the substance persisting through the hundreds or even thousands of pages that may, considered together, be thought to have some consistency, and perhaps in consequence some value, however transient, however dependent on the research of others.

One of the things that became quite clear to me as I listened to these and other papers at Warwick was that there are a great many contradictions in my work, which has now extended over several decades and has never been controlled by a comprehensive intellect. Another was that there is, all the same, something that persists from those remote days I spoke of earlier, when it seemed that something new was needed, and when, as I believe, something new really came about and gave a semblance of shape or pattern to individual thoughts, even helped to give expression to the little one could call one's own – what somebody at the conference almost, if not quite, called 'the carnal kernel', what

Stevens called 'the presiding personality', which would be much too grand a phrase if one did not remember that very small children display, through the mad vagaries of their daily behaviour, a quality, recognisable with affection by parents and more dispassionately by others, that might warrant the use of the term.

The shape of that personality is, as I've suggested, something to be discerned by others. But I will confess that as I look back at the experience and read the papers there is one imputed trait that occupies me more than any other; so as I conclude I will qualify a little what I said about it earlier, perhaps displaying as I do so an inconsistency that might, in charitable constructions, seem part of a larger consistency. For I find myself wondering whether Patrick Parrinder (and another speaker, not represented here) can have been right after all to find in much of what I have written a displaced religiosity, the cult of a 'secular surrogate'. Perhaps my first response was a stock secularist reaction, a reflex prompted by a need to conceal a blush, a sense of having been found out. It must be possible that we are still in the mourning period for God, whose absence is our unacknowledged subject. However, if that is so it applies equally to us all. I was brought up in the Church of England and keep a faint absenteeist affection for it, but in fact (and this may be a sign of mourning) I have come to think of all religion as likely to be corrupting, and believe it important that we should be able to recognise this fact, if it is agreed to be one, while at the same time understanding to what an enormous degree we still live, think, and read under its shadow, as indeed the whole world does, though we are obliged as clerical sceptics to eschew violent fundamentalisms, false pieties, false consolations.

That is why it seems proper to be a little sad about what we, and especially, in these circumstances, I, try to do. Our interpretations lack all hope of that kind of success, the success of salvation, access to the kingdom. There is not a lot to be genuinely cheerful about, and it does at times appear that since – not if, as in the original formulation – God is dead, absolutely anything goes; but we know it doesn't. Charity and hope survive, at any rate, especially charity; even this book is an example of its action. On no very compelling occasion a number of gifted, generous and serious lecturers and listeners, who might well have spent the time more pleasantly and more profitably, attended to me instead; and so, in an appropriate fit of genial melancholy, and with a due sense that an end is nigh, I offer my warmest thanks to all who contributed to a moment of critical celebration I cannot bring myself to regret, and promise never to mope about.

Two
Essays in Interpretation

7

The Location of Utopia: Narrative Devices in a Renaissance Fiction

Dominic Baker-Smith

Is he deep, this Thomas More?
(Yesimin-Volpin 1961, 'The Raven', 53)

Thomas More's *De Optimo Reipublicae Statu*, better known as *Utopia*, was issued by the Louvain printer Thierry Martens late in 1516. There is something deeply ironical about the way in which the place of the approved title has been usurped by the name of More's fictitious island, since for much of its career his *libellus aureus* has been subjected to the inflexible glare of literal interpretation. In Utopian terms literal interpretation means focussing on Book II, the actual account of the island society, and treating this as a series of reformist proposals discreetly decked in camouflage. From this vantage point More's work is a fiction in the highly restricted sense that it adopts a veneer of make-believe either so as to alleviate intellectual drudgery on the part of the reader (a medicine of cherries) or to secure the author an escape route in the event of official disapproval. The extraordinary thing is that this way of reading the text – the prescriptive reading as we might call it – asserted its dominance at a very early date. This may well have something to do with the increasingly grim tone of intellectual discussion which sets in during the 1520s, and certainly More himself reacted to this new atmosphere in a pessimistic way:

I saye therfore in these dayes in whyche men by theyr owne defaute mysseconstre and take harme of the very scrypture of god, vntyll men better amende, yf any man wolde now translate Moria in to Englyshe, or some workes eyther that I haue my selfe wryten ere this . . . I wolde not onely my derlynges [Erasmus'] bokes but myne owne also, helpe to burne them both wyth myne owne handes. . . . [1]

Here in 1532 it is important to see what More is not doing: he is not rejecting his earlier work, or that of Erasmus, but he is declaring it inopportune – 'vntyll men better amende'. The time is out of joint and so is the art of interpretation. In the fury of polemic which burst over Europe after Luther, the pleasure of the text was to be found in kinds of reassurance, and the appeal of a fantastic island inhabited by rational men might outweigh that of any anatomy of current abuses. Sir Philip Sidney's reservations about *Utopia* arise from his aristocratic dislike of the Utopian polity, and it is clear that for him this is the essence of the book. His contemporary Francesco Sansovino, whose *Del Governo et Amministratione di Diversi Regni et Republiche* (Venice, 1578) describes the systems of France, England, Turkey, Lucca, Nuremberg and other states, includes without further comment 'Del Governo della Republiche d'Utopia'. This concentration on the second book which marks all discussion of More's book until modern times is a symptom of a literalism expressed by the Reverend Ferdinando Warner in his introduction to the work in 1758:

There is no doubt, I think, but that All his own Notions of Government were recommended under this ingenious Fiction of a Commonwealth: And if in some Instances of his Conduct afterwards, he seemed evidently to counteract them, it may be supposed that he had seen Reason to change his Sentiments, upon further Knowledge, and more experience of Men and Things. (Warner 1758: 145)

The veil of fiction is extremely thin. In the light of this understanding of *Utopia* as – to take the subtitle of the 1743 Glasgow edition – 'A Philosophical Romance', it is not surprising to discover its appropriation by the radical cause. In *The German Ideology* Marx and Engels class More with the Levellers, Owen, Thompson and Watts as an early example of English communism, while to William Morris *Utopia* was 'a necessary part of a Socialist's library'. Karl Kautsky's remarkable socialist analysis of the book in 1888 endeavours to disengage it from the precedent of Plato's

Republic, noting that More's essential modernity, induced by his exposure to mercantile capitalism, derives from recognition of the great socialist principle 'that man is a product of the material conditions in which he lives' (Kautsky 1927: 171–2). Thus the tendency of the prescriptive reading is quite simply to focus attention on the description of Utopian society, treating its fictional aspects as little more than a didactic aid which can be dispensed with by the perceptive reader. In such a reading the first book and the closing lines of the second merely provide a frame and induce through their satirical edge a receptive disposition towards the exemplary account of More's ideal polity.

For a truly 'literary' reading of *Utopia*, one that is which pays due attention to the rhetorical devices which operate within the text, we have to wait until modern times. To anyone concerned with the history of interpretation this is a rather disconcerting fact to face, yet if we admit that some readings of a text will strike us as more persuasive, more expressive of its potential for meaning, than others, then we have to accept that such readings may go underground for periods of time, if not for perpetuity. What is so striking about the *fortuna* of More's work is the speed of its decline into a partial reading, and modesty suggests caution about its reappraisal in our own time.

There are some signs, however, that More would not have been surprised by the fate that overtook his work, almost in his own lifetime. He had, after all, read the *Phaedrus* and knew the warning of Socrates about the loss of authorial control once words were trapped in writing, so that the composition drifts all over the place, getting into the wrong hands, 'And when it is ill-treated and unfairly abused it always needs its parent to come to its help, being unable to defend or help itself' (Plato 1961: 275e). It was, of course, just such a pessimistic view of hermeneutic stability that prompted More's 1532 retraction of his earlier works, but there are grounds to suppose that even while *Utopia* was in the press his hopes were not substantially more sanguine.

Consider, for example, the letter that he sent to Erasmus on 31 October 1516, which bears directly on matters of interpretation. The first issue concerns reactions to Erasmus' version of the Greek New Testament, published that summer; John Fisher, the Bishop of Rochester, is in favour of it but others, notably a group of Franciscans, are hostile and they have conspired 'to read what you write in a very different frame of mind'. They have taken an oath, More adds with suitable hyperbole, 'that they will read right through [your works] with the greatest care, and not understand anything'. This Phaedrian anxiety about misreading is still present in More's subsequent remarks about the *Epistolae Obscurorum Virorum*, the brilliant anti-scholastic satire which had appeared a year earlier in reaction to the bitter clash between the pioneer Hebraist Johannes Reuchlin and the Cologne theological faculty. As the letter reports, everyone was enjoying them but, More is careful to observe, for different reasons: 'the learned as a joke and the unlearned in all seriousness'. It is that seriousness or failure to appreciate the basic irony which interests More and he expresses some regret at the title of the book since the incongruity of its reference to 'obscure men' may alert the unwary. Without that clue, he argues, within a hundred years pedants dazed with their own learning would have 'failed to detect the long nose of scorn, had it been longer than any rhinoceros's'.[2] They would, in other words, have read the text literally, as would indeed happen to *Utopia*.

It is interesting that More should have had misreading so much in mind at this time. The manuscript of *Utopia*, under its original name of *Nusquama*, had been sent to Erasmus early in September and he was seeing to its final preparation in consort with a mutual friend, Pieter Gillis, the Petrus Aegidius of More's text. Part of the plan, to which the latter part of More's letter alludes, was the collection of a body of prefatory material, primarily in the form of congratulatory epistles from men of note. This made up the so-called *parerga*, the ornaments added to the text. But the function of these ornaments is not simply to bear witness to the standing of the author; some of them have a direct bearing on how we should approach the text – they are in effect interpretative controls. The earliest of these is the preface which More wrote himself and addressed to Gillis. Since the surviving correspondence shows only a minimum of collusion between the parties, we must assume that More had already advised the others of his intent and this had been confirmed by the preface. In fact, the character of Gillis' additions strongly suggests that he had a privileged insight into More's plans and it is hardly likely that Erasmus would have been unaware of them either. When we look at the circumstances surrounding the composition of *Utopia* these strengthen the impression of a circle of initiates, fully alert to the kind of book More had in mind.

In July 1519, less than three years after the publication, Erasmus informed Ulrich von Hutten, a co-author of the *Epistolae Obscurorum Virorum*, that More wrote *Utopia* backwards, starting with Book II and adding the first book later as opportunity arose. In other words he began with the account of the Utopian polity, a fantastic republic set in an undiscovered island, and then wrote the frame which might be said to mediate that fantasy to a world which the reader can identify, based as it is in an Antwerp garden where More and Gillis listen to the account of Raphael's travels. The idea that More described the communitarian state of Utopia during a lull in his duties as a negotiator in the Low Countries and then followed it with a narrative which placed it – in both fictional and moral terms – during his spare moments as Wolsey's factotum in London has a strong logical coherence.[3] What is less persuasive is the suggestion that More began with an ideal society and then attached to it a satirical survey of European politics as an afterthought. There seems no reason to suppose that he did not have his strategy in mind from the outset; *Utopia* is, after all, an episode in a long tradition which reaches back to Plato and has evolved largely in response to the challenge of his *Republic*.

If we are to arrive at some recognition of the rhetorical controls that More built into the work before it began drifting away (as Socrates had warned it would), then it is useful to consider what the reader of the first edition in 1516 had to encounter as the pages were turned. First the title, *De Optimo Reipublicae Statu Deque Nova Insula Utopia*, at once places the book in its tradition, pointing back to its Platonic origin; at the same time the description of the author as 'Londinensis civis & Vicecomitis', citizen and under-sheriff of London, links this tradition to a specific set of circumstances. On the reverse of the title-page Martens printed a woodcut of the amazing island, a device which gave the fantasy a seductive semblance of reality. Next, facing this, and functioning as ontological ballast to the fiction, comes the Utopian alphabet, followed by a tetrastichon in that tongue and a hexastichon by Raphael's nephew, 'poeta laureatus'. The reader then encounters the series of commendatory letters and verses which culminate in More's prefatory letter to Gillis. Later editions saw a considerable expansion of the *parerga*, notably the letter from

Guillaume Budé to Thomas Lupset which is printed together with
an additional letter from More to Gillis in the second edition
printed in Paris in 1517. But it is not difficult to distinguish
between those materials which are, quite simply, commendatory
and those which connect in a vital way with the interpretation
of the text. And these latter we can limit to the contributions
made by More, Gillis and (conceivably) by Erasmus, the inner
circle of collaborators.

We are thus faced by a series of concentric circles. At the centre
stands the remarkable island, the setting for an experiment in
political suppression of the ego. But this is described by the
Portugese traveller Raphael in an Antwerp garden in the year
1515 in the presence of Pieter Gillis, Thomas More and his secretary John Clement. Again, we only hear Raphael's words
through the report written by Thomas More some time after the
event, supposedly when he had returned to London. This process
of transmission by which we hear of the island through two
stages of report bears some resemblance to that by which the
realm of Platonic ideas finds shadowy duplication in terrestrial
forms. If the ideas suffer dilution they nevertheless engage with
an identifiable and historical world in a way which is intriguing.
Thus the exemplary fiction of Book II is surrounded by a frame
of narrative circumstances based in an Antwerp garden, and this
in turn leads out to More's prefatory letter and the response of
his correspondent Pieter Gillis. Each move out from the centre
places the Utopian vision in closer proximity to the compromises
and confusions of the real world: so, in the garden, Raphael's
account of Utopian values is met with reserve and polite resistance; once we move beyond the text proper and into the *parerga*,
the dominant issue becomes the status of the work, the kind of
reality that it can claim in the setting of contemporary Europe.
And if we can describe the enterprise as an emanation of utopian
ideas into the order of common experience, then there is also
the return journey in the mind from Europe to the archetype.
Renaissance literature, marked as it is with the impress of rhetoric, persistently dwells on the relationship between ideal and
actual, between golden and brazen worlds; the unusual feature
of More's book is its critical focus on this traffic between imagination and performance.

If the title draws our attention to the Platonic debate *de optimo
reipublicae statu*, it equally alerts us to the book's status as a travel

narrative *de nova insula utopia*. Now the travel narrative had its own particular association with Lucianic satire, a point that we shall examine in a moment, but in the year 1515 it also had a unique topicality. More was thus able to exploit both the traditional, ironic use of travellers' tales and contemporary interest in the newly discovered lands to the west. Travel literature has an obvious tendency to refer back to the familiar, either laying bare its faults or indicating alternative social arrangements. It is a commonplace that the first visitors to the New World interpreted their experiences in the convenient categories that they took with them: Columbus had read Sir John Mandeville. The kind of fantasy travel literature which Mandeville represents gave to the genuine explorers a compelling image of virtuous Indians who anticipate many qualities of the Utopians, as in Mandeville's folk of the Isle of Bragman,

> where that ben gode folk and trewe and of gode lyvynge after hire beleve and of gode feyth. And all be it that thei ben not cristned ne have no perfyt lawe, yit natheless of kyndely [natural] lawe thei ben full of all vertue and thei eschewen all vices and all malices and all synnes. For thei ben not proude ne covetous ne envyous ne wrathfull ne glotonous ne leccherous. Ne thei don to no man other wise than thei wolde that men diden to hem. And in this poynt thei fulfillen the X commandementes of god, And gif no charge of aveer [avarice] ne of ricchess. And thei lye not ne thei swere not for non occasioun, but thei seyn symply ye and nay, For thei seyn he that swereth will disceyve his neyghbore; And therefore all that thei don thei don it withouten oth. (Mandeville 1919–23: 194; on discovery narratives see Hahn 1978)

This Houyhnhnm-like state of the Bragmanians is very similar to that of the Utopians, and it does bring out the manner in which older tales fused with the new reports on the Indies to provoke speculation about the natural state of man. Even while the accounts of Vespucci and Waldseemüller ran off the presses, Mandeville's *Travels* had four editions between 1496 and 1510. And it was probably in the latter year that the first English language account *Of the newe landes* was published in Antwerp by Jan van Doesborch.

It is instructive to keep this blend of fantasy and objective report in mind when examining Utopia's claim to actuality. The reader turning from the map of the island to the Utopian alphabet facing it is strongly persuaded to suspend disbelief. This addition can probably be attributed to Pieter Gillis, together with the tetrastichon in Utopian and the hexastichon by Raphael's nephew Anemolius. Two words in the transliteration of the tetrastichon catch the eye as offering some purchase to understanding, *'gymnosophaon'* and *'gymnosophon'*. In the Latin translation these are rendered as *'philosophia'* and *'philosophicam'* in the claim made by the island that 'I alone among all lands, without the aid of *philosophy*, have manifested to mortals the *philosophical* city' (More 1965: 18).[4] However, the use of words that provide a link with the fabled gymnosophists of the East, the sages of Indian wisdom, evokes precisely the blend of myth and report which is so fertile in More's fiction.

The verses by Anemolius which follow may be by Gillis as well; what is certain is that they are by someone intimate with More's scheme. Leaving aside the play on Ou-topia (no-place) and Eu-topia (happy place), the most interesting point is the direct comparison with Plato's republic: what he merely sketched in words the new island actually demonstrates. Again, one is nudged towards the distinction between 'philosophy' and the 'philosophical'. The allusion is to that point at the end of Book IX of the *Republic* where discussion turns on the location of the ideal city. This is a crucial discussion for More, since it relates to the issue of involvement or non-involvement in the political life; it was a theme that had interested him at least since his translation of the *Vita* of Giovanni Pico della Mirandola in 1504. As the *Republic* makes clear, debate over the active or contemplative lives cannot be separated from the issue of perfectibility. Can a rational society be achieved? If not, how is it possible to justify involvement in a political world tainted by irrational motives? It is at this point in the *Republic* that Socrates asserts that the wise man may participate in the politics of 'his own city', but not, perhaps, in those of the city of his birth. Glaucon clarifies the point,

> 'I understand . . . You mean the city whose establishment we have described, the city *whose home is in the ideal*, for I think that it can be found nowhere on earth.'
> 'Well', said I, 'perhaps there is a pattern of it laid up in

heaven for him who wishes to contemplate it and so beholding to constitute himself its citizen.' (Plato 1930: 592a-b)

The phrase of immediate relevance is that in italics, literally 'the city which is laid down in words' (*tē en logois keimenē*). Plato touches here, in a tantalising way, on the problematic nature of fictions: the reflective politician is committed to participation in an imaginary community or *polis*. Even more tantalising to the student of More's *Utopia* is the way in which the book's original title, *Nusquama* appears to echo Marsilio Ficino's translation of this very passage from the *Republic*, 'quae verbis solum, in terris vero nusquam, ut arbitror existat' (Plato 1517: fol. CCLXV^v; the point is made in Nagel 1973: 173). Does Utopia exist only in words? Of course it does. But what could be said to distinguish it from Plato's handling of the theme '*de optimo reipublicae statu*' is that it offers a fictional rendering of the ideal community in action. This is the whole point of the verses by 'Anemolius', that Utopia surpasses Plato's city because it exhibits a working model of the just state.

But to limit the fictional strategy of *Utopia* to this embodiment of a desirable polity, precisely the reading of a majority of readers who have been hypnotised by Book II, is to disregard the most subtle – and the most Platonic – of More's devices. This we can summarise as the engagement of the reader in the process of authentication. In the *Republic* the pattern (*paradeigma*) of the ideal city is laid up in heaven; while Glaucon doubts the possibility of realising a comparable city on earth, Socrates evades the issue: the important point is not whether such a city exists or will exist, but that it is in a sense an option for the wise man who will contemplate it and 'constitute himself its citizen'. We are at that problematic juncture where the idealising imagination engages with the exigencies of history.[5]

More, in concert with Erasmus, had engaged in a careful study of Lucian in the period 1505–6. This was undertaken to develop his Greek and one result was the *Luciani opuscula* printed at Paris by Josse Bade in the latter year. It would not be surprising if his first encounter with Plato's *Republic* had relied on a Latin version like Ficino's, but by 1515 More was well able to use the Greek text and his approach to it would inevitably have been coloured by his knowledge of Lucian. In fact it would be fair to say that the Platonic influence on *Utopia* is closely bound up with Lucian's own adoption of Platonic motifs in such dialogues as *The Ship* and *A True Story*. Lucian's innovatory handling of the dialogue form gained much of its ironic force from the fact that dialogue had traditionally been the preserve of philosophical authors. His use of sophisticated narrative games and fantastic inventions directed attention to the subjective element in any reading of 'reality'. In satirical terms he played with the human propensity for comforting self-deception, and it was this aspect of his work which attracted More. In *A True Story*, a narrative with obvious relevance to *Utopia*, Lucian's traveller commences the account of his journey with a contemptuous attack on travellers' tales, those concoctions of falsehood and deception. While Odysseus is picked out as a guide and instructor in this kind of charlatanry, the narrator finds it hard to condemn the extravagances of travel writers since lying has become commonplace, even among philosophers. Now this reference to lying philosophers has been seen as a dig at Plato's use of the dream of Er, the soldier who returns from the dead to describe the post-mortem fate of the soul at the close of the *Republic* (614b ff.). It can hardly be coincidental that the sailing of Raphael to strange new lands is compared to that of Ulysses or Plato. Once Lucian's narrator arrives at the Isles of the Blest he visits the Elysian fields and meets the famous dead – all but one, that is. Plato is nowhere to be found: 'it was said that he was living in his imaginary city under the constitution and laws which he himself wrote' (Lucian 1913–67: I, *A True Story*, 319–21). This can only be an ironical allusion to the words of Socrates and Glaucon about the ideal city in the *Republic*. By contemplating the non-existent the philosopher does, all too literally, 'constitute himself its citizen'. Thus it is as well to recognise that while Lucian is an important influence on the writing of *Utopia*, More uses him to open out issues first discovered in Plato; narrative games direct the reader towards a serious question, the location of the ideal order within ordinary experience. And, very much in the spirit of his classical models, More thrusts the issue off the page, as it were, and deposits it in the reader's lap.[6]

The fecundity of More's text is a consequence of its instability. If we leave out of consideration Raphael's whole account of the fantastic island then the remainder of the fiction, from the opening dispute over the *vita activa* to the letters added by More and Gillis to the *parerga*, is set to blur the reader's sense of the boundaries between fact and fiction. The precise location of Utopia, a parody of the ontological issue raised by Socrates' ideal city in the *Republic*, is one of the topics designed to disturb our response. Thus Gillis' letter, to all appearances the last part of the fictional entity to be completed[7] and one of the first to be encountered by the reader, addresses the question of the island's position only to confess that someone, 'who had, I suppose, caught cold on shipboard', coughed at the critical moment when Raphael had revealed it. More, for his part, had been distracted by a servant and missed it as well. The only hope is to ask Raphael again, but where is he? Dead according to one report; another claims that having returned to his homeland he became disenchanted and set out for Utopia again. It is worth noting that the second rumour describes the alienation of the Platonic sage whose politics are those of the ideal city and not those of the city of his birth.[8] He is consumed with longing for a place which the reader has yet to encounter.

More's letter to Gillis is an example of intricate narrative irony. There are at least three Thomas Mores that the reader has to contend with: the participant in the discussion at Antwerp, the writer of the letter who has also dutifully recorded the words of that discussion, and by implication the author, the under-sheriff of London. If we take the garden-scene as the first narrative, then Raphael's recollection of Utopia is an anachrony, a step back into the temporal sequence of Vespucci's final voyage to the New World. More's letter to Gillis coincident with the completion of the record of the Antwerp discussion is written 'after almost a year', thus transporting the reader to another and more immediate temporal sequence. In fact if we take *Utopia* as a whole, inclusive of the letters, we are confronted by a remarkable example of what Gérard Genette would classify as narrative metalapsis (Genette 1972: 234–5), a situation in which characters within the narrative sequence move out into non-narrative levels. Its effect is always to perplex, to stimulate reflection on our standards of objectivity. The letter to Gillis shows More's highly sophisticated and post-Lucianic ambition to provoke the reader with tantalising fictions. Typical is the issue of the bridge at Amaurotum: as More recalls it, it is 500 paces in length, but John Clement, his secretary who had been present at Antwerp, insists it is 300. Only one person can settle the matter, the elusive Raphael. And only he can locate the island, a matter of increased urgency now since there is a theologian planning to evangelise the inhabitants. Can Gillis contact him by word of mouth or letter?

To the reader who has progressed through the prefatory letters, therefore, the eventual encounter with Raphael in Antwerp after Mass at Notre Dame is a relief to curiosity. Not only does the setting recall the opening of the *Republic* in the port of Piraeus after a religious festival, but Raphael's credentials have a Platonic ring. His sailing has, according to Pieter Gillis, 'not been like that of Palinurus but that of Ulysses or, rather of Plato'. Forewarned by Lucian, we may be tempted to take a wholly negative view of these precedents. But it is possible that this association with the author of the *Republic* has a more complex significance than that suggested in *A True Story* by the absentee from the Elysian fields. Raphael's credentials are presented by Gillis in a brief speech of introduction (More 1965: 48–50) which reveals his preference for Greek over Latin, his sacrifice of his patrimony so as to retain freedom to travel, and his actual journeying with Amerigo Vespucci. Now the preference for Greek will be no great surprise, and the abdication of his patrimony appears to be lifted almost verbatim from the biography of Pico della Mirandola (More 1931: I, 'The Life of John Picus Erle of Myrandula', 6a-b). The travels with Vespucci are carefully confined to 'the last three of those four voyages which are now universally read of', an insider joke since the well-informed already suspected what later study has confirmed, that Vespucci's first voyage was a hoax. It is typical of More's entwining of fantasy with objective report that he inserts his fictional traveller to 'No-place' into an authentic expedition and dissassociates him from a voyage which never took place.[9] On the fourth voyage, which lasted from May 1503 to May 1504, Vespucci sailed some 260 leagues from Bahia and built a fort at the modern Cape Frio in Brazil; there he left 'twenty-four Christian men . . . being part of the crew of the *Capitana* that was lost' (Vespucci 1894: 55). One of the historic twenty-four is transformed by More into Raphael, who then sets off on his travels. These are left as vague as possible, but he does state that he spent five years among the Utopians before moving on to Taprobane (Sri Lanka) where Sir John Mandeville had surfaced from his fantastic wanderings. Leaving aside the period in Utopia, his other travels cannot have been swift and it is unlikely that we should picture him returning to Europe much before 1511. The later the better, of course, since it brings us closer to the narrative set in Antwerp in '1515'.

Lucianic games maybe, but games which are fundamental to More's destabilising of our ordinary perceptions. If, as I have suggested, a central part of the fictional strategy is to obscure the bounds between mental and historical events, then the Platonic motive for it can be sensed in our traveller's own name. Hythlodaeus has its origin in the Greek terms *huthlos*, 'nonsense', and *daios*, 'cunning'; the familiar rendering of this characteristically Lucianic combination is 'skilled-in-nonsense'. Witty, no doubt, and disturbing for us who rely on his testimony, but the name offers no direct clue to interpretation of the narrative. Once again, however, guidance may be found in the *Republic*. Early in the first Book Socrates engages in argument with Thrasymachus, the voice of moral scepticism and power politics. Indeed, the whole argument of the *Republic* ripples out from this initial clash. Thrasymachus is a noisy and abusive speaker who wastes no time in attacking Socrates' idea of justice:

> And don't you be telling me that it is that which ought to be, or the beneficial or the profitable or the gainful or the advantageous, but express clearly and precisely whatever you say. For I won't take from you any such drivel as that! (336d)

'Drivel', or 'nonsense', is the interesting word: *huthlos*. If Raphael is skilled in nonsense then his nonsense must be the nonsense of Socrates, the talk about 'that which ought to be', a world of ideal justice beyond the contamination of *realpolitik*. If we think back to Socrates' contrast between the city founded on words and the actual political community then it is clear that Raphael, named after an archangel, the heavenly physician sent down to earth to guide Tobias, is our witness to just such a political community.

That does not of itself provide any answer to the problem: Raphael's intrusion into a world co-extensive with the historical reality of the reader is countered by his refusal to participate in the political world of under-sheriff Thomas More, ambassador from the 'invincible' King of England to His Serene Highness of Castile.[10] We are not offered any formula for justice but if we attend to the text we are both intrigued and unsettled; a process of introspection is initiated. And that, no doubt, is as it should be. H. D. Rankin has remarked of the Platonic city, 'If the *Republic* cannot be realised in stone, earth and institutions, and Plato had doubts about such a realisation, it can affect individuals as an instrument of social philosophy' (Rankin 1964: 138; on Plato's approach to fiction see Gill 1979). Any close examination of the means by which report of Utopia filters through to Renaissance Europe, and to our own time, can only undermine the literal reading which seemed once so dominant. It is the instability of the text which proffers the more compelling reading, both in Plato and in More, at the point at which philosophy drifts off into fiction. This was, of course, always present as a potency in dialogue and the fact that More develops it so richly can be attributed in part to his Lucianic approach to the *Republic*. For in the end, as the humanist polemic against the scholastics reiterated, concepts do not easily transform into conduct. *Utopia* is, before all else, a fiction, not a blueprint; not an enchiridion, but an imaginative response to the irony of our subjunctive situation. If, as Frank Kermode has argued, we only read a classic because we believe it says more than its author meant (Kermode 1975a: 80), then we may have to acknowledge cases where part of the meaning is to mean more than is meant. More's attitude to the reader provokes a surplus of signification, and as a result his work hovers outside the reach of any definitive reading, for it is only the closed text which no longer calls for our participation. Criticism, no less than literature, operates within a context and it is a revealing comment on our own time that we have re-learned to respond to the multivalency of the Renaissance text.

Notes

1. *The Confutation of Tyndale's Answer* in More 1978: III 179. 'Moria' is the *Encomium Moriae* or *Praise of Folly*.
2. Letter 481 in Erasmus 1974ff: IV, 114–17. 'Nose' (*nasus*) is proverbially associated in Roman satire with wit or the capacity to read irony.
3. The classic presentation of this case is in Hexter 1952. For Erasmus' letter to von Hutten, see Letter 999 in Erasmus 1974ff, VII, 23–4.
4. The distinction is presumably between 'philosophical' as a quality and 'philosophy' as a pedagogic technique.
5. This is the dilemma of being in what Frank Kermode calls the 'middest', from which we reach out, 'desiring these moments of significance which harmonize origin and end' (Kermode 1967: 48).

6. 'Plato seems on the whole reconciled to leaving the just state as an ideal, whereas he wants individuals actually to improve by reading the *Republic* and using it as an ideal to which to conform themselves.' (Annas 1981: 187)

7. Erasmus requested the letter on 17 October (Erasmus 1974ff: IV, no. 477) and Gillis' response is dated 1 November. The book was published by January.

8. *Republic* 592b; the same disenchantment is the fate of the enlightened who have seen the light of the sun but have to return to the shadow world of the cave, 516e–517e.

9. See Vespucci 1894: xxv; I am grateful to Dr H. C. Porter for alerting me to this point.

10. Again it can hardly be chance that in the 1515 *Adagia* Erasmus includes *invictus* and *serenissimus* among the 'magnificent lies, that must be added to royal titles' (Erasmus 1703–6: II, 871A).

8

'Why should he call her whore?' Defamation and Desdemona's Case

Lisa Jardine

> *Emil.* Why should he call her whore? who keeps her com-
> pany?
> What place, what time, what form, what likelihood?
> > Shakespeare *Othello* 1965: IV. ii. 139–40
> > (All references are to the Ridley Arden edition)

This piece is part of a larger project on the relationship between cultural history and textual studies, taking as its focus the texts of the works of Shakespeare.[1] It is also the piece of work with which that enterprise began – I was prompted to want to reconsider the nature of the relationship between history and text criticism specifically by what was happening in work on *Othello* and in particular on Desdemona. The work began as a polemical intervention, but has, as it has developed, been shaped (and, I hope, mellowed) by my own growing understanding of the complexity of the issues, and my admiration for many of the practitioners in the field of 'historical' Shakespeare studies.[2] I can think of no more appropriate piece of work to offer as a tribute to Frank Kermode, whose own *Renaissance Essays* (1971) offer an exemplary practice in drawing together history, scholarship and criticism into a single coherent account of renaissance textuality.

My concern in this work is to use the textual traces of early modern social relations as the point of encounter with early modern agency – specifically the agency of those whose point of view has tended to be excluded from dominant cultural production (non-élite men and all women). My proposal is that the social relations in the community, as conveyed to us in the 'shaped' accounts which come down to us, position the self (the subject) as the intersection of overlaid maps of acknowledged interpersonal connections. This in turn can helpfully sharpen our response to the dramatisation of interpersonal relations on the Elizabethan and Jacobean stage, if we regard stage dramatisation as the focusing of otherwise inchoate 'experience' into socially constructed units of meaning, for the purpose of clear and distinct transmission of plot to audience. So the present piece of work is not just offered as one more novel way of enhancing our reading of Shakespeare's texts; it is proposed as a very particular way of recovering some sense of connection between the textual and the social – recovering, perhaps, a distinctively *cultural* dimension in early modern textual production.[3]

The shift towards such a cultural dimension has come, in my own case, from a sense of limitation within textual studies. Specifically, in some recent 'historical' work on *Othello*, a commitment to textuality has seemed to carry the consequence that the critic is no longer to be held responsible for distinguishing verbal suggestions of Desdemona's guilt which enter the play as interpretations or anticipations of her actions, from the 'tale' (the construction as plot, in the text) of those actions themselves. The result has been that Desdemona has come increasingly regularly to be 'read' as guilty by association (with what had been said of her), and her death has been presented as punishment (ideologically and individually), instead of tragic injustice.[4] In my view, methodologies which erase the agency of any main protagonist so effectively from the interpretation are fundamentally flawed.[5] It is one thing to suggest that, textually, female figures are deprived of the power and authority to control the interpretation and evaluation of their actions (that texts place them permanently in the object position in the narrative); it is quite another to continue to sustain the traditional historical view that the lived experience of women down through history has been as objects.

In seeking to develop a methodology which would restore subject status (subjectivity, even) to the female figure in history, one significant objective seemed to be to find some means of distinguishing in a text between casual verbal formulations involving women, and what I shall specify as *events* in which women participate. Here I take *event* to be a configuration of circumstances and persons which was perceived as having a shape, so that it carried a shared meaning for the early modern community: although our access to such a configuration is necess arily via surviving textual remains which give it shape, we are able (I shall argue) to distinguish such an event as socially and culturally meaningful in the flow of incidents and social inter-actions.[6] Take, as an extreme case of the former, the following piece of scurrility on Iago's part, in the opening scene of Act II of *Othello*:

> *Iago.* [*Aside.*] He takes her by the palm; ay, well said, whisper: as little a web as this will ensnare as great a fly as Cassio. Ay, smile upon her, do: I will catch you in your own courtes-ies: you say true, 'tis so indeed. If such tricks as these strip you out of your lieutenantry, it had been better you had not kiss'd your three fingers so oft, which now again you are most apt to play the sir in: good, well kiss'd, an excellent courtesy; 'tis so indeed: yet again, your fingers at your lips? would they were clyster-pipes for your sake . . . [*Trumpets within.*] The Moor, I know his trumpet.
>
> *Cassio.* 'Tis truly so.

Othello II.i.167–79

Here lewd innuendo at Desdemona's expense enters the text without on-stage acknowledgement; and the overly-courteous Florentine Cassio's reply adds to the joke, as he apparently assents to the implied unchastity of her behaviour ('The Moor, I know his trumpet'/*Cassio.* ''Tis truly so'). None of us, I think, imagines that this piece of wordplay weighs very heavily in the balance of the play's developing value-system; indeed, we do not imagine that the figure Cassio, on the stage, has heard the pun. Yet the play on words is there (as it is also, at equivalent moments, in *Troilus and Cressida* and in *The Merchant of Venice*), and in the increasingly intricate games that Shakespearean critics play with the text, it is made increasingly to count as part of a case against Desdemona – a case for making Desdemona take the critical blame.[7]

Play on words in itself does not damage a reputation; innuendo alone does not shift the emphasis from potentiality for blame (an incautious marriage, provocative behaviour) to blameworthiness. Reputations are damaged by harmful accusations made under socially significant circumstances. At the other pole of the scale of cultural meaningfulness for which I am concerned to construct a methodology stands substantial *defamation* – an offence against an individual which had consequences, historically, in the community, which was an *event* with a kind of concreteness and stability to which we are able to give our critical attention, in a specifically historical sense (and making such a distinction is, for me, crucially what it means to read Shakespeare historically).

If we treat Desdemona simply textually – as a 'representation', in a uniformly illuminated discourse (without the light and shade of historical context) – then the vectors of agency (who acts, and upon whom) will necessarily end with her as object to some male subject.[8] Yet, in history, agency is a dynamic, in relation to women and to men (both women and men have acted, have been acted upon). It is this historical *agency* which I am concerned to retrieve, in theory as well as in practice. The distinction between scurrility and an accusation which requires a formal hearing (offensiveness and substantial offence) is designed to retrieve the category of agent, as the intersection of a set of social relationships and cultural expectations.[9] To understand what happens in *Othello*, I shall argue, it is important to distinguish an offensive remark or gesture (of the kind which remains all-too accessible and current) from what was once an indictable offence (but one which, as an integral part of the system of social relations of the early modern period, we no longer recognise).[10] It does not just matter *that* a woman is called 'whore', it matters *when* and *where* she is.[11]

If we fail to sustain that dynamic relationship between history and text, we may mistake the shared textual conventions of a period for an authentic Renaissance subjectivity (because separate subjects share access to matching cultural conventions). That in turn may be taken as evidence as to the intrinsic nature of the event these conventions represent (the closest to the 'real' to which the textual can give us access).

The lure of such a textual 'authenticity' can be illustrated with an example which turns out to be particularly relevant to Desdemona's case in *Othello*. A recent article on *A Midsummer Night's Dream* juxtaposes a passage from the private diary of Simon Forman, which draws attention to the biological femaleness of the ageing Queen (dated 1597, when Elizabeth I was in her sixties) with two passages of description of the Queen from the journal of Hurault de Maisse, ambassador extraordinary of King Henri IV of France (also dated 1597):

I dreamt that I was with the Queen, and that she was a little elderly woman in a coarse white petticoat all unready; and she and I walked up and down through lanes and closes, talking and reasoning of many matters. At last we came over a great close where there were many people, and there were two men at hard words. One of them was a weaver, a tall man with a reddish beard, distract of his wits. She talked to him and he spoke very merrily unto her, and at last did take her and kiss her. So I took her by the arm and put her away; and told her the fellow was frantic. And so we went from him and I led her by the arm still, and then we went though a dirty lane. She had a long, white smock, very clean and fair, and it trailed in the dirt and her coat behind. I took her coat and did carry it up a good way, and then it hung too low before. I told her she should do me a favour to let me wait on her, and she said I should. Then said I, 'I mean to wait *upon* you and not under you, that I might make this belly a little bigger to carry up this smock and coats out of the dirt.' And so we talked merrily and then she began to lean upon me, when we were past the dirt and to be very familiar with me, and methought she began to love me. And when we were alone, out of sight, methought she would have kissed me.[12]

The descriptions of the Queen's appearance by de Maisse are also from a private journal:

She was strangely attired in a dress of silver cloth, white and crimson, or silver 'gauze', as they call it. This dress had slashed sleeves lined with red taffeta, and was girt about with other little sleeves that hung down to the ground, which she was for ever twisting and untwisting. She kept the front of her dress open, and one could see the whole of her bosom [*gorge*], and passing low, and often she would open the front of this robe with her hands as if she was too hot. The collar of the robe was very high, and the lining of the inner part all adorned with little pendants of rubies and pearls, very many, but quite small. She had also a chain of rubies and pearls about her neck. On her head she wore a garland of the same material and beneath it a great reddish coloured wig, with a great number of spangles of gold and silver, and hanging down over her forehead some pearls, but of no great worth. On either

side of her ears hung two great curls of hair, almost down to
her shoulders and within the collar of her robe, spangled as
the top of her head. Her bosom [*gorge*] is somewhat wrinkled
as well as [one can see for] [sic in text] the collar that she
wears round her neck, but lower down her flesh is exceeding
white and delicate, so far as one could see.

As for her face, it is and appears to be very aged. It is long
and thin, and her teeth are very yellow and unequal, compared
with what they were formerly, so they say, and on the left
side less than on the right. Many of them are missing so that
one cannot understand her easily when she speaks quickly.
Her figure is fair and tall and graceful in whatever she does; so
far as may be she keeps her dignity, yet humbly and graciously
withal.[13]

[In a second audience, the Queen appeared] clad in a dress of
black taffeta, bound with gold lace, and like a robe in the Italian
fashion with open sleeves and lined with crimson taffeta. She
had a petticoat of white damask, girdled, and open in front,
as was also her chemise, in such a manner that she often
opened this dress and one could see all her belly, and even to
her navel [mistranslation of: *luy voyait-on tout l'estomac jusques
au nombril*]. Her head tire was the same as before. She had
bracelets of pearl on her hands, six or seven rows of them. On
her head tire she wore a coronet of pearls, of which five or six
were marvellously fair. When she raises her head, she has a
trick of putting both hands on her gown and opening it inso-
much that all her belly [*estomac*] can be seen.[14]

The critic maintains that juxtaposition of these passages shows
how 'the virginal sex-object' of Forman's dream 'corresponds with
startling accuracy to descriptions of Elizabeth's *actual* appearance
in 1597' (my emphasis). And in a revealing comment on what is
meant by 'actual' in relation to the Queen's appearance as
described here, he observes:

Elizabeth's display of her bosom signified her status as a
maiden. . . . Like her bosom, Elizabeth's belly must have fig-
ured her political motherhood. But, as the French ambassador
insinuates, these conspicuous self-displays were also a kind of
erotic provocation [my emphasis]. The official portraits and

courtly blazons that represent the splendor of the Queen's immutable body politic are nicely complemented by the ambassador's sketches of the Queen's sixty-five year old body natural. His perceptions of the vanity and melancholy of this personage in no way negate his numerous observations of her grace, vitality, and political cunning. Indeed, in the very process of describing the Queen's preoccupation with the impact of her appearance upon her beholders, the ambassador demonstrates its impact upon *himself* [author's emphasis]. (Montrose 1983: 64)

The 'erotic provocation' belongs, I am suggesting, to the text, and its cultural conventions – the shaping in the telling which refracts and intensifies 'experience' into expression – not to the event (that is, to any of the Queen's many public appearances).[15] What the two 1597 accounts of the physically female Elizabeth share is a common set of motifs denoting sexual availability. Both texts dwell on a prominence of breast and stomach (ambiguously prominent, though not necessarily naked), which takes the eye of the observer, and troubles decorum in its possibilities for suggestiveness (most clearly to be seen in the obscene fecundity of woodcut 'whores' of the period).[16] In the case of the Catholic Hurault de Maisse's two descriptions, glimpses of female flesh – neck, throat, and (in veiled decolleté) suggestions beyond – cannot be accommodated to his version of female decorum. The detailed richness of the dress, furthermore, in conjunction with the suggestions of indecency, reinforces the anxiety about 'whoredom' (since finery and extravagant dress was customarily associated with prostitution).[17] In the case of the Forman passage the whore/harlot connotations are readily mobilised when 'Queen' is heard (in the familiarity of tone of the account) as 'quean' (prostitute).[18] Forman's dream fantasy of female 'power' overwhelmed, inverts the culturally dominant iconic versions of Elizabeth as Diana (chaste goddess), as Penthesilea (virgin amazon warrior), as phoenix (reproducing without a mate), all of which iconographically stress chastity as her *virtù*, and occlude as far as possible her 'actual' sex.

What is interesting about this example (from an article by a critic for whom I have a great deal of respect) is that while it invokes history, it slips, at the point of comparison between the two accounts, into an exercise in intertextuality, and the critical mistake (equating 'actual' with 'textual' versions of Elizabeth) is a direct consequence. Textual 'equivalence' (the words weighing equally),[19] I suggest, does not automatically confirm that there is a common historical 'actual', in which both texts are grounded. In this case the discourses are undoubtedly shared: both texts make use of contemporary cultural versions of 'woman spoken badly of' (specifically, spoken of as *fallen* woman – harlot, whore).[20] But then, the *occasion* for both accounts is the same: the appearance in public, in a position of authority rather than of deference, in her own right, of an unmarried woman – in early modern terms an intrinsically indecorous event, and one to which the two early modern authors respond in the kind of unseemly terms which they consider are licensed by her (the Queen's) breach of acceptable female behaviour.

Forman's erotic dream-encounter with the Queen seems to tell us more about Forman's own preoccupations than about Elizabeth;[21] the Sieur de Maisse's recorded observations are more complicated in their relation to the occasion to which they give expression – the preoccupation with visible flesh which shapes his description of the Queen's appearance is structured by conventions of decorum which are, perhaps, the ambassador's response to the fundamental lack of *respectability* involved in a woman's occupying the throne of England (unthinkable under French Salic law), and suggestions of her as 'harlot/whore of Babylon' in reaction to her further public prominence as head of the English church.[22] Neither text gives us (the twentieth-century reader) access to Queen Elizabeth as historical subject and agent.

There are two reasons why I have considered this example to be important enough to treat it at some length. One is that the culturally constructed figure of the whore or harlot, as a response to a 'forward' woman, which stands behind this example is particularly appropriate (in its yet more culturally specific form of 'whore of Venice') when we come to look at *Othello*. The other is that what surfaces very clearly in this example is a tendency in textual criticism to privilege for analysis texts which are concerned with desire and sexuality. And the very plausibility of the critical case made suggests that the temptation to claim two culturally homologous textual versions of 'woman spoken badly of' as 'actual' is then particularly strong. Here, I think, the 'historical' becomes troublingly entangled with the theoretical version of subjectivity in which subjectivity is the unconscious, and which takes the self to be constructed in discourse – a discourse in which unconscious desire is uttered in an endless process of aspiring towards a fulfilment which is permanently deferred. This version of subjectivity allows the 'shaping fantasy' of the Forman and Sieur de Maisse texts to be 'actual', not in the sense that that was how Elizabeth 'really' was, but in the sense that Elizabethan male subjects expressed (and therefore consciously experienced) their selfhood in those (explicitly sexual and desirous) terms.

But, strikingly, distinctions in female agency in history seem to have a strong tendency to collapse into a transhistorical textual identity when we concern ourselves as critics with utterances which centre on woman's sexuality. Or, to put it another way, if we require discoursing subjects to produce themselves in terms of desire, in order to recognise those subjects as persons in our modern sense, then we seem already to have disadvantaged early modern women.[23] This tendency is a marked one in *Othello*, a play in which sexually-charged utterances concerning women play a remarkably prominent part in the action.

In *Othello* three women, of three distinct social ranks, figure prominently in the plot. Desdemona is the daughter of one of Venice's most senior and influential citizens. Bianca is a Venetian courtesan – a woman of substance who supports herself and her household by her liaisons with men of rank (notably Cassio, Othello's second-in-command).[24] Emilia is wife of Othello's third-in-command, Iago, and personal maid to Desdemona.[25] As women playing active roles within the community the three are occupationally distinct. All three are wrongfully accused of sexual misdemeanour in the course of the play; all three, though unequal in their rank-power, are equally vulnerable to a *sexual* charge brought against them: although the incidents which provoke the slander may be presumed to be of separate and distinct types (as befits the differing social situations in which the three women find themselves), they yield the identical slur, the identical charge of sexual promiscuity – the most readily available form of assault on a woman's reputation.[26] Each of the three takes the accusation (once made) extremely seriously; but the ways these accusations are *dealt with* by the women themselves have very different consequences, and this is crucial, I shall argue, for a 'historical' understanding of the outcome of the plot. In the substantial part of this paper I shall propose an alternative approach to the 'defamatory' in *Othello* as part of a general argument for the need to consider the relationship between text and cultural context in 'historicist' approaches to Shakespeare.

The Ecclesiastical Court records which survive for England in the early modern period contain a profusion of examples of cases in which individual women believed their reputations had been harmed by imputations of unchastity, and what they felt it neces- sary to do about them. To be more precise: the depositions laid in defamation cases in the Ecclesiastical Courts (throughout England, though I shall use the Durham records because of their comparative accessibility) show us how it was expected that a *story would be shaped* in relation to public accusations of unchastity – the sort of occasion, the nature of the accusation, the circum- stances of the incident, and above all how these were put together as a 'convincing' tale for the presiding clerical official. Throughout the period, ordinary people who had been publicly accused of social misdemeanour sought restitution in the Ecclesi- astical Courts (the courts which had jurisdiction over violations of acceptable practice in domestic, marital and sexual matters).[27] The offended party made depositions (sworn statements) which if substantiated in court led to the offender's doing public penance, paying a fine, or (in extreme cases) being excommunicated. The charges of adultery, whoring, bastard-bearing, scolding, petty theft, etc. were, however, such that if the defamation were allowed to stand the person defamed (the offended party of the records) stood in danger of being charged in their turn in the courts. In other words, the defamation, if it went unchallenged, could became an 'actuality'. I shall argue that we can use the evidence of the Ecclesiastical Court records to make good sense of what does and does not happen with regard to such accu- sations in *Othello*.[28]

One of the conclusions to emerge from these records is that 'when women defended their reputations through defamation suits in the ecclesiastical courts, they were more concerned with their reputation for chastity, not for submissiveness, obedience or being a good housewife. . . . [By contrast] [m]en worried about insults to their social position, their honesty or sobriety as well as about their sexual behaviour'.[29] In a sample survey of the York records, for example, 90 per cent of cases involving a female plaintiff involved her sexual reputation (Sharpe 1980: 15). Ritual sexual banter, including lewd mocking rhymes and fairly explicit romping at weddings, was an acceptable part of social practice (see Ingram 1985: Roper 1985a; Roper 1985b). But there was a point at which it was understood that lewd talk became defamation – when the accusation, circulating publicly, endangered the individual's reputation. The impact of defamation is most graphically illustrated by citing some cases (here taken from the Durham records).

On 26 October 1568, Margaret Nicholson ('singlewoman') made a deposition against Agnes, wife of Robert Blenkinsop, claiming that she, Margaret, had been defamed as follows:

> Hyte hoore, a whipe and a cart and a franc hood, waies [woe is] me for the, my lasse, wenst [wilst thou] have a halpenny halter for to goo up Gallygait and be hanged?[30]

On 7 December 1568, Ann Foster made a deposition against Elizabeth Elder:

> That the wifes of the Close wold say that she was a spanyell hoore. (Durham 1845: 89)

Here the *circulation* of the defamatory accusation is the substance of the accusation, but (by implication) it emanates from Elizabeth Elder. Janet Steilling lodged a complaint against Margaret Bullman for defamation which shows how the charge of 'whore' is apparently substantial, where other charges of dishonesty are not. In this case Agnes Wheitley (wife of Robert Wheitley, of Segefield, aged thirty-three years) made deposition on Steilling's behalf as follows:

> As this examinate was commyng forth with her skeill she hard Bullman's wyffe caul Styllynge 'noughtie pak' [baggage, worthless person (according to the OED), but often 'whore']; who answered, 'What nowtynes know you by me? I am neyther goossteler nor steg [gander] steiler, I would you knew ytt.' And then Bullman's wyff said 'What, noughty hoore, caull thou me goose steiler?' 'Nay, mayry, I know thee for no such' saith Stillinge wyffe, 'but I thank you for your good reporte, whills you and I talk further.' (Durham 1845: 104)

In this deposition it appears that mutual accusations of thieving take second place to the central slandering 'naughty hoore' by Bullman against Steilling.[31]

A case in which the shaping of the tale is more obviously a crucial element is the one brought by Katherine Reid against Isabell Hynde, in 1569. Two depositions were made in this case, both on behalf of Katherine Reid, the woman against whom the defamation has been uttered. It will be clear that the accused woman, Isabell Hynde, is the more vulnerable of the two, and has no-one (perhaps) to speak on her behalf. The first deposition is made by Agnes Dods ('late wife of Edward Dods of Newcastle, shipwright, aged 23 years' [a widow?]):

> She saith that, the weik before Easter last past, one George Dawson and the said Isabell was in this examinate's house, what other certain day this deponent cannott depose, at which time the said Isabell spoke to a baster [bastard] litle boy of the said Isabell, which the said George bygatt of hir and put to this examinat to boor [board], thes words, 'Thow shall not caule Katherine Reid mother, for she caul me hoor, and I never maid fault but for this christen soull, and they will nott dytt [stop] ther mowethes with a bowell of wheit that wold say she had bore a barne in Chirton.' – She said the said Dawson, that shulde mary the said Katherin, was present.

Here the scenario is explicitly socially fraught: the slander is perpetrated by the unwed mother about her ex-lover's wife-to-be (in the presence of the woman with whom her child boards, while she herself works to support him). The second deposition shows how by repetition it is reinforced and becomes more serious. This deposition is made by Helinor Reid ('wife of John Reid of Newcastle, merchant, aged 26 years' [sister-in-law of Katherine Reid]):

> She saith that the said Katherine haith been sick thes 2 last yeres, and for the most part this twelmonth haith bein in house with this examinat, hir brother's wyf. And that the said Kathren toke on very hevylye for that she had gotton knowled that the said Isabell had slandered hir, and that she had borne a barne in Chirton. Whereupon this deponent saith 'Suster Kathren, be of good cheir, and cast not your self downe again for any such talk; And, tor ease of your myend, I wyll myslef

goo and question hir of hir words.' And therupon this examinat went to Mr Th. Clibborn house, and the wench Isabell was out a doores. And to [until] she came yn this deponent was opening the matter to hir dame. And at last the said Isabell came in, to whome hir dame Clibborn's wyfe said, 'Thou hast brought thyself in troble with this good wife's suster,' pointing to this examinat then present, and said, 'Thy M^r will not be in troble therwith.' And the said Isabell maid answer, 'What, Katherine Reid?' 'Yea,' saith this examinat, 'she will have you to answer the sklander that ye have maide upon hir, which was that she had borne a barne in Chirton.' And the said Isabell answered, after many folish words, that that which she had sayd she would say ytt again, for that she had one wytnes for hir. (Durham 1845: 90–1)

The point in invoking these depositions is not that they are 'documentary', but that as texts they are explicitly *purposive* – they shape the story told to a desired outcome. As this last example shows particularly clearly, they are told to the clerk so as to 'make a case': someone's good name has to be shown to have been damaged, by an accusation which must be shown to be false (what would happen to Katherine Reid's engagement, if Isabell Hynde's defamation were allowed to stand?). The apportioning of blame is constructed into the telling: the deponent for the person slandered acts as character witness for them, and endeavours to show that the slanderer is unreliable.[32] What helps our understanding of the case against Desdemona in *Othello*, is that the depositions show how some ostensibly verbal incidents between individuals, as they spill over into the community space (the village green, the pump, outside the house)[33] become recognised as events, which generate particular expectations on the part of the audience (for the local community is surely both onlookers and audience): whatever the audience thought heretofore, the event in question introduces competing versions of fault and blame, which must now be resolved in order that the individuals concerned may be reintegrated into the community.

In *Othello* the crisis point in the play's presentation of Desdemona comes in Act IV, scene ii, when Othello publicly defames Desdemona, and Emilia repeats and circulates the defamation (thus reinforcing and confirming it). The seriousness of the incident is explicit, in strong contrast to the earlier easy, casual impugning of Desdemona's honesty amongst male figures in the play, in private, and in her absence:

> *Oth.* Impudent strumpet!
> *Des.*   By heaven, you do me wrong.
> *Oth.* Are not you a strumpet?
> *Des.*   No, as I am Christian:
>   If to preserve this vessel for my lord
>   From any hated foul unlawful touch,
>   Be not to be a strumpet, I am none.
> *Oth.* What, not a whore?
> *Des.*   No, as I shall be sav'd.
>   *Enter EMILIA*
> *Oth.* Is't possible?
> *Des.* O heaven, forgiveness.
> *Oth.*   I cry you mercy,
>   I took you for that cunning whore of Venice,
>   That married with Othello: you, mistress,
>   That have the office opposite to Saint Peter,
>   And keeps the gates in hell, ay, you, you, you!
>   We ha' done our course; there's money for your pains,
>   I pray you turn the key, and keep our counsel.
>   *Othello* IV.ii.81–96

When Othello accuses Desdemona of unchastity he sends Emilia away, giving her expressly to understand that the conversation between himself and his wife is to be private and *intimate* – 'Leave procreants[34] alone, and shut the door, / Cough, or cry hem, if anybody come' (IV.ii.28–9). It is her premature return which results in her *over*hearing Othello call Desdemona whore. But once the defamation has been accidentally uttered Emilia's outrage on her mistress's behalf consolidates it:

> *Emil.* Alas, Iago, my lord hath so bewhor'd her,
>   Thrown such despite, and heavy terms upon her,
>   As true hearts cannot bear.
> *Des.* Am I that name, Iago?
> *Iago*   What name, fair lady?
> *Des.* Such as she says my Lord did say I was?

> *Emil.* He call'd her whore: a beggar in his drink
>   Could not have laid such terms upon his callat.
>
> (IV.ii.117–23)

'Speak within doors', cautions Iago – 'speak lower; "you don't want the whole street to hear" ', reads Ridley's note – underlining the fact that the charge *has* moved from the intimacy of the bedroom to the public space (IV.ii.146). And the very forms of Emilia's repetition of this 'slander' (IV.ii.135) indicate first the seriousness of the accusation, and secondly the necessity for formally rebutting it:

> *Emil.* Why should he call her whore? who keeps her company?
>   What place, what time, what form, what likelihood?
>
> (IV.ii.139–40)[35]

This is technical defamation, which invites direct comparison with the cases in the Durham records. In historical and cultural terms this is the point in the play at which Desdemona's culpability becomes an 'actual' issue, in the sense that the depositions in the Ecclesiastical Court records suggest: the verbal has been constituted as *event* in the community by virtue of the circumstances of utterance, its location in public space, the inclusion in its performance of persons not entitled to hear what is uttered in privacy or intimacy. Just as the tale is told so as to enhance these features of the alleged *causa diffamationis* in the records, so Act IV, scene ii of *Othello* is shaped, I am suggesting, so that the audience at this point is party to a slander, 'audiently' uttered, and hears it repeated and circulated.[36]

The point is reinforced in the play by what immediately follows: Emilia reminds Iago that (as the audience already knows) Othello was once suspected of sexual misdemeanour with Emilia ('it is thought abroad, that 'twixt my sheets / He's done my office' (I.iii.385–6; also II.i.290–4)). But now she specifies that in that case she too was a victim of a defamation:

> *Emilia* Why should he call her whore? who keeps her company?
>   What place, what time, what form, what likelihood?
>   The Moor's abus'd by some outrageous knave.
>   Some base notorious knave, some scurvy fellow;
>   . . . Oh, fie upon him! Some such squire he was,

That turn'd your wit, the seamy side without,
And made you to suspect me with the Moor.

(IV.ii.139–48)[37]

Unlike the noblewoman Desdemona, Bianca and Emilia understand the need actively to counter defamatory utterance against
their reputation. In Act V scene i (and surely in deliberate juxtaposition with Desdemona's defamation?) Iago accuses the courtesan Bianca of keeping a bawdy house, and Emilia publicly calls
her strumpet; Bianca's retaliation is immediate:

Iago This is the fruit of whoring; pray, Emilia,
  Go know of Cassio where he supp'd to-night:
  What, do you [Bianca] shake at that?
Bian. He supp'd at my house, but I therefore shake not.
Iago. O, did he so? I charge you go with me.
Emil. Fie, fie upon thee, strumpet!
Bian. I am no strumpet, but of life as honest
  As you, that thus abuse me.
Emil.   As I? faugh, fie upon thee!
Iago Kind gentlemen, let's go see poor Cassio dress'd;
  Come, mistress, you must tell's another tale.

(V.i.115–24)

Bianca, in spite of her 'profession', retaliates against the slander-
ous 'strumpet'.[38] Bianca is uncomfortably 'like' Desdemona at this
point in the play: both women of independent spirit (and means),
both *Venetian* women of some rank and status, both accused of
being 'whores of Venice', when Venetian whores were a recognisable *topos* of literature and art, both associated negatively with
Cassio's Florentine manners and 'proper manhood'.[39] Textually a
critic might note their 'equivalence'; but there are considerable
consequences to their occupying entirely different rank positions
in the community, with differing sets of social relations.

I am proposing that Desdemona's case is altered from this
point forward in the play – in the telling of the tale of Desdemona's relations with a community which includes the play's
audience – not because of any alteration in Desdemona's own
conduct, but because she has been publicly designated 'whore'
in terms damaging enough to constitute a substantial threat to
her reputation. From this point on there is no casual innuendo,

no lewd comment on Othello's wife's behaviour or supposed sexual appetite. Desdemona's two remaining scenes focus on her now supposedly culpable sexuality, culminating in her suffocation on her bed, in a state of undress – a whore's death for all her innocence.[40]

Desdemona's defamation has no substance at all; at the moment of her own death Emilia testifies to her mistress's chastity: 'Moor, she was chaste, she lov'd thee, cruel Moor, / So come my soul to bliss, as I speak true' (V.ii.250–1).[41] Yet in spite of her private protestations of innocence, Desdemona does nothing formally to restore her now 'actually' impugned reputation. It might be said that she does nothing because she does not know of what she is accused (reminding us that calling your wife 'whore' is common abuse, whatever the offence):[42] 'If haply you my father do suspect / An instrument of this your calling back [to Venice], / Lay not your blame on me', she says, whilst begging Othello forgiveness on her knees (IV.ii.45–7). She cannot even bring herself to utter the word used against her ('Am I that name, Iago?' 'What name, fair lady?' 'Such as she says my lord did say I was?'; 'I cannot say "whore": / It does abhor me now I speak the word').[43] In striking contrast to the innocent Desdemona's inaction, the worldly Bianca recognises the affront, and its damaging consequences, and retaliates.

Many critics have observed that Othello treats Desdemona as a prostitute in IV.ii. Indeed, the scene is often described as the 'brothel' scene. But that, I am arguing, is once again to miss the *distinctions* between shaped and meaningful events, and the persisting innuendo and suspicion which shrouds the action of the play from the moment Desdemona marries against her father's wishes, and for love of a man whose 'ugliness' (ethnicity) makes it clear she can be drawn to him by lust alone. 'Leave procreants alone' may be lewd talk, it may be unworthy of a man of Othello's standing in relation to his wife, but it does not have bulk and density as the uttering of the words 'I took thee for that cunning whore of Venice / That married with Othello' does, 'audiently'. Whether or not Emilia physically enters, or whether she simply and pedantically circulates the defamatory utterance (like the wives of the Close in one of the examples I gave from the Durham records), it is from that moment an accusation in public space.

To sharpen this last observation a little more: there is one further, curious deposition in a case of defamation in the Durham records, which we may usefully set against this account of *Othello* IV.ii. In the early 1570s John Hunter, 'of Medomsley, husband-man, aged 50 years' who *'partes bene novit a suis cunabulis'* (knew the parties well as neighbours), made a deposition on behalf of the supposed utterer of a defamation, in the case of Helen Johnson, wife of Simon Johnson, against George Allenson, as follows:

> Upon his consciens he beliveth that the said Elinour is a veri honest woman, and so named and reportyd within the towne and parish of Medomsley of all the inhabitors there, saving hir own husband, who, beinge a very suspecious man, haith some tyme audiently caulde the said Elinor 'Skott's hore'.
>
> He saith, upon his oothe, that he never harde the said Allenson say at any time any such wordes as is articulate. Mary, he saith, that, about St. Elenmas last past, to this examinate's remembrance, the said Helen [alias Elinour] Johnson, by report, satt downe of hir knees in the church porche of Medomsley, upon a sonday or hallydaye, after service, when many people were assembled in the church yarde; at what tyme the said George Allenson came to this examinat, being then talking with one John Stevenson, of Bierssyde, and requierd this examinate and one Androo Hunter to here what he, the said Allenson, wold say, and examon the said Helen upon which had satt down in the kirke porch, and asked a vengeance of hym, the said George. At whose request this examinate and the said Androo went with the said George to the aforesaid Helyn Johnson, and in the presence of 30 persons moo, then, this examinate and Andro Hunter questioned and examoned the said Helene, what fault he had maid hir or hir husband to ax a vengeaunce upon hym, the said George Allenson? to whom the said Helyn answerd and said then, 'whye dids thowe caule me — hoore?' and then the said Georg aunswerd hir, the said Helyn, and said, 'Thou knowist best whither thou art a hore or noo: thou was never my hoore'. And she, the said Helyn, still said that the said George had cauld hir so. And then the said Allenson offerd to make amends yf she culd bring in aither honest man or woman that wolde prove thoise wordes. 'Yeis', quodth the said Symon, 'Thou caulde hir hoore to my face at the well grein'. And then aunswerd the said George and said,

'Loke, what I caulde hir afore, that will I caull hir againe'; and so the parties departyd. Examined whither he, this examinate, haith harde the said George caule the aforesaid Symon cookhold or noo, he aunswerethe negatively.

Signum + JOHANNIS HUNTER.

The deponent testifies that 'the said Elinour is a veri honest woman', but suggests her reputation is damaged by the fact that 'hir own husband, . . . beinge a very suspecious man, haith some tyme audiently caulde the same Elinor "Skott's hore" ' (and perhaps the suggestion is that this leads to *others* repeating the slander). 'Audiently' (presumably the clerk's interpolation – it comes from an educated vocabulary)[44] – captures perfectly the way in which words uttered in the privacy of the home are altered as they are 'heard' in public – whether deliberately, or *overheard*. It is the spilling-over of private exchange into a public space ('Thou caulde hir hoore to my face at the well grein [green]') which alters the nature of the incident, and turns it from verbal abuse into event in the communal sphere.

If we read *Othello* in this way, locating our analysis at the disciplinary interface between history, culture and text, we (the twentieth-century explorers of the past) begin to see a web of social relations, a mesh of interpersonal tensions, given meaning by the social events which rendered incipient feeling actual and acknowledgeable in the community. The shape of the tale becomes structurally significant, as it matches the shapes of other tales, told in the early modern community to other, more occasional, judgmental ends. We do not thereby access 'truth' or 'reality', but we do begin to recognise the shared cultural conventions where 'lived experience' was given expression and acknowledgement. So the process can (I maintain) yield a submerged intensity and explicitness in interpersonal feeling which can helpfully position our twentieth-century attention, can perhaps give us back a point from which to respond to culturally significant incidents which no longer have meaning in this early modern sense. This, at least, is what I am arguing in the present case.[45]

And in conclusion, I want to suggest that if we allow a historical reading to direct us towards substantial defamation as the crux of the plot in *Othello*, then we are also led towards a revised reading of the instrumentality of Othello's 'jealousy'.

I suggest that once the substantial defamation stands against

Desdemona, Othello murders her *for adultery*, not out of jealousy.[46] If we retrace the play to Act III, scene iii, we find jealousy contrasted both with *ignorance* of dishonour on the part of a husband, and with *certainty*. Jealousy is the humiliating condition of *doubt* in relation to your own honour and your wife's obedience. It is linked from the outset, by Iago, with 'good name':

> *Iago* Good name in man and woman's dear, my lord;
>   Is the immediate jewel of our souls:
>   Who steals my purse, steals trash, 'tis something, nothing,
>   'Twas mine, 'tis his, and has been slave to thousands:
>   But he that filches from me my good name
>   Robs me of that which not enriches him,
>   And makes me poor indeed.
> *Oth.*   By heaven I'll know thy thought.
> *Iago* You cannot, if my heart were in your hand,
>   Nor shall not, whilst 'tis in my custody:
>   O, beware jealousy;
>   It is the green-ey'd monster, which doth mock
>   That meat it feeds on. That cuckold lives in bliss,
>   Who, certain of his fate, loves not his wronger:
>   But O, what damned minutes tells he o'er
>   Who dotes, yet doubts, suspects, yet strongly loves!
>   . . .
> *Oth.*   Think'st thou I'ld make a life of jealousy?
>   To follow still the changes of the moon
>   With fresh suspicions? No, to be once in doubt,
>   Is once to be resolv'd . . .
>   I'll see before I doubt, when I doubt, prove,
>   And on the proof, there is no more but this:
>   Away at once with love or jealousy!
>
> (III.iii.159–96)

Later in the scene Othello reiterates the view that cuckoldry is not theft until it is public knowledge ('Let him not know't, and he's not robbed at all' (III.iii.348–50)). And what he demands of Iago is knowledge, to end his doubt (and his jealousy):

> *Oth.*   Villain, be sure thou prove my love a whore,
>   Be sure of it, give me the ocular proof . . . [47]
>   Make me to see't, or at the least so prove it,

That the probation bear no hinge, nor loop,
To hang a doubt on:

                                                        (III.iii.365–72)

In the crafted narrative of the play, Othello's doubt is ended,
and with it his jealousy, when a case of defamation is perpetrated
against Desdemona, and the case is not answered – 'She turn'd
to folly, and she was a whore' (V.ii.133).[48] From that point he
acts with complete certainty of her guilt.[49] 'It is the cause [the
case, adultery]', he says, as he prepares to murder her (V.ii.1–3),
and as he murders her, his cross-examination is couched in the
terms of the lawcourt: 'If you bethink yourself any crime . . .
solicit for it straight'; 'take heed of perjury'; 'confess'; 'O perjur'd
woman'; 'He hath confess'd . . . That he hath . . . us'd thee . . .
unlawfully'.[50] In other words, doubt has given way to certainty
– a certainty built not on 'ocular proof', nor even on the misinter-
pretation of his eavesdropping on Cassio, far less on the persist-
ence of Iago's lies. Certainty, for Othello, the certainty that
entitles the cuckolded husband to seek retribution upon his
wife,[51] hinges on that substantial defamation, perpetrated by
Othello himself – who 'beinge a very suspecious man, haith some
tyme audiently caulde . . . [his wife] "hore" '.

Finally, let me return to that matter of agency, and its retrieval
for those traditionally excluded from the historical account. The
present case conveniently illustrates the fact that what I am concerned to do is to find a way of including the possibility of
agency, a reciprocity of activity such as we experience ourselves.
As I said earlier: 'In history, agency is a dynamic, in relation to
women and to men (both women and men have acted, have
been acted upon). It is this historical *agency* which I am concerned
to retrieve, in theory as well as in practice.' In my exploration of
Othello I have not been able to give back to Desdemona power
to accompany her activity – but I have, I believe, repositioned
our attention in relation to the events which take place on the
stage so that representation no longer overwhelms the interpersonal dynamics of an early modern community to which the text
gives expression.

Notes

1. *Reading Shakespeare Historically* (forthcoming).
2. In the first version of this paper, in which I took issue directly with a number of 'new historicist' critics who had, I alleged, overlooked problems with gender in their treatment of power and authority in the Elizabethan and Jacobean drama, I chose to focus my attention on Louis Montrose's (then recent) article, ' "Shaping Fantasies": figurations of gender and power in Elizabethan culture' (1983). Since then I have had several valuable discussions with Louis Montrose on this and other topics, and my respect for his work has grown. I have come very much to regret that I initiated the discussion in public debate, without observing the courtesy of informing Montrose in advance, or offering him the opportunity to reply to my criticisms. In the ensuing rumpus the possibilities for constructive debate from within what I believe to be a shared general framework of political commitments and beliefs were severely hampered. For that, I consider that I owe Louis Montrose a formal apology here.
3. For a similar insistence on studies like the present one as part of an emerging inter-discipline, rather than a series of borrowings by literary studies from adjacent disciplines, see Mullaney 1988: x-xii.
4. Most infamously in Tennenhouse 1986: 127.
5. In this respect, the present work is of a piece with other work in social history and textual studies which focuses attention on the way in which categories of person outside the dominant elite have been excluded from traditional historical types of explanation. See e.g. the introduction to Wrightson 1982: 11.
6. I am conscious that such a type of investigation is crucially related to recent work in social anthropology. See, in particular, Turner and Bruner 1986, especially Bruner's introductory essay, 'Experience and its expressions' (3–30). I am extremely grateful to Bill Sherman for drawing this volume to my attention, and for his extremely astute comments on a draft of the present article.
7. The play on words is never, as far as I am aware, commented on by editors of the play, though it is precisely the same joke as the one at Cressida's expense in *Troilus and Cressida* (IV.v.54–63): '*Ulysses*. Fie, fie upon her! / There's language in her eye, her cheek, her lip – / Nay, her foot speaks; her wanton spirits look out / At every joint and motive of her body. / O, these encounterers, so glib of tongue, / That give accosting welcome ere it comes, / And wide unclasp the tables of their thoughts / To every ticklish reader: set them down / For sluttish spoils of opportunity / And daughters of the game. *Flourish. All.* The Trojan's trumpet'. Kenneth Palmer's footnote in the Arden edition runs: 'Delius is obviously right: it is for Hector's trumpet that the Greeks have been waiting. A. P. Rossiter (*Angel with Horns*, 1961, p. 133) suggested the 'knavish device' of aural ambiguity – the cry could certainly be heard as *The Trojan strumpet* – but the trumpet call is what modulates the scene,

from facetious comment and moral distaste, on the one hand, to serious chivalric action, on the other' (Shakespeare 1982: 247–8). In other words, Palmer both acknowledges the innuendo, and brushes it aside as irrelevant. See also *Merchant of Venice* V.i.122 (and the insinuating response, 'We are no tell-tales madam').

8. See Kappeler 1986. This is also, I think, what Coppelia Kahn (1981) highlights in her work on the pressure of male fantasy as a deterministic discourse in Shakespeare's plays.

9. Retrieve, because the pursuit of such an 'agent' as the residual trace of 'lived experience' in text and document has been the constant goal of Left criticism committed to the theoretical positions of Raymond Williams and E. P. Thompson; but most of this work has not been done on early modern material. See Swindells and Jardine 1989.

10. There is a nice example of just this distinction in *Hamlet*. During the 'Mousetrap' performance, after the Player Queen has declaimed long and passionately on the wickedness of second marriage ('In second husband let me be accurst; / None wed the second but who kill'd the first' (III.ii.174–5)), a topic naturally bound to offend Gertrude, Claudius asks Hamlet, 'Have you heard the argument [do you know the plot of the play]? Is there no offence in't?' 'No, no', replies Hamlet, 'they do but jest – poison in jest. No offence i' th' world' (III.ii.227–30). Offensive, possibly; but no *real* crime is committed.

11. There is a literature going back some way on 'slander' in this play and others, but I am arguing for a more precise distinction than has hitherto been made between utterance (text) and occasion (what I am calling 'event').

12. Rowse 1974: 20. Rowse comments that this dream 'has a wider, an anthropological significance: it throws a shaft of light, as nothing else that I know, into the erotic stimulus *that the menfolk derived* from having a Virgin Queen upon the throne' (my emphasis). This seems to me right – it is men who 'derive the erotic stimulus' from any event in which the Queen figures. Forman's dream cit. Montrose 1983: 62–3.

13. de Maisse 1931: 25–6. The French text is unavailable in print, but fortunately large extracts are reprinted in Prevost-Paradol 1855. The relevant passage here runs: 'Elle avait le devant de sa robe en manteau ouvert et luy voyoit-on toute la gorge et assez bas et soudvent, comme si elle eust eu trop chaud, elle eslargissoit avec les mains le devant dudict manteau . . . sa gorge se montre assez ridée, autant que (la laissoit veoir) le carcan qu'elle portoit au col, mais plus bas elle a encore la charnure fort blanche et fort déliée autant que l'on eust peu veoir' (*Journal*: 240, 241; *cit.* Prevost-Paradol 1855: 151). 'Gorge' here surely means 'throat' rather than 'bosom' (see Robert and Huguet dictionaries), since the elaborate choker-necklace she wears largely conceals it. English text cit. in part Montrose 1983: 63.

14. de Maisse 1931: 36–7; the relevant passage in French runs: '. . . Une

robe dessous de damas blanc, ceinte et ouverte devant, aussy bien que sa chemise, tellement qu'elle ouvrait souvent cette robe et luy voyait-on tout l'estomac jusques au nombril . . . elle a cette façon qu'en rehaussant la teste elle met les deux mains à sa robe et l'entrouvre, tellement qu'on luy veoit tout l'estomac' (*Journal* 256: *cit.* Prevost-Paradol 1855: 155). It is not clear here whether what is revealed is decolleté or stomacher (on the dress of black taffeta, over which the over-dress of white damask is worn) but it is clear that de Maisse is disturbed by the gestures of *revealing*. In a third audience Elizabeth once again wears an embroidered over-dress, this time over a white dress embroidered with silver, 'Echancrée fort bas et le sein descouvert; *Journal* 279; *cit.* Prevost-Paradol 1855: 168). At the fourth and final audience, 'Elle estoit ce jour-là habillée de toile d'argent comme de coustume, ou gaze, que nous appelons en françois; sa robe estant blanceh et la sapronelle de soye d'or de couleur viollette. Elle avoit une très-grande quantité de bagues sur elle tant sur la tête qu'au dedans de son collet, à l'entour des bras et aux mains, avec une très-grande quantité de perles, tant autour du col qu'en bracelets, et avait deux carcans, un à chaque bras, qui estoient de fort grand prix' (*Journal*: 316; *cit.* Prevost-Paradol 1855: 180–1). In this last case Elizabeth's dress is clearly high-fronted (since the 'very great quantities' of jewels around her neck hang over her collar); it is anything lower than this which draws the ambassador's attention. English of first passage cit. in part Montrose 1983: 64.

15. In fact, it turns out to belong to the twentieth-century English translation of de Maisse's diary, far more than to the original French, although one would still want to take note of Hurault de Maisse's difficulty with the breach of decorum (in his terms) of a woman of Elizabeth's age receiving him with *anything other* than a gown which entirely concealed her body.

16. See for instance the illustrations in Roper 1985a. 'Respectability' is probably a good term, historically, to describe what is going on (undermining it) in the late sixteenth-century passages describing Elizabeth.

17. See Roper 1985a: 20. And see in particular Diane O. Hughes's compelling account of Italian sumptuary laws assigning extravagant dress *exclusively* to prostitutes as badge of their trade, and as a disincentive to 'honest' women's wearing lavish clothing (Hughes 1986). See also polemicists like Stubbs, who also suggest that all women who wear extravagant dress are potentially whores. Warren Boutcher gives me another example from Florio's translation of Montaigne's *Essais*: Florio renders Montaigne's description (in the essay 'De l'institution des enfans') of Angelique, 'vestue en garce, coiffée d'vn attifet emperlé' as 'disguised and drest about the head like vnto an impudent harlot, with embroyderies, frizelings, and carcanets of pearles' (French from Montaigne 1872–1900: I, 198; English from Montaigne 1603 sig. H3ʳ). The English makes finery inappropriate for rank figure for 'impudent harlot[ry]'.

18. The soiled smock of the Forman passage is a standard euphemism for sexual (or at least moral) laxity and sluttishness, see e.g. *Piers Plowman*.

19. Throughout this paper I use 'equivalent' in inverted commas, to remind the reader that when words 'weigh equally' it may not mean that there is an *identity* between the events the text recalls.

20. And that is the point the critic wishes to make in the article in question. So although I am drawing attention to problems for my way of approaching Shakespeare historically, in this kind of justa-position, I am not commenting on the argument in the context of an investigation of 'figurations of gender and power' which argues the case that the Queen's 'pervasive [female] *cultural presence* was a condition of the play's imaginative possibility'.

21. Rowse (1974: 66–7) gives us a clear indication of what kinds of 'event' *did* occasion it: 'That morning Forman arrested Sefton [a cleric, with whom Forman was engaged in protracted lawsuits] for the money he had lent him, "and I had a silver bowl for my money". When Forman went to the Queens Attorney, "he entreated me to stay the matter. After I went to Avis Allen [with whom he is sexually involved]." He was with her the next day, and on the 20th, "but did not halek [have sex] but spake with her". He himself put the question whether it were best to leave her or no, "and not to continue her love in hope", i.e. of marriage. It was at this time, 23 January 1597, that he had his suggestive dream of the Queen'.

22. See the Lutheran whore of Babylon woodcut in Roper 1985a.

23. Here it is instructive, as so often, to listen to the anthropologists. In 'Can the concept of the person vary cross-culturally?', Shweder and Bourne summarise the problems encountered by western analyses of non-western selves (citing Geertz on Bali, Read on the Gahuku-Gama, and Dumont on India) as follows: 'How are we to interpret this widespread mode of social thought in which the individual is not differentiated from the role [with intentional theatrical connotations], and where the person achieves no abstract, context-independent recognition?' (Shweder and LeVine 1984: 168) See also Michelle Rosaldo, 'Towards an anthropology of self and feeling': 'Cultural idioms provide the images in terms of which our subjectivities are formed, and, furthermore, these idioms themselves are socially ordered and constrained. . . . Society . . . shapes the self through the medium of cultural terms, which shape the understanding of reflective actors. It follows that in so far as our psychology is wedded to our culture's terms in its accounts of people elsewhere in the world, it is unlikely to appreciate their deeds' (Shweder and LeVine 1984: 150). Scrutinising the textual remains of early modern England, we search for subjectivity in our own cultural terms, and fail to appreciate women's deeds.

24. Although the text is not *explicit* as to Bianca's place of origin, I would argue that it is crucial to the play that Bianca might be described as a 'whore of Venice' (the phrase used by Othello to insult Desdemona, and a popular Renaissance 'type'). Bianca has

a household in Cyprus and is Cassio's established courtesan. For a near contemporary account, incorporating all the popular stereotype features, see Coryate 1611; repr. 1905: I, 401–9. On Venetian courtesans see particularly Santore 1988; Barzaghi 1980; Chojnacki, 1976.

25. This is an alteration of the source story, in which Emilia's rank is higher. The social distance between them is carefully charted in the play in their relationships to the talismanic handkerchief. The intricately embroidered piece is a gift to Desdemona from Othello (who had it from either his mother or his father – in either case it draws attention to Desdemona's acquisition of wealth/goods with marriage (see Spufford 1984)); finding it by chance, Emilia decides to have the work copied to please her husband, who (she thinks) admires it – an act of service which confirms her subordinate, serving status; passed to Bianca by Cassio with the request that *she* copy the needlework, the gentlewomanly but morally dubious courtesan is outraged (not just that Cassio might have another mistress, but that she be taken for a servant, or a casual prostitute (see Roper 1985a) for the association with needlework)).

26. Apart from the claim that Desdemona has committed adultery with Cassio, Emilia has been accused of adultery with Othello, and Bianca (although professionally a courtesan) is accused of running a bawdy house and *whoring* by Iago and Emilia (see below).

27. By 'ordinary' I mean to indicate the fact that the middling sort (women and men) had regular recourse to the Ecclesiastical Courts in this period. See Herrup 1987; Sharpe 1984: ch. 2, 'Courts, officers and documents'; Ingram 1976.

28. On defamation depositions see Sharpe 1980. I am grateful to Jim Sharpe for verbal comments on a draft of this paper delivered at the 1987 HETE conference at Canterbury. See also Hair 1972: 256–8; Ingram 1976; Marchant 1969; Haigh 1975; Dunhill 1976: 49–51.

29. Amussen 1985: 208. Amussen's article usefully shows the gendering of offences against the social in the Norfolk records. Sharpe (1980: 27–8) suggests that in the York records the discrepancy between female and male sexual slurs arises only in the seventeenth century: 'A total of 1,638 cases for defamation are known to have entered the Consistory court in the 1590s, of which 49 per cent involved male plaintiffs and 51 per cent female. 565 such cases entered the Consistory in the 1690s, of which only 24 per cent involved male plaintiffs'.

30. Durham 1845: 89. By contrast, on 4 May 1568 Jasper Arkle of Gosforth made a deposition for defamation against Martin Atchuson, claiming that Atchuson had said publicly 'that he wittinglye solde one stolne shepe skyn in the towne of Newcastell' (89). I am extremely grateful to Keith Wrightson who launched me on the ecclesiastical court records, and continues to give me advice and support in the project of bringing together literature and history in the early modern period.

31. The OED gives as instance of the use of the obsolete 'naughtie packe', the 1540 translation of Vives' *Instruction of the Christian*

Woman: 'Call hir a naughtie packe: with that one woorde thou haste taken all from hir, and haste lefte hir bare and foule'. For the 'whore' insinuation in the original 'noughtie pak' see e.g. Lilly 1867: 194: 'At Maydstone in Kent there was one Marget Mere, daughter to Richard Mere, of the sayd towne of Maydstone, who being vnmaryed, played the naughty packe, and was gotten with childe, being deliuered of the said childe the xxiiij. daye of October last past, in the yeare of our Lord 1568, at vij. of the clocke in the afternoone of the same day, being Sonday' (the child is a monstrous birth, revealing the mother's sinful behaviour). I am grateful to Carolyn Whitney-Brown for drawing my attention to this example. Ian Archer confirms for me that in the Bridewell records the phrase 'naughty pack' is consistently used as a synonym for 'whore', e.g. Bridewell Court Book I, fol. 62: Lewse Hochyn, 'a naughty packe' committing whoredom is punished, and Ellyn Holt, 'a lewd, naughty pack' who 'as a "bribyng drab" went in the name of Nicholas Williams of the Chamber with whom she dwelt, to a butcher for a shoulder of mutton and a breast of veal', likewise (Ian Archer, personal communication, November 1987).

32. See Davis 1988a for a similar argument about pardon tales. Where depositions survive for the supposed slanderer (see, for example, above, pages 141–2), the invariably try to undermine the character of the person supposedly defamed.

33. There is a striking example in the Durham records of the inside/outside the house boundary being breached, and drawing 'outsiders' into a case of wife abuse (then, as now, customarily treated as 'private') (Durham 1845: 97–8):

> Ex parte Agnetis Carr adversus Thomam Carr, maritum suum. WILLIAM BAYKER, of the city of Durham, yoman, aged about 40 years. This examinate was in Durham that present day, when the parties and all their compeny cam home with them frome their mariadge here to Durham, wher they dwelt as man and wif togither, by the common report of the people. Mary, this examinate was not present at their mariadge. he saith that he belyvith that Thomas Carr, articulate, haith not used nor entretyd the said Agnes, his wyf, as an honestman ought to have doon; for this examinate was personally present at one tyme enspeciall when the parties had bein at the lawe, and the said Thomas then commanndyd to take hir, the said Agnes his wyfe, home with hym, and to use hir as he aught to doo; and immediatlie after ther home commynge quietly togither, according as their were commandyd, this examinate, and one John Woodmose, was doon to the market-place, and commyng by the said Carr's doore, the said Agnes was Wepinge and sore lammentyng, sainge that hir said husband Thomas wold not suffer hir to tarye that night with hym in his house here in Durham, but commandyd hir then, being towerd night, to goo to Feildehouse, which she said she wolde nott. And at this examinate's coming home he founde the

said Agnes in his owne house in the Balye. And, after moche talke that this examinate and his wyf had with hir, this deponent came doon in the streit again to hir said husband Thomas Carr, and reasoned with hym, mervalinge moch that he wold not use and intreit his said wyf accordinge as he was commandyd. And was then well content, saing yt was not well doon to put hir out of his house towerd night frome hym self, which Thomas Car gave this examinate so light and short annswers in such angre and greiff, that this examinate therupon thougth veryly, and yett doith, that he, the said Thomas, had much misused his wyf; and further to this article he canott depose upon his own knowledg. Mary, the said Agnes, with weping eies, haith affirmed all the resydew of this article to be trew to this examinate and his wyfe, saing, hir said husband had not used hir as his wyfe, nor wolde sufer hir aither to gyve hym meat and drinck, or take hir self any, but used [her] worse and a servannt, and had his meat gyvon by a youngwoman one of the said Thomas maid servaunts. Signum + W. BAIKER.

34. 'Would-be copulators', according to Ridley's Arden note.
35. It is also telling that it should be Emilia who circulates the defamation, like the 'wifes of the Close'. As the 'low' female servant character in the play, she both loyally supports her mistress, and contributes to her undoing (as also in the 'willow' scence).
36. Desdemona's oath on her knees (but only to Iago) that she has never been unchaste 'either in discourse of thought or actual deed' (IV.ii.155) further emphasises the seriousness of what has happened.
37. Ridley, the Arden editor, comments: 'This disposes of any idea that Iago's suspicions of Othello . . . were figments, invented during momentary 'motive-hunting' and dismissed. They have been real, and lasting, enough for him to challenge Emilia' (Shakespeare 1965: 159). For the early twentieth-century critic also, apparently, occasions for sexual jealousy are 'actual' as long as they are produced as 'actual' defamation. On Ridley's general tendency to betray deep-seated patriarchal attitudes see Jardine 1983: 119–20.
38. An interesting piece of supporting material comes here from Santore 1988. Julia Lombardo goes to court against a public charge of 'whoring', which is at odds with her comparatively elevated status as courtesan (and would imply loss of important privileges).
39. Thus the defamation links back to the first part of this paper. In Jardine 1983 I noted the intrusion in the 'willow scene' of the observation, 'This Lodovico is a proper man', which reintroduces the sensual and 'flaws the "innocence" which a modern audience looks for in Desdemona' (75). The secondary sense of 'proper' (a *manly* man) harks back to I.iii.390–6, where it is Cassio whom Iago describes as 'a proper man', and therefore susceptible to an accusation of adultery: 'After some time, to abuse Othello's ear, /

That he is too familiar with his wife: / He has a person and a smooth dispose, / To be suspected, fram'd to make women false'.

40. I consider the careful counter-currents of innocence, essential for the final tragic denouement ('Let nobody blame him, his scorn I approve'), in Jardine 1983: 184–5.

41. It is particularly poignant that at the opening of IV.ii – immediately prior to the defamation – Othello entirely disregards Emilia's careful laying of evidence by testimony, that she has never seen Desdemona behave suspiciously with Cassio, ending, 'if she be not honest, chaste, and true, . . . the purest of her sex / Is foul as slander' (IV.ii.17–19). At this point in the play (*before* the 'case' against Desdemona has been framed as a defamation) such testimony is not sufficient to Othello's jealous demand for 'ocular proof'.

42. See, for instance, V.ii.230, where Iago's response to Emilia's testimony against him is the insult, 'Villainous whore!'

43. This further highlights the dramatic intensity of the accidental *overhearing* by Emilia: since Desdemona cannot bring herself to utter the word 'whore', *she* would never have circulated the charge – as Emilia so energetically does – outside the hearth. This genteel decorum also ensures that from this point on Desdemona is no longer vulnerable to the suspicion of implicit 'knowingness' which was part of the pervasive innuendo of the earlier part of the play (contrast II.i.109–66 with V.iii.35–105, where Emilia is 'knowing' and Desdemona refrains (apart from that first, triggering reminiscence in 'That Lodovico is a proper [sexy] man')). See Jardine 1983: 119–20, 75. It has been suggested to me that the decorum of her rank requires that one of her male kin act to clear her name; that it would indeed be unseemly for her to lodge the kind of deposition (as it were) that the rural artisanal woman pronounced. This suggestion is supported by the fact that after Desdemona's death it is specified (irrelevantly, in terms of other plot concerns) how isolated and remote Desdemona was from the protection of any male kin (Gratiano and Lodovico are specified in the *dramatis personae* as brother and kinsman to Brabantio, respectively), apart from her husband: '*Othello* 'I scarce did know you, uncle, there lies your niece . . .' *Gratiano* 'Poor Desdemona, I am glad thy father's dead; / Thy match was mortal to him, and pure grief / Shore his old thread atwain' (V.ii.205–7). In Act IV.i Lodovico is involved in the incident in which Othello strikes his wife – another type of 'inside' domestic incident between man and wife which once 'outside', the court records show, may require formal action (see above, note 33). But he does not intervene, in spite of his elaborate sustaining of courtesy towards Desdemona, when Othello has dropped all 'good forms' (IV.iii.3–5).

44. I take it that in all the depositions we can detect the clerk's framing of the testimony to court norms.

45. For a carefully argued account of exploration of the past through

'document' and literary text which agrees with my own see, most recently, Davis 1988b.

46. Natalie Davis points out that in early modern France 'jealousy' is a demeaning emotion, which is therefore never admissible as justification when male supplicants make pleas for pardon in letters of remission in the public records (*Fiction in the Archives*, 1988a: 'A peasant wife threw stones at her husband's lover "de chaulde colle", but also "by force of jealousy" ("par force de la jallosie"), thereby mentioning an emotion which men did not admit in slaying their adulterous wives or their wives' lovers. A husband merely said, with a merchant apothecary of Tours, that he "had previously forbidden his wife the company of the said Estienne". Honor and obedience were at stake for him, not demeaning jealousy.') I am extremely grateful to Professor Natalie Davis, who commented on an early draft of this paper, and allowed me to see the relevant sections of *Fiction in the Archives* in manuscript. On the punishment of adultery in early modern England see Thomas 1978. It does not matter, for my argument, that Othello *himself* perpetrated the defamation (though see the Helen Johnson case above); it is not archival verisimilitude I am after, but clues to what the community (the audience) would have expected to happen once a defamation was 'audiently' made.

47. On the contemporary debate about the comparative status of 'ocular proof' and testimony in the English lawcourts of the period see Langbein 1974; Langbein 1977; Bellamy 1984. I am extremely grateful to Professor Katharine Maus for drawing my attention to the discussion of 'ocular proof' in law, and clarifying its relevance to *Othello*.

48. And again, 'Iago knows / that she with Cassio hath the act of shame / A thousand times committed; Cassio confess'd it' (V.ii.211–13).

49. On the two senses of 'conviction' (being convicted, and clinching the case) in the context of doubt and certainty in the lawcourts, see K. E. Maus, 'Proof and consequences: inwardness and its exposure in the English renaissance' (in press).

50. V.ii.passim. See particularly the point at which Othello recognises that without the certainty, Desdemona's death would be murder, not, what Ridley in the note to this passage calls, 'impersonal justice': 'O perjur'd woman, thou does stone thy heart, / And makest me call what I intend to do / A murder, which I thought a sacrifice' (V.ii.64–5). On adultery as 'unlawful' see L. Jardine, 'Reading Shakespeare historically: *Hamlet* and unlawful marriage' (in preparation).

51. For an *English* audience, Othello is nonetheless *guilty* of murder in killing his wife as retribution for her adultery, since English law specified that murder by a husband of his adulterous wife could only be excused if it took place in the first flush of anger. See Davis 1988a: ch. 2.

9

Sherlock Holmes and the Adventure of the Dancing Men and Women

Alastair Fowler

Modern criticism of the detective story has one starting point in Frank Kermode's W. P. Ker lecture of 1972, which filtered implications of earlier work by Raymond Queneau, Michel Butor and Roland Barthes to a clarified form. Kermode talked of a generic specialisation, whereby one element of narrative undergoes elephantiasis, so that the reader's main object becomes interpreting clues or solving problems – in fact, 'hermeneutic activity':

> Clearly this emphasis requires, to a degree much greater than in most stories (though all have hermeneutic aspects) the disposition, in a consecutive narrative, of information which requires us to ask both how it 'fits in', and also how it will all 'come out'; and this information bears up an event, usually a murder, that precedes the narrative which bears the clues. (Kermode 1983a: 56)[1]

This might be qualified by genre. Crimes usually precede detection in police fiction; but in 'mysteries' like Raymond Chandler's, the detective may be hired first. And Conan Doyle's Sherlock Holmes stories often begin at a stage when the crime (if any) only impends. These are hardly classic detective stories; yet the idea of a hermeneutic task proves valuable to their interpreter in unexpected ways.

Of Conan Doyle's art, the first thing to observe is the degree of subtlety. It is a far more sophisticated art than has usually been supposed. Even the structure of a Sherlock Holmes story is relatively complex: a recent comparison of Conan Doyle's use of narrators to Nabokov's by no means exaggerates. (Barolsky 1987: 73) Detective fiction generally involves two interpretative activities, the detective's investigation and the reader's attempts (hampered by narrative subterfuges) at the same problem. But Conan Doyle commonly has at least three investigations, since the narrator, Watson, also takes a hand (not all visible); sometimes with more success than the reader, but always with less than Holmes. Even although Watson may exploit hindsight, his limitations control, for the reader, the pace of hermeneutic activity. For Holmes often chooses not to confide in him – 'I confess that I was filled with curiosity, but I was aware that Holmes liked to make his disclosures at his own time' (Doyle 1981: 'The Dancing Men', 65). Kingsley Amis has perceptively remarked that Watson's 'not quite always unqualified' admiration achieves the result of portraying Holmes 'at exactly the right distance and in exactly the right light'. (Doyle 1974: Introduction) But Watson's narration achieves almost as much in another mediation: between the reader's desultory puzzling and the great detective's intense investigations. And other characters too engage in hermeneutic construction – not only police detectives like Martin, but stationmasters, doctors, servants. Holmes's society is one of ordinary people making sense of things.

For Conan Doyle's investigative reader, the problems to be solved are imaginary and intellectual. Yet part of the pleasure of our association with Holmes depends on his also enjoying the intellectual problems his cases present. He is always on the lookout for 'interesting' cases with 'unique' features. His seductive theoretical interests can sometimes be detected, indeed, breaking out outrageously. When a fresh example turned up of the dancing men cryptograms that were 'killing [Elsie] by inches', Holmes 'rubbed his hands and chuckled with delight' (Doyle 1981: 63). Holmes's intellectual interests have to be reconciled, however, with the interests of clients and others. His investigations are not pure enquiries, but interactions of pure and impure, theoretical and practical, technical and human factors.

Much of the tension derives from such conflicts of interest; as when Holmes realises a blunder ('I've been a fool') and must break off research for a suspenseful race against time. And if the race is lost, he feels guilty for pursuing theoretical certainty to the point of endangering his client. I almost said 'patient'; for conflict between scientific interest and human solicitude charac

terises medical 'cases', too. There is much in Owen Dudley
Edwards' contention that Conan Doyle wrote from a conviction
about the inhumanity of contemporary medical practice.
(Edwards 1983: 200; cf. Accardo 1987) Certainly Holmes, no less
than Dr Conan Doyle, is a professional – a point repeatedly
emphasised: 'the whole incident may appeal as a remarkable
professional study' (74); 'Holmes preserved his calm professional
manner' (65). But even this hardly broadens the reference far
enough; for reading of symptoms belongs to a more general
interpreting of life, and Conan Doyle's readers join Holmes in
similar inferences as they compose events into a narrative that
makes sense, at each stage forming a provisional domain of
assumptions to be revised at the next.

Particularly interesting from this point of view is 'The Adventure of the Dancing Men', since it contains the subsidiary hermeneutic task of interpreting cryptograms. Holmes's breaking of
the cipher stands, in fact, as an icon of the investigation as a
whole. The profusion of texts in the story is remarkable (although
by no means without parallel in the Sherlock Holmes canon).
Besides Watson's everpresent notebook ('I have fulfilled my
promise of giving you something unusual for your notebook'
(82)), there is the letter from America burnt by Elsie (59); seven
cryptograms (one of composite authorship); an eighth by Holmes
himself; Hilton Cubitt's transcriptions (one encapsulated in a
letter); a reported letter of Elsie's; three telegrams; Holmes's
working papers in solution of the code; and literary subtexts
present by allusion, especially Poe's 'The Gold-Bug'. It is natural
to enquire whether the cryptograms may not contain self-reflexive
analogies with the story or the investigation.

The source of the dancing men cipher, like the source of the
Nile, has had many discoverers. We hear that it was invented
by the son of one Cubitt, proprietor of the Hill House Hotel at
Happisburgh in Norfolk, where Conan Doyle stayed; that it
appeared in the St Nicholas magazine; or that it came from the
'alphabet of Hermes' in Albert Mackey's *Encyclopedia of Free-
masonry* (1874) (of interest, surely, to Conan Doyle the occultist).
(Baring-Gould 1968: n. 16) But the cipher's point lies not in
sources so much as a functional relation to the cipher of 'The
Gold-Bug'.

Poe's story is an indispensable subtext of 'The Dancing Men'.
In both tales, decipherment comes in flashback, long after the

real-time solution has brought a first denouement (discovery of the treasure; Holmes's attendance at Ridling Thorpe Manor soon after Cubitt's death). Poe conceals Kidd's cryptogram until the flashback; motivating this deception as Legrand's practical joke on the narrator (which the latter repeats on us). But Watson honestly follows the sequence he experienced; since he could not decipher the dancing men cryptograms, and Holmes would not help him (65). The anticlimactic structure obviates suspense, but allows the decipherment to become a retrospective microcosm of the investigation. In both stories, the coda of decoding is like the explanatory recapitulation – the Metamenusis, as Knox calls it (1954: 108) – that completes the classic detective story. At the same time, there are striking contrasts between the two detectives' methods.

Legrand's 'rationale' is rigorously deductive, and could be repeated in real life, at least with similarly doctored messages. (Poe 1984: 591) Thus TH.RTEE is 'immediately suggestive of the word "thirteen" ' (590). By contrast, Holmes's professedly scientific method is in practice notoriously hard to follow. For the five letter word he says 'might be "sever", or "lever", or "never" ', there are actually twenty-seven other alternatives (Doyle 1981: 76; Baring-Gould 1968: n. 13); he can justify choosing 'never' only on grounds of contextual probability. Context is again relied on for the 'combination which contained two E's with three letters between', which, 'it occurred' to Holmes, 'might very well stand for the name "ELSIE" '. But why assume a name at all? Similarly, Holmes 'could only make sense' of A. ELRI.ES (77) by assuming the missing letters to be T and G. Add to these guesses mistakes in encipherment, and it is no wonder that readers emulating Holmes have felt the decipherment to be too like life by half.

Both detectives stress the cipher's simplicity, mixing arrogance with patronising encouragement. Legrand makes out 'the very simplest species of cryptograph': he has 'solved others of an abstruseness ten thousand times greater' (Poe 1984: 567, 591); while Holmes claims to know 'all forms' (!) of secret writings, and boasts authorship 'of a trifling monograph upon the subject, in which I analyze one hundred and sixty separate ciphers' – although the dancing men are 'entirely new' to him. The dancing men cipher is 'easy enough', in fact, for Edward Woodland and Fletcher Pratt to suggest that it is only a simplified version – a token surrogate – of the more high-powered cipher that put the great detective to 'intricate and elaborate calculation' (see Baring-Gould 1968: n. 13). But if the cipher as Watson gives it is so simple, why should its decipherment elude exposition? Why does Holmes not solve it by steps as repeatable as Legrand's?

Two contrasting answers suggest themselves. One might take its departure from the views of poststructuralists like M. Pouffe. Conan Doyle, an inferior artist to the great Poe, has garbled the cipher; this, like other elusivenesses in his text, betrays an area concerning which his ideology remains aphatic. The other approach might assume that Conan Doyle was as capable of standing on Poe's giant shoulders as Holmes (in 'Milverton') on Watson's, and that the descents from the rigour of Legrand are quite likely to have been deliberate. After all, Conan Doyle considered 'The Dancing Men' his third best story: for him, at least, it was not casual work.

To pursue this second approach thus involves acknowledging the relevance of Conan Doyle's artistry. It calls for knowledge of his *oeuvre*, and of his place in a tradition – the tradition of Poe and Stevenson – that sanctioned expending the classic resources of authorship on peripheral, unofficial genres. In this view, an artist such as Conan Doyle was not likely to have fallen short of his model unnecessarily. Elsewhere, after all, he seems able at will to construct brilliant arabesques of inference, cadenzas of reasoning, bravura passages of deduction.

Indeed, Sherlock Holmes stories generally begin with a supererogatory demonstration of method, exemplifying deduction through a series of 'inferences, each dependent upon its predecessor and each simple in itself' (56). Motivated by Holmes's wish to present his credentials to a new client, the demonstration 'really' serves to establish his character to new readers. But it also introduces a paradigm of the 'scientific' method with whose inadequacy many of the later Sherlock Holmes stories are concerned. In 'The Dancing Men', this theme becomes almost explicit. Not only is the demonstration here to Watson himself (and thus thinly motivated), but it takes the form of the very 'trick' of Dupin's that Holmes scorns in 'A Study in Scarlet' – 'that trick of his of breaking in on his friends' thoughts with an apropos remark after a quarter of an hour's silence is really very showy and superficial.'[2] Here, Holmes contemptuously explains 'with the air of a professor addressing his class' how, if 'one simply knocks out all the central inferences and presents one's audience with the starting point and the conclusion, one may produce a startling, though possibly a meretricious, effect' (Doyle 1981: 56). The effect is nevertheless one he cannot resist repeating.

This homage to Poe by no means implies unqualified admiration for scientific method on Conan Doyle's part. Holmes may profess the method, but it is not the way his cases are solved – as Watson, with his talk of Holmes's 'curious faculties' (86) seems aware.

'The Dancing Men' presents extreme instances of this contradiction. Holmes talks, indeed, about his science, and his cryptology is superior to Legrand's as regards adequate samples (75) and the rank ordering of letters by frequency (ETAOINSHRDL, not EAOIDHNRST as Legrand supposes). But deductive method hardly dominates his actual practice. As we have seen, he guesses 'NEVER', arrives at 'ELSIE' by 'a happy thought', and makes sense of 'ELRI.ES 'by supposing'. Unlike Legrand's, Holmes's deciphering is a multifaceted process, combining inference, intuition, inspiration, chance, mistake and recourse to external knowledge; just as in the larger investigation, where he draws on 'knowledge of the crooks of Chicago' (77). Throughout Holmes depends on assumptions, so that readers, not always able to draw on the relevant domains of assumption, must sometimes be shut out like Watson. Not being in Holmes's confidence, however, lets them share another aspect of the investigative experience: confrontation of mystery. Prevented from following the investigation conspectively, readers are mystified, even if (like Watson) perceptive here and there. Holmes's exclusion of his faithful friend is thus one of Conan Doyle's masterly ways of fostering identification with Watson. And Holmes himself, after all, is often less than triumphant. In 'The Dancing Men', breaking the cipher brings only 'surprise and dismay', and failure to prevent a tragedy.

Assumptions – especially wrong assumptions – are the stuff of 'The Dancing Men'. Its hermeneutic task entails not only making sense of the facts, but working out from exiguous hints what the right facts to assume are. Almost as with Hawthorne, narrative bricks must be made with little factual straw. And always readers have to follow Watson in resisting complete identification with Holmes.

The first construction of the case may be regarded as what 'the servants say' (67). On this assumption, two shots were fired, one killing Hilton Cubitt and the other wounding Elsie. To the impartial local surgeon 'It was equally conceivable that he had shot her and then himself, or that she had been the criminal, for the revolver lay upon the floor midway between them'. But to Martin and the servants it was not equally conceivable. As the stationmaster reports, they assume the foreign lady's guilt: if her life can be saved it will be 'for the gallows'.

At one stage Holmes himself may have assumed Elsie's guilt. When 'It fills [him] with hopes' (64) to hear that Elsie has been replying to Abe Slaney's messages, this is probably because he expects her to give away the 'secret' – which he also advises Cubitt to ask her about directly (60). But the cryptograms reveal something of Elsie's innocence and guilt; and Holmes goes to Norfolk with a new assumption. Friend of the establishment and enemy of criminals, he tends to assume the guilt of the latter; and his knowledge of Chicago crooks, in particular, prepares him 'to find that [Slaney] might very rapidly put his words [ELSIE PREPARE TO MEET THY GOD] into action'. Holmes evidently thinks this expectation fulfilled, to judge by his vague continuation: 'I at once came to Norfolk . . . to find that the worst had already occurred'. When he notices the bullet hole in the window sash, and deduces the firing of a third shot, Holmes's new assumption seems vindicated: Slaney ('the most dangerous crook in Chicago') must be the murderer.

Inspector Martin, changing front, is eager to make an arrest (76). His new-found assumption of Slaney's guilt may be ironically highlighted, for when the American says 'I guess the very best case I can make for myself is the absolute naked truth' (80), he is cautioned (not charged): – ' "It is my duty to warn you that it will be used against you," cried the inspector, with the magnificent fair play of the British criminal law.' Legally, 'will be used' was as valid as 'may be used'; but it was not the customary formula. Martin evidently sees no need to specify a charge of murder, nor to envisage the truth's not all being used against Slaney.[3]

But the case, like the decipherment, turns out to have something of a false bottom. Perhaps maturer consideration, certainly Slaney's surprise and grief at hearing of Elsie's wounding, qualify Holmes's view of the Chicagoan. He 'sternly' charges Slaney not with murder but with 'bringing about the death of a noble man and driving his wife to suicide'.

With uncharacteristic negligence, Ronald Knox remarks that in Sherlock Holmes stories 'all criminals are model criminals' (Knox 1954: 113). In fact almost the reverse is true: they tend to be ordinary people, or at least people with ordinary feelings. Although Conan Doyle was no shallow idealist, as the medical stories show he thought well of human nature. 'The deeper strata are good' (Doyle 1903: 'The Surgeon Speaks', 243). Here, Slaney is shown as a grieving lover rather than a professional killer. In his own view he has 'nothing to hide . . . the man had his shot at me, and there's no murder in that' (79); and in the reader's too, perhaps, Slaney's guilt may be palliated by his passion, and his American valuation of what amounts, after all, to a shootout. Nevertheless, the court finds him guilty of murder, doubtless on grounds of constructive malice; for he is condemned to death (a penalty later commuted). His criminal record will have counted against him – significantly Holmes is made to say 'That is your record in this business . . . and you will answer for it to the law' (80).

It is not immediately clear what Holmes means by Slaney's 'driving' Elsie to attempted suicide: her motivation must be inferred. How much was guilt at her own part in 'bringing about the death of a noble man' by keeping her 'guilty' secret? How much, perhaps, at a residual attachment to Slaney? And how much apprehension about English society's probable verdict on one with her pedigree? Although Holmes suppresses this point, an entire social culture conspired against Elsie. When she tried to tell Hilton her secret, she never got beyond talk of the Cubitts' 'reputation in the county, and our pride in our unsullied honour' (62). For such pride, and for his share in a society where the truth is hard to tell, Holmes's client seems not entirely blameless. And the story diffuses guilt even further, to the great detective himself. For on reading Cubitt's last letter, Holmes says 'we have let this affair go far enough'; implying that he could have intervened sooner. Two motives for delay seem likely, and probably both are to be supplied. Holmes may have refrained out of delicacy, giving Elsie a chance to settle the affair discreetly without harming his client's all-important honour. (Holmes was similarly discreet in the Milverton affair.) Or he may have awaited a full understanding of the case; working as usual towards a theatrical disclosure.

Holmes's comparative failure in 'The Dancing Men' contrasts strikingly with Legrand's total success in the denouement of 'The Gold-Bug'. Legrand may behave madly – with 'a nervous *empressement* which alarmed me and strengthened the suspicions already entertained. His countenance was pale even to ghastliness, and his deep-set eyes glared with unnatural lustre' (Poe 1984: 567): treasure may seem to have obsessed and 'demented' the narrator's 'unfortunate companion' (567, 577): but this is a false appearance, created by Legrand as a joke. And the landscape descriptions that assist the erroneous construction? The 'dreary' region of melancholy, with crags of guilt impending and 'deep ravines' which 'gave an air of still sterner solemnity to the scene'? All this evocation of a mood of malaise is the narrator's joke on the reader. The outcome reveals a perfectly rational Legrand, who turns to practical account even the *scarabaeus caput hominis* – the previously unknown death's head beetle that has seemed an obsessing 'maggot' (his 'whole intellect seemed to be absorbed by "de bug" '). Dropped through the orbit of the skull – linking it with the remaining, buried parts of the divided skeleton – the beetle of death becomes a means of finding treasure.

The story's anamorphic structure (Legrand mad: Legrand sane) is apparently trivialised, when the suggestions of morbidity turn out to be a pointless joke. Otherwise, one might be inclined to see the search for buried treasure as signifying pursuit of identity, selfhood, or an integrated soul.[4] (Decipherment would be abreaction of what had been repressed with violence.) But deep interpretation seems undercut by Legrand's joke – unless that, too, is to be internalised, as the detective-hermeneut's evasion of the narrator's rationality. Was Poe capable of such symbolism? Details like his insistence on the treasure's (and the bug's) being 'real gold', 'solid gold', with the gratuitous information that 'there was no American money' (580), certainly suggest awareness of a psychological dimension. And recent work suggests that Poe was more aware of unconscious repression than has been supposed (see Wuletich-Brinberg 1988). The story's closure – the sinister question about Kidd's violence in suppressing the truth – surely aims at more than a last frisson of horror. But, writing when he did, Poe felt an overwhelming need for concealment.

'The Dancing Men' arouses fewer doubts as to artistic control.

Here, successive assumptions are not mutually destructive, but lead in a consistent direction. And Poe's overt psychologising is avoided. For all his emulation of the farouche Virginian, Conan Doyle thought him 'not altogether a healthy influence': without 'countering qualities' Poe might become 'a dangerous comrade' (Doyle 1912: 121). In his own less romantic fiction, Conan Doyle follows a more social route, scouting the 'perilous tracks' and 'deadly quagmires' of Poe's introspection. But the route need not be that of 'classic realism'. And if Conan Doyle thinks Poe 'devoid of humour', yet in his own composed way he takes quite as tragic a view of life. In Sherlock Holmes stories, appearances of morbidity are not explained away as jokes, but hint at a reality beyond the control of science.

'The Dancing Men' is not the only case in which Holmes arrives too late to avert 'the worst'. Although his method is vindicated theoretically, he often enough fails to prevent a tragic outcome. Tragedy, indeed, commonly supplies the generic mechanism of Conan Doyle's machines of death. Thus, in 'The Dancing Men' Holmes's enquiries have the inexorability of Oedipus', as he successively implicates Elsie, Slaney and Cubitt, while conspicuously failing to admit his own responsibility. At last Holmes triumphantly congratulates himself on 'a remarkable professional study' that has left his client dead. Here one may suspect satire of the callously complacent theorising Conan Doyle hated in the medical establishment. But to stress this aspect is to miss the story's complexity; for in another mood (as in the train to Norfolk) Holmes's guilt, or at least sense of failure, can bring him to 'blank melancholy' ('Seldom', says Watson, 'have I seen him so utterly despondent'). Such depression has to do with Conan Doyle's own sense of man's 'tragic destiny'.[5] Understanding is always an eaten apple – retrospective, belated, inadequate. By contrast with Poe's enquiring closure, therefore, Conan Doyle's presents a final image that transcends understanding: Elsie's life of expiatory caring.

From this viewpoint, one can understand the eponymity of the dancing men, the story's most memorable image. These scribbled 'forerunners of so terrible a tragedy' connect guilt with childhood, through their suggestion of 'a child's drawing'. The seeming childishness of the cryptograms is stressed so repeatedly as to extend the distribution of evil, while curiously intensifying it. The effect is not merely a sense of horror at discovering that what 'would pass as a child's scrawl' belongs to Slaney's 'dangerous web'. Less explicitly, there is a sinister impression of infantile malice. One recalls that the surgeon in Conan Doyle's 'A Medical Document' was only once frightened: by the 'malignancy' of an ambiguously mature 'infant'. (Doyle 1903: 154)

The vague menace of the dancing men grows ever more imminent, with the inexorability of night following day, as the chalk-mark sites alternate between bright sundial and black toolhouse. The dancing men dance, it seems, a *Totentanz*. (The secret knowledge of evil that Elsie and Slaney share includes, it seems, knowledge of mortality, the wages of sin.) But the toolhouse and sundial suggests also the interaction of technology and time, art and nature – not merely the *circuit de la parole* round-dance but the whole choresis of man's fatal history. As stories such as 'The Third Generation' show, the problem of evil – 'the sins of the Creator' – much exercised Conan Doyle. Here, the ancestral origin of the cipher (Elsie's father invented it for 'the Joint', his criminal organisation of seven, that is, all of us) indicates one answer unambiguously: evil is inherited. Conan Doyle repudiated the Calvinistic doctrine of total depravity, however; inheritance of social circumstances and tendencies may be more to the point. Elsie, who (like everyone in Conan Doyle's view) is good at heart, tries to repudiate her criminal connections. But she succeeds only temporarily; her origin is not to be denied. Indeed, failure to confess her link with 'the Joint' is precisely what falsifies her relationships and precipitates tragedy.

I hope these suggestions have been arrived at without violent decentring. Still, they can hardly be called obvious. Conan Doyle's is an economical, understating art, as his muting modulations of 'The Gold-Bug' repeatedly reflect. For Poe's landscape of horror, he substitutes the ordinary wasteland of Norfolk. Holmes in his despondency misses altogether the 'few scattered cottages' and 'enormous square-towered churches' that interest Watson – signs of depopulation, of former glory. But the reader should not overlook these indications of social change, nor the contrast between the flat landscape and Poe's subjectively horrid crags. Yet if Conan Doyle provides 'counteracting qualities', he is by no means mocking Poe. He profoundly admired 'the master of all' in the short story, and regarded 'The Gold-Bug' as one of Poe's two stories of perfect excellence – for proportion and perspective 'I don't see how either of those could be bettered'

(Doyle 1912: 114). In fact (a hard fact, perhaps, for some) Conan Doyle thought of Poe, much in the way he thought of Stevenson, as a classic writer. Thus he observes that 'all treasure-hunting, cryptogram-solving yarns trace back to . . . "The Gold-Bug" ' (Doyle 1912: 115). In emulating such a 'classic' model, finesses, economical allusions, and ironic intertextualities were appropriate, just as in the canonical 'great tradition'; so that 'The Dancing Men' also has to be approached through its (extracanonical) tradition.

So regarded, it may become itself a classic, although perhaps of a distinct type. This warrants treating it seriously, and allows Catherine Belsey (1980: 116) to relate it, quite legitimately, to interests of feminism. It is not deficiency of art in Conan Doyle's stories, nor 'the limits of their own project', that opens the door to her particular hermeneutic activity.

Kingsley Amis has pointed out that the Sherlock Holmes tales are properly 'adventure stories involving a crime, or an apparent crime, and concentrating attention on a detective, his friend and chronicler, and the relations between the two' (Doyle 1974: Introduction, 8). And one might add that Conan Doyle's best 'yarns' (as he called them) are 'tertiary' adventures, in which features of the 'secondary', or conscious, adventure form are reused as material for symbolic applications, and every clue becomes a potential clew of metaphoric yarn. Allowing for the lower profile of their effects, they resemble in this way the stories of Hawthorne and Stevenson.

The principal features of 'The Dancing Men' are symbolic, signifying not so much through the representative action of 'classic realism' as through recall of analogues in congeners like 'The Gold-Bug', through modulation of the genre's repertoire. A generic frame of reference informs our inferences, and each allusion to Poe is potentially meaningful. Thus the decipherment, paradigmatically, can refer to the investigation at large, and can draw attention to assumptions underlying Holmes's procedure. Again, in 'The Gold-Bug' the decipherment reveals a secret of ancient aggression, which remains as an object of enquiry. But Conan Doyle applies this potently vague symbol rather differently. His decipherment leads not to a dead pirate's crime, but a living woman's history of criminal association.

As in Poe, disclosure of the secret reveals conflict – as much internal, in Elsie's case, as social. This conflict, precipitated by the surfacing of her past, is a clash between violently contrasted cultures – as often in Conan Doyle. Here, he dramatises the clash in a gunfight between a noble East Anglian and a Chicago criminal; thus externalising, perhaps, the disparities straining the Cubitts' unlucky marriage. Qualities sundering Elsie and Hilton link her to her former love; it would not be surprising if her feelings were mixed when she restrained her husband 'with convulsive strength' from pursuing Slaney. It crossed Cubitt's mind for a moment 'that perhaps what she really feared was that he [Slaney] might come to harm'. Yet at the same time he is certain of Elsie's loyalty – as Slaney testifies, 'she would have nothing to do with anything on the cross' (Doyle 1981: 81). Cubitt's social standing raises this high moral line of Elsie's still higher: she is fatally incapable of expressing her conflict and telling her secret, because 'there is not a man in England who ranks his family honour more highly'. The resulting conflict charging their relations is symbolised in the catastrophe. For Conan Doyle renews Poe's question about the unfathomable extent of aggression ('perhaps a couple of blows with a mattock were sufficient . . . – who shall tell?'), by making it an issue how many shots were fired at Ridling Thorpe Manor. Perhaps a couple of shots were sufficient? Well, two sounds of shots were. But contributing to one of these reports was Slaney's third, simultaneous shot, the result of aggression provoked by Elsie's attempt to pay him off. And motivating this, in turn, was her wish to conceal her guilty secret, her criminal father. Holmes's client remained unaware of any fault in himself; and so did Holmes – enough that Cubitt, having promised not to speak, was as good as his word. But Conan Doyle the campaigner for women's rights knew how much wives could be silenced and oppressed by the elevation of 'family honour'.

A remaining subtextual feature, Kidd's treasure, is utilised less obtrusively still. Gold only surfaces in 'The Dancing Men' in connection with Watson's train of thought, deduced by Holmes: 'it was not really difficult, by an inspection of the groove between your left forefinger and thumb, to feel sure that you did not propose to invest your small capital in the goldfields' (56–7). Watson's cautious bearishness is perhaps to be contrasted with Cubitt's rash foreign investment, not in the goldfields, but in a wife who might turn out a gold-digger. Cubitt said he 'would spend [his] last copper to shield' Elsie (60). And she, for her part, was prepared to pay Slaney notes from her specifically silver purse. (Was it silver of faithfulness, or the reprobate silver of Jeremiah 6: 30?) She herself constitutes the treasure Cubitt and Slaney fight over; whether treasure of pure gold, is one of the story's questions.

She comes, like Kidd's treasure, with a guilty secret; but then buried selves are always partly 'evil'. Exhumation before renunciation. Is not Elsie's repentance 'devoting her whole life to the care of the poor' presented a little perfunctorily? Only in terms of realism. No one can deny the virtual death to her old life that her attempted suicide symbolises. Moreover, she is only partly responsible for the tragic denouement. Inherited ills, as we have seen, played their parts; Slaney; Holmes; and Cubitt with his sense of racial superiority.

Only Watson seems free from the diffused taint of guilty responsibility. But is even his refraining from investment in gold quite innocent? How far was his decision overcautious? How far nationally prejudiced? And how far an indication of Conan Doyle's negative judgement on the British gold-diggers in the Rand?[6]

From this approach, assessments of 'The Dancing Men' take on an altered appearance. In particular, Pierre Macherey's conclusion (that Conan Doyle silences the woman's voice involuntarily) loses any attraction it may have had.[7] For in 'The Dancing Men' the supporter of the rights of women seems well able to express their perspective. And elsewhere he does so, sometimes, with searing intensity – in the symbolism of stories like 'Lady Sannox', for example, or in the anecdote of the policeman's compulsory couvade in 'A Medical Document'. Like the handcuff on the bleeding policeman, the 'woman question' constantly chafed at Conan Doyle. Thus, as early as 1888 Holmes was fascinated by Irene Adler, the careerist with 'the mind of the most resolute of men' who excelled him in the art of professional disguise ('A Scandal in Bohemia'). For him she was always 'the woman'. And in 'Doctors of Hoyland' the woman question – again posed by a successful woman careerist – receives the realistic treatment Macherey desiderates. Departure from 'classic realism' was not forced on Conan Doyle simply by his taking up the woman's point of view.

The Sherlock Holmes stories, written for a somewhat different audience, had to appear amusing detective adventures, and so have come to seem to some a 'limited project'. Throughout his fiction, however, Conan Doyle wrote symbolic romance; and he developed the form as an eloquent means of expressing social ideas. Admittedly, the surface features leading readers to his serious content have very low profiles. But 'The Dancing Men' illustrates how much it was possible for Conan Doyle to convey, even in a detective adventure.

The later Sherlock Holmes stories call for as much critical attention as that demanded by Robert Louis Stevenson's – which is as much (although distinct in mode) as with a canonical Conrad tale. In approaching these stories we cannot sustain the usual division between, on the one hand, a canon of 'high' works suitable for literary criticism, on the other 'low' uncanonical writing to be quarried for examples supporting social or political generalisation. These are too well-written for that, and merit attention as literature. Frequently they present additional qualities that have little directly to do with social ideas: that elude, indeed, criticism of existing sorts. It seems almost impossible to approach their pleasures – pleasures of being baffled by bizarre impenetrable puzzles rather than of solving them; of detecting rather than apprehending; of anticipating the unexpected – without curtailing them.

Notes

1. Throughout the present paper, I am indebted for many suggestions to Paul Barolsky and Wallace Robson.
2. See Edwards 1983: 141. Accardo (1987: 27) notes that the demonstrations follow the lecturing style of Conan Doyle's professors at Edinburgh.
3. The form of the caution itself would have been legally acceptable, but probably not customary (for this information I am indebted to Susan Kreitman).
4. On meanings of 'the treasure hard to attain' archetype, see Jung, 1953: 113–14.
5. See, e.g., 'The Third Generation', in Doyle 1903.
6. On Conan Doyle's ambivalence towards the Boers in 1899, see Carr 1949: 146.
7. Macherey and Balibar 1978. The common error of supposing Conan Doyle ambivalent on the woman question may have arisen from his dislike of the 'anarchic' suffragette movement.

10

The Pater of Joyce and Eliot
Richard Poirier

According to its author, Frank Kermode, the 'main topic' of *Romantic Image* (1957) has to do with 'that "esthetic image" explained in Thomist language by Stephen Daedalus in the *Portrait of the Artist as a Young Man* and he almost immediately indicates that St Thomas shares the honours with Walter Pater. Stephen's description of 'epiphany', he remarks, is 'the Joycean equivalent of Pater's "vision" ' (Kermode 1957: 1–2). The 'Joyce industry', as Kermode calls it five years later in the title essay of *Puzzles and Epiphanies* (1962: 87), has yet to venture much beyond this merely initial point in the argument of *Romantic Image*, and even when critics refer now and again to Stephen as a Paterian artist, there are seldom any explanations – short of a few references to his theories of 'luminous stasis' – of what it more pertinently means to call him one. As Kermode goes on to suggest, the connections between Pater and Joyce, discoveries of which depend necessarily on a more intense reading than Pater normally receives, are intricate and substantial. They constitute one of the vital links between the 'nineties' and the literary modernism of the first two decades of this century, a conjunction which Eliot was determined to suppress. Eliot's trashing of Pater, combined with his attempted appropriation of Joyce in '*Ulysses*, Order, and Myth' (Eliot 1975), were part of an effort to make Pater and the poets whom Yeats called 'the tragic generation' seem merely eccentric and, in any event, outside the main English tradition. From the beginning, Kermode has brilliantly, and against a determined critical consensus, set out to remedy this situation.

In doing so he draws attention to neglected and essential aspects of Pater which are at work in modernist literature. A bit later in the opening chapter of *Romantic Image*, for example, he comments on how 'to our great benefit, Pater in *The Renaissance* and *Marius the Epicurean* and James in "The Art of Fiction" and in his practice, insisted on the moral value of what is highly organised and profoundly apprehended, in life and in art' (Kermode 1957: 11–12). He is suggesting that Pater's impingement on modernism, as it might be represented by Joyce, included his tough awareness of the cost of arriving at or trying to hold onto ecstatic moments and, especially, of finding the right words to represent them. Pater is concerned, that is, as much with the formal disciplines required if one is to achieve intensifications of experience as he is with the intensifications themselves. This, I take it, is what Kermode has in mind when he says that for Pater art 'is the only true morality' (1957: 20).

So conceived, Pater becomes a figure of much greater consequence to Joyce and Eliot than he is usually thought to be, and thus to any revaluation of literary modernism. With a few distinguished exceptions,[1] however, critics tend to ignore or trivialise the role of Pater in these equations, and it is given only a casual nod in the best books on Pater himself, like Wolfgang Iser's estimable *Walter Pater: The Aesthetic Moment* (1960; trans. 1987). Indeed, Pater is a provocative example of how a writer, even when fortunate enough to find a critic sensitive to the historical ramifications of his work, can still be denied the place he has earned in 'the tradition' if to put him there means that the tradition has to be reconstituted.

This is as much the fate of Pater with respect to Joyce, Eliot, and the modernism associated with them, as it is the fate of Emerson and William James with respect to twentieth-century American poets like Frost and Stevens, both of whom are still being disfigured by interpretations slavishly geared to the standard modernist and post-modernist lines of succession. Lines of succession are, to be sure, altered now and then, and there are always disagreements among its fiduciaries, but these seem designed actually to prevent the proper investitures of prodigals like Emerson and Pater. To give them their due would badly disrupt the chronologies and periodisations in which the various modernisms, including 'paleo' and 'post', briskly succeed one another. About such chronologies and periodisations Kermode was as sceptical in the mid-sixties, with the opening section of *Continuities* called 'The Modern', as he is now in the late eighties, with the chapter called 'Canon and Period' in *History and Value*.

Revisions in favour of Pater and Emerson would mean, among other things, that Eliot's version of modernism would be seen as mostly eccentric and self-serving; it would mean that the proponents of deconstructive theory would be seen less as innovators than, properly, as a subject for the sociology of knowledge. It would mean the emergence of historicisms less specific and insular than the kind now called 'new'. Pater, who refers to Jonathan Edwards, most assuredly read Emerson, and would himself, in turn, probably have been read by William James, as we know he had been by Henry. Pater, Emerson, William James together provide in my view an alternative criticism and pedagogy to currently prevailing ones, as I have argued at some length in *The Renewal of Literature* (1987). In the absence of that alternative it seems unlikely that a writer as gushy as Pater, in the cartoon versions now held of him, could have had a profound influence on Joyce, or that a writer as perpetually hopeful as is a misread Emerson could have strongly influenced Stevens, or that a poet as down home as Frost could all the while be indebted, in poem after poem, to William James.

The neglected, not too much to say the shunned aspect of Pater, no less than of Emerson, is the darker, skeptical one which questions the ideas which he is better known for advancing. Pater, like Emerson, fears getting lost altogether in the flood of free sensation to which he inevitably wants to respond; he finds in literature, or more particularly in the inferrable activity of writing, a reminder of the need for form, for discipline even while these work against imaginative freedom. Rigour and self-restraint in the use of language is especially necessary, so it is implied, in a situation where the collapse of cultural institutions, including the institutions which derive authority from a God long rumoured to be dead, is treated by the likes of Emerson and Pater not as a bad but as a good omen. Reading and writing provide a form in which it might be possible to shape an idea of the self when the self can no longer be substantiated by concepts like God, the soul, or immortality. Reading and writing depend, however, on words, and the trouble with words is that when they are thought to have no authority behind them except the authority of usage, they can become overwhelmed with connotation. Because of this, they can then betray any attempt to hold them to a particular purpose. The self created in words may quickly disappear, provoking a need for reconstitutive performative acts, like turns of voice or figure. It is a possibly frightening situation. Not everyone wants 'success in life' when, to get it, you must, as in the Conclusion of Pater's *The Renaissance* (1984: 60), 'burn always with this hard gemlike flame'. And those who most yearn for that kind of success are always in danger of merely spontaneous combustions. To concentrate on 'burning' is to know how quickly you can burn up; it is to come to the stark realisation that you can be consumed wholly within biological life, to face extinction without memorial. It is, with Pater, to become obsessed with the absoluteness of death.

When referring to Pater's sense of a necessary discipline, I have in mind the particular form of it which he calls '*ascêsis*'. The word and its variants can be found in almost everything he writes. In the Preface to *The Renaissance*, for example, he speaks of 'the charm of *ascêsis*, of the austere and serious girding of the loins of youth' (Pater 1984: 20), and in his essay 'Style' he defines its literary manifestations as 'self-restraint and renunciation' (108). Pater is famous for recommending the maximum degree of intensity in response to experience; yet you will notice his equal insistence on nearly the reverse. That is, in order to produce and sustain this intensity there is need for a high degree of calculated self-curtailment. The position is fraught with difficulty, even contradiction. On the one hand, considerable individual self-trust is required by the desire to maximise the intensity of a feeling; on the other, this intensity depends on self-erasure, so that there will be a minimum of obstruction to the ceaseless changes and accelerations of pure temporality. As Iser notes, 'it is only through the onward movement that our inner world can be enriched with the precious momentary impressions of experience that come and swiftly go. The transitoriness of these moments makes us increasingly conscious of the shortness of our lives' (Iser 1987: 30).

Pater's total commitment to art as an activity is understandable when, as he argues in *The Renaissance*, 'art comes to you proposing frankly to give nothing but the highest quality to your moments as they pass, and simply for those moments' sake' (Pater 1984: 62). Art does not redeem the time or offer any kind of redemption. Instead, as he writes of the school of Giorgione, it gives us the illusion of 'exquisite pauses in time, in which, arrested thus, we seem to be spectators of all the fullness of existence, and which are like some consummate extract or quintessence of life' (Pater 1986: 165). The vocabulary – 'exquisite' and 'consummate extract' – is not meant idly or to characterise merely the feelings of the observer. It points rather to artistic performance or, as he says earlier in the same sentence, to the 'admirable tact' by which the artist separates 'ideal instants' from a 'feverish, tumultuously coloured world'. This requires a kind of impersonality which Eliot, never one to credit his predecessors, sets up as an artistic ideal. The artist as a person achieves only such immortality as is vouchsafed anyone else; beyond that he or she can continue to exist only in those performative functions in the work which can afterward be located, as traces of presence, only by particularly responsive readers. It is hoped that these traces will 'arrest' us, as they might the artist, within the passage of obliterating time. The poetry and essays of Stevens are suffused with this sort of Paterian (and Whitmanian) yearning for a life after death in the poems left behind.

But we are here concerned with the Pater found in Joyce. It is found partly in the shared expectation that through the design of a work of art the artist might hope to claim a measure of immortality. This becomes in the writings of both of them a design more specifically of the older artist upon any younger versions of himself. The older artist desires, that is, to cleanse and recompose himself as a young man, and in the process to attenuate the linkages of the later self to an earlier version which by hindsight seems always to have been doomed. In this Pater and Joyce are especially alike. In his late autobiographical story 'The Child in the House', Pater speaks, for example, of 'a certain design he had in view, the noting namely, of some things in the story of the spirit – in that process of brain building by which we are, each one of us, what we are' (Pater 1984: 1). It is made clear that the 'design' is actually being fulfilled in the very writing of the story and therefore in our reading of the story. The writer is here reconstituting and recomposing his younger self in the person of Florian, and the word 'house' refers to more than a place of residence. It refers also to the mind and physical being of this younger self and to the physical being of the older one in whom the child still lives. The narrator is, as a writer, fulfilling the Socratic function described in *Plato and Platonism*: 'to flash light into the house within, its many chambers, its memories and associations, upon its inscribed and pictured walls' (quoted in Iser 1987: 25). The child in the house is, then, two different persons: first, it is the child in its own mind, which is already to some extent written upon by his surroundings, including the physical house which helps mediate all his impressions; and second, it is the child who, at the later time of the story and its composition, still exists in the mind of the writer, the older artist. The writer, unlike any version of the child, is aware of multiple mediations of all the experience that is now held in his, the writer's, mind, and with this awareness comes a recognition of the limitations on freedom of experience. This recognition is something that the child as child, in any of *its* manifestations, could not have known about, or known only vaguely and intermittently.

In Pater, no less than in Joyce of *A Portrait*, the projected 'design' of the older artist is not, then, merely an imposition on experience; rather it partakes of, participates in, above all repeats those 'designs' or inscriptions which shaped the younger version and, at least to some extent, still therefore persist in the older one. The authorial 'design' is not intended merely to disclose the disorderly contents of a younger self and to give it shape as a *bildungsroman*. Quite the reverse. The older artist now sees that all experience, even as it comes to the mind of the infant child, was already 'designed' or mediated; the superiority of the older artist to the younger one is simply his capacity now to recognise that this was the case, to see patterns which were not visible to the younger self who felt very often in the presence merely of confusions or disorderliness. The older artist knows that experience is always and forever mediated by the forms of language by which it is brought to consciousness, and this includes even the language he is now using.

By virtue of this recognition Pater can be said to discover for himself, and for Joyce, an essential component of modernism attributed by criticism more exclusively to Joyce alone. From the outset, *A Portrait*, no less than 'A Child in the House', shows that experience is mediated by writing, and this long before the writing done later on by the older artist. Within the first 300 words of *A Portrait* the experience of the artist as an infant is filtered to him through various media: the opening lines are a story of a 'moo cow' being told to him by his father; he then hears a song and tries to sing it; he is made to dance while his mother plays the piano; he is introduced to the symbolic colours on the brushes of Dante's press; he is intimidated with nursery rhyme words which will recur in his later experiences at college – 'Apologise,/Pull out his eyes'. And still within this compass he

is moved from games at home to games at school, to the play-
grounds of Clongowes. There, as throughout the rest of this
novel and, with some notable exceptions, *Ulysses*, he tries to keep
out of the games others play while pretending to be in them. It
is here, in the form of emotional trauma, that his theory of
aesthetic detachment begins to take shape, and not in any later
readings of aesthetic theory. 'He kept', as Joyce says, 'on the
fringe of his line' (Joyce 1957: 8).

Interpreters have frequently pointed out that the terms which
at this juncture impress themselves on the boy's mind help determine the language by which Joyce represents Stephen's subsequent experience. Thus, 'cold', associated with wetting the bed
and guilt, becomes connected with the water of the Clongowes
ditch and, later, the sea, the flow of matter into which he falls.
Analysis has recorded these repetitions many times over. Words
are shown thereby to be less the instruments of liberation that
he takes them to be, than a source of entrapment in past experience; and continually, as the novel progresses, words frustrate
his declarations of intensity and of freedom. Recall his ecstatic
walk by the sea in chapter 4 where his Icarian vision is
accompanied by the cries of children at play, 'O, Cripes, I'm
drownded!' (169), referring back to the boys at Clongowes who
shouldered him into the slime of the ditch. So, too, with respect
to Stephen's aesthetic theories in the next chapter; these are often
read as if Joyce subscribes to them, as if intellectual-philosophical
talk is somehow free of the slippages and ironic pressures at
work everywhere else in the language of the book. In fact it
doesn't matter whether or by how much Joyce *might* subscribe
to any of Stephen's theories, because what the structure of the
book puts into question is the degree to which Stephen's articulation of them can ever be less than embarrassing. Joseph Buttigieg is one of the critics who is especially perceptive about
Stephen's theorising in his recent *A Portrait of the Artist in a
Different Perspective*, no affront intended by him to Hugh Kenner's
laudable essay of 1948, 'The *Portrait* in Perspective'. Stephen's
articulation of theory, his wording of it – not to be confused with
the same theories worded differently – is a confused mishmash
of Pater and Aquinas wherein his terms carry destructive connotations from earlier and, by him, suppressed moments in the
story. The patterns of the book require that the reader recall what
the young artist is anxious to forget.

Citations of repetition in *A Portrait* are by now so familiar as to have become rather stale. I mention them only as easy examples of the technique by which Joyce shows, despite Stephen's declarations, that it is impossible with respect to any object to 'see that it is that thing which it is and no other thing' (Joyce 1957: 213). There can be no virgin womb of the imagination, because the imagination only knows itself thanks to the words that have already possessed and fertilised it. The implications for language are made embarrassingly evident to Stephen well before *Ulysses*, as when he tries to compose his vilanelle near the end of *A Portrait*, just after his announcement about the virgin womb. The phrases that prosaically intrude upon his poetic fashioning have nothing to do with virgins. Just after the third stanza of the poem as later completed, he lapses into compositional ruminations: 'Smoke went up from the whole earth, the vapoury oceans, smoke of her praise. The earth was like a swinging swaying censer, a ball of incense, an ellipsoidal ball' (218). Any attentive reader will recall that only a few pages back the phrase 'ellipsoidal balls' played a part in the 'rude humour' of Moynihan during a lecture in mathematics. When the professor, quoting from a poem by W. S. Gilbert – Stephen has yet to learn that everything is a quotation – refers to 'elliptical billiard balls', Moynihan 'leaned down towards Stephen's ear and murmured "What price ellipsoidal balls! Chase me, ladies, I'm in the cavalry!" ' (192). Even though Stephen will eventually complete the poem, the frustrations of his efforts at this point, and in immediate proximity to his theorising about the imagination, is an encapsulated illustration of how, by these quietly managed repetitions, Joyce denies Stephen the exercise of power over language which he too easily proposes to exert.

Stephen's recommendations of detachment and withdrawal in the interest of artistic gestation result less from intellectual rigour than from compulsions, the repetition compulsion so to speak, made evident as early as Clongowes. He is compelled to separate himself from the games others play and, especially, from what he calls, at another point, 'the sordid tide of life' (98), a tide, he says, that moves within as well as without him. Joyce's images of tides and streams is everywhere anticipated in Pater, often in phrases that catch his curious revulsion from the flow he also desires, as when, in the 'Conclusion' to *The Renaissance*, he speaks of 'the delicious recoil from the flood of water in summer heat'

(Pater 1984: 55). The same image of tides, flows, and floods is conspicuous in Emerson and in William James, in writers, that is, who exult in the stream of consciousness but who, for that reason, discover within this image there is a movement inevitably and irresistibly towards oblivion.

One fails to do any sort of justice either to Pater or to Joyce by asking simply if Stephen is a failed Paterian, or if *A Portrait* is in part a fictional substantiation of Eliot's criticism of Pater. The essential question is whether or not there can ever be such a thing as a successful Paterian, one who is not depressed and defeated by his own perception of the role of art and of the artist. The question, as I want to argue, was asked first and most starkly by Pater himself, and Joyce's portrait of Stephen is to be read, I think, less as a critique of Pater than as an assimilation and deep understanding of him. Eliot adopts Joyce's reading of Pater for his own uses only by refusing to understand it.

The 'Conclusion' to *The Renaissance* written in 1868 was withdrawn by Pater from the second edition and then, when restored to the third edition, revised in the hope of making its skepticism less subject to attack. There is no escaping even now its powerful denial of fixed principles and its tough-minded willingness to let the idea of the self become unfixed and floating. It is an alarmingly vivid account of solipsism and its dangers, these being a total transfer of objects into the impressions one has of them, a divestment of the 'solidity with which language invests them' (Pater 1984: 59). The passage, which concludes with the image of the 'continual vanishing away, that strange, perpetual weaving and unweaving of ourselves', looks toward one of *The Imaginary Portraits*, which will be considered presently, named 'Sebastian Van Storck' and beyond that to the portrait of Stephen Daedalus, especially his fragmentation into the self-cancelling assemblage of allusions and sentiments which characterise his language in the first three chapters of *Ulysses*. Here, also, Pater anticipates the image of the 'tide' within as well as without, though he never calls it 'sordid':

> Or if we begin with the inward world of thought and feeling, the whirlpool is still more rapid, the flame more eager and devouring. There it is no longer the gradual darkening of the eye and the fading of the colour from the wall, – movements of the shore-side, where the water flows down indeed, though

in apparent rest – but the race of the mid-stream, a drift of momentary acts of sight and passion and thought. At first sight experience seems to bury us under a flood of external objects, pressing upon us with a sharp and importunate reality, calling us out of ourselves in a thousand forms of action. But when reflexion begins to play upon those objects they are dissipated under its influence; the cohesive force seems suspended like some trick of magic; each object is loosed into a group of impressions – colour, odour, texture – in the mind of the observer. And if we continue to dwell in thought on this world, not of objects in the solidity with which language invests them, but of impressions, unstable, flickering, inconsistent, which burn and are extinguished with our consciousness of them, it contracts still further: the whole scope of observation is dwarfed into the narrow chamber of the individual mind. Experience, already reduced to a group of impressions, is ringed round for each one of us by that thick wall of personality through which no real voice has ever pierced on its way to us, or from us to that which we can only conjecture to be without. Every one of those impressions is the impression of the individual in his isolation, each mind keeping as a solitary prisoner its own dream of a world. Analysis goes a step further still, and assures us that those impressions of the individual mind to which, for each one of us, experience dwindles down, are in perpetual flight; that each of them is limited by time, and that as time is infinitely divisible, each of them is infinitely divisible also; all that is actual in it being a single moment, gone while we try to apprehend it, of which it may ever be more truly said that it has ceased to be than that it is. To such a tremulous wisp constantly re-forging itself on the stream, to a single sharp impression, with a sense in it, a relic more or less fleeting, of such moments gone by, what is real in our life fines itself down. It is with this movement, with the passage and dissolution of impressions, images, sensations, that analysis leaves off – that continual vanishing away, that strange, perpetual, weaving and unweaving of ourselves. (Pater 1984: 59–60)

Stephen Daedalus, 'weaver of the wind' as he calls himself in the opening chapter of *Ulysses*, sounds, in the account I am giving of him, as if he were entirely a function of language. He is of course also a novelistic character sufficiently portrayed so that he can be imagined independently of the words only by virtue of which he exists. And yet for Joyce he principally is, to recall Henry James' phrase, a compositional resource. That is, he is 'used' within a larger inquiry into the way language, under certain cultural conditions, tends to dissolve the objects, including the selves, to which it is supposed to give solidity. This may happen in any work of literature, but it happens in *A Portrait* by repeated design, as in Stephen's efforts at poetic or theoretic composition.

Joyce's portrait of Stephen is most significantly Paterian, then, not when Stephen is mouthing familiar Paterian phrases or when these are used to describe him ('A soft liquid joy like the noise of many waters flowed over his memory and he felt in his heart the soft peace of silent spaces of fading tenuous sky above the waters. . .' (Joyce 1957: 225).) He is most significantly Paterian when he comes to grief, and it is grief which Pater himself has already compellingly described. I have argued elsewhere that Eliot's essay of 1930 entitled 'Arnold and Pater' is mostly owed, though Eliot never mentions it, to Joyce's *Portrait* and the opening three chapters of *Ulysses* (Poirier 1987: 6–9); it now seems to me that Eliot was only able to find there what he most wanted to use and that he left behind all the best of it. He took only so much of Pater as served the polemical-religious purpose of the moment. The spectre of tides, of things being made to flow into one another, was especially disturbing to Eliot, so that when he describes this process as it occurs culturally, and in a movement generated, so he supposes, by Arnold and Pater – 'Religion becomes morals, Religion becomes art' – it is with obvious misgivings. 'The total effect of Arnold's philosophy', he writes, 'is to set up Culture in the place of Religion, and to leave Religion to be laid waste by the anarchy of feeling. And Culture is a term which each man not only may interpret as he pleases, but must indeed interpret as he can. So the gospel of Pater follows naturally upon the prophecy of Arnold' (Eliot 1978: 387).

Eliot is quite likely being instructed here by the kinds of appropriation of religion into art instigated by Stephen throughout the last sections of *A Portrait*, and which are made no less abundantly by Marius and by Pater's Florian in 'The Child in the House'. Stephen, while telling Cranly that he does not believe in the Eucharist and admitting that he fears it may indeed be 'the body and blood of the son of God' (239, 243), is simultaneously anxious, for purposes of art, to hold on to the form and vocabulary of transubstantiation. Similarly, he wishes to take the place of a young priest, whom he observes with a young woman, not only in her regard but in the confessional: 'To him she would unveil her soul's shy nakedness, to one who was but schooled in the discharging of a formal rite, rather than to him, a priest of the eternal imagination, transmuting the daily bread of experience into the radiant body of ever-living life' (221). Surely it took no great critical effort, nor does it constitute any but the most elementary reading of Pater, to remark as Eliot does that *Marius the Epicurean* is a document of that moment in history when 'Religion became morals, religion became art, religion became science or philosophy' (Eliot 1978: 393), or for that matter when religion became sex and politics.

A difference between Eliot and Joyce in their reading of Pater (which *A Portrait* and *Ulysses* can be taken in part to be) is that Joyce attributes a pathos to Stephen's Paterian position and refuses ever wholly to dissociate himself from it. He seems to recognise, as Eliot cannot afford to do, that Pater was fully aware of the risks, deprivations, and loss of self-hood that might follow along, with an exhilarating sense of liberation, from his aesthetics. This is the aspect of Pater which Eliot represses while, as Louis Menand (1987) and Perry Meisel (1987) have shown, he remains heavily indebted to him, even in phraseology, for his idea of impersonality. He is equally indebted, I would add, for other notions, like the suspect claim that in the modern age the poet must perforce become more 'difficult' and allusive than he had hitherto been obliged to be. It seems equally obvious, too, that in Eliot's poems, early and late, there is at work something like Pater's *'ascêsis'*, an expressed yearning for a principle of order that can account for a riot of disturbing because uncontrollable impressions. As an inferable presence in Joyce's work, Pater is understandably less impressive than is the Pater inferable from *Marius* or from the *Renaissance*, but he is never the cardboard and patronised figure of Eliot's essay. 'I have spoken of the book as of some importance', Eliot pompously remarks of *Marius*. 'I do not mean that its importance is due to any influence it may have exerted. I do not believe that Pater, in this book, has influenced a single first-rate mind of a later generation' (Eliot 1978: 392). Such a remark requires no comment, especially given the self-protective evasiveness of the phrase 'this book', as if *Marius* were somehow, from a writer of monotonous consistency of tone and substance, importantly different from any of his other writings. When Eliot goes on to remark that Pater's 'view of art, as expressed in *The Renaissance*, impressed itself upon a number of writers in the "nineties", and propagated some confusion between life and art which is not wholly irresponsible for some untidy lives' (ibid.), it only reminds us that Pater's own life was tidy to a degree almost pitiable, and that his writing, even as it preaches ecstasy and stimulation, managed, especially in *Marius*, to bear the marks of continuously suppressed, controlled, sedated passion. His stories in particular are full of the most elaborate mediations in the telling, with multiple buffers between the writer, especially when he characterises himself within the story, and any earlier version of himself.

As I see it, Pater's writing is most interesting, and also most important to Joyce, when it exhibits contradictory impulses: an acute need for exercises of control and discipline, along with an equally acute impatience with anything that might get in the way of the flow of sensation and impression. Pater's efforts to work within this contradiction help make him a seminal figure in the modernist situation as it is sometimes and, I think, most persuasively described. That situation is one in which the illusion has at last been given up that the self can be satisfactorily understood by an appeal to various forms of external authority. While this to some may represent a loss it represents to others a considerable gain. It makes people freer than they have ever known themselves to be, releasing them to the play of desire, speculation and sensation. It encourages them, otherwise unassisted, to enter what William James would later call, after Emerson, the stream of consciousness.

But even those who take this as an opportunity admit to a number of perplexities. First, if you do not already have a confident sense of self how then do you choose to attend to some sensations or experiences and not to all of them at once? Second, if you do let all of experience come at you indiscriminately, how do you keep from unravelling altogether? We noted awhile back that in his 'Conclusion' to *The Renaissance* Pater speaks of the self as a constant process of weaving and unweaving. This occasions yet another question. How do you get control of the pattern of weaving and unweaving so that it, too, is an experience and not merely an accident? Here, the answer would appear to be an anticipation of Hemingway or the James of 'The Moral Equivalent of War'. In the absence of religious faith and the devotional exercises that can go with it, you turn to more personal exercises like James' mountain climbing or the connoisseurship of Hemingway or you imagine, as did Gertrude Stein long before Mailer, an analogy between conducting a war and your own composition of a work. Pater's taste for the martial arts in his stories is, in that regard, only incidentally homoerotic.

His ideal of discipline seems mostly to be located, as to a degree it is also for these others – as it is everywhere for Joyce – in literary technique, in an idea of style as described in his essay on that subject in *Appreciations*. This raises yet another question. If discipline or self-curtailment or *ascêsis* is to be exercised in style, then to what end? If you do not have a soul to save then, without a soul, what instructs you to bother with efforts to compose the self, if only momentarily, within the flow of sensations? Perhaps the answer, as already mentioned, is that only by exerting some degree of control can you increase the intensity of such moments, cramming each of them with a maximum amount of felt intensity. But why *write* in order to do this? Why not stand on your head? It appears that writing, in the absence of God or soul, is the one form of discipline that might, again, offer some prospect of immortality, an arrest to the otherwise uninterrupted flow toward death. Style offers Pater the best way known to him by which to create structures that can, at least for the duration of the writing and reading, substitute for anything more permanent.

I am trying to describe a dilemma at the heart of Pater's philosophy of art and his own efforts to deal with this dilemma. The discipline of style serves a double purpose, one of which seems to frustrate the other. On the one hand the discipline is necessary to ensure that any given moment is exploited to the fullest, whether it be a moment of perception or of writing; on the other, because this discipline involves a degree of self-curtailment, of impersonality in the service of style, it thereby threatens to dissolve the very subjectivity which he wishes to enhance, to unweave or shatter the participating self. Pater does not evade this difficulty, and his efforts to cope with it are partly responsible for some of the murkiness of his writing. He tends abruptly to enter words or phrases of qualification into an argument that is heading another way, and to do so in subordinate parts of his sentences, as if to hide them from anyone but himself; or he will make assertions which cannot be reconciled with positions he famously adheres to, as in the last paragraph of 'Style' where, he says, the distinction between great art and good art depends 'not on form but on matter'. At his best, however, he is impressively scrupulous about the negative and self-defeating possibilities in his own philosophy of art. In evidence there is, notably, 'Sebastian Van Storck', a story included in *Imaginary Portraits* of 1887 and published the year before in *Macmillans*.

It is a powerful and disturbing work, unique on a number of counts. First, it is the only one of the *Imaginary Portraits* with a fictional rather than an historical or mythological hero, and though it does contain historical figures, including various Dutch painters of the seventeenth century and a cameo appearance by Spinoza, it is clear that in this instance Pater wants a form loose enough to allow a lot of personal intrusions and ruminations. He manages to bring into the story, as if for inspection and testing, ideas less critically elaborated in both the previously published *Marius* and *The Renaissance*. Second, it is for Pater unusually bleak, as compared, say, to the later 'The Child in the House'. And third, while the Pater of 'The Child in the House' echoes throughout the Joyce of *A Portrait*, especially at points where Stephen is enthusiastically anticipating his artistic emergence, 'Sebastian' anticipates the defeated Stephen and, more important still, the crises which, in Joyce's book, are shown to lurk just beneath the exuberant rhetoric of the Paterian artist. Sebastian is not as 'Paterian', in the popular understanding of that term, as Marius or as Florian, either when Florian is a child or when he is the older narrator of his story; for that matter he is not as Paterian, again in the popular sense, as is Stephen at the end of Chapter 4, 'singing wildly to the sea, crying to greet the advent of the life that had cried to him' (170). Sebastian more nearly resembles the Stephen after Chapter 4, the increasingly detached, prideful, and theoretical intellectual of Chapter 5, a young man obsessed with the sea and, nearly, a hater of his kind in the first three chapters of *Ulysses*.

Sebastian, that is, prefigures Stephen's destiny in an aggravated form and his metaphorical fall into the sea of matter. Before even introducing him, Pater depicts a situation bound by the same parameters that will encompass Stephen's: a stifling domesticity, art, and the sea. That's Holland for you, and Ireland too.

'The Dutch had just begun to see', Pater remarks, 'what a picture their country was' (Pater 1984: 67) – art informing them about their lives and their landscape. From the very first line, which refers to a winter scene by Adrian van Velde, to the end, where it is revealed that Sebastian has destroyed the one portrait done of him (by Isaac van Ostade), Dutch art and artists are evoked at every turn. And at every turn they are put in contrast to the other constant element in the determination of Dutch landscape, namely 'the sea which Sebastian so much loved' (70). Sebastian has already tired of art and turned away from those domestic refinements which Stephen assiduously tries to recover, if only for a time, after the collapse of family fortunes. 'The arts were a matter he could but just tolerate. Why add, by a forced and artificial production, to the monotonous tide of competing, fleeting experience?' (68) He prefers a quite different 'tide', the obliterating sea which will reduce everything to a *tabula rasa*, an 'empty place.' (69) Pater writes that 'In his passion for *Schwindsucht* – we haven't the word – he found it pleasant to think of the resistless element which left one hardly a foot-space amidst the yielding sand' (71). *Schwindsucht* can refer both to consumption – the artist's disease of the nineteenth century – and to renunciation and self-curtailment. In either case it raises the spectre of a gradual refinement of self out of existence, a grotesque extension of Stephen's idea of a God-like impersonality. And he is like Stephen, too, when, in relation to family and especially his mother, it is said that

> All his singularities appeared to be summed up in his refusal to take his place in the life-sized family group (*très distingué et très soigné*, remarks a modern critic of the work) painted about this time. His mother expostulated with him on the matter: – she must feel, a little icily, the emptiness of hope, and something more than the due measure of cold in things for a woman of her age, in the presence of a son who desired but to fade out of the world like a breath – and she suggested filial duty. 'Good mother', he answered, 'there are duties toward the intellect also, which women can but rarely understand.'(74)

Like Stephen, Sebastian is a theoretician of detachment, with a taste for authorities, and while he cites Spinoza and not Aquinas, it is to much the same effect as Stephen's Thomism.

' "Things that might have nothing in common with each other cannot be understood or explained by means of each other" ' (77), he copies into his notebook. These notebooks are a version of Stephen's self-absorbed diary, with which *A Portrait* concludes. Even more to the point, Sebastian's theories are, like Stephen's, forced into embarrassing and sometimes invalidating proximity to the recordings of daily experience. Speaking of the notebooks, Pater observes that

> The volume was indeed a kind of treatise to be: – a hard, systematic, well-concatenated train of thought, still implicated in the circumstances of a journal. Freed from the accidents of that particular literary form with its unavoidable details of place and occasion, the theoretic strain would have been found mathematically continuous. The already so wary Sebastian might perhaps never have taken in hand, or succeeded in, this detachment of his thoughts; every one of which, beginning with himself, as the peculiar and intimate apprehension of this or that particular day and hour, seemed still to protest against such disturbance, as if reluctant to part from those accidental associations of the personal history which prompted it, and so become a purely intellectual abstraction. (76–7)

Sebastian dies in a flood when a dyke gives way, apparently while he is attempting, in an uncharacteristic gesture of human solidarity, to rescue a child. Because he loved the sea, as Stephen does not, he might have welcomed his fate within it, a possibility Stephen finds loathsome. There are, that is, differences. And yet the language which accounts for the relationship of each of them to the sea, the conceptual framework in each case, is markedly similar to the other. Recall, for instance, Stephen's disappointment in Chapter 2:

> How foolish his aim had been! He had tried to build a break-water of order and elegance against the sordid tide of life without him and to dam up, by rules of conduct and active interests and new filial relations, the powerful recurrence of the tide within him. Useless. From without as from within the water had flowed over his barriers· their tides began once more to jostle fiercely above the crumbled mole. (Joyce 1957: 98)

Sebastian's resolve, when he goes to the sea for the last time, had already been phrased similarly by Pater:

> Here he could make 'equation' between himself and what was not himself, and set things in order, in preparation towards such deliberate and final change in his manner of living as circumstances so clearly necessitated. (Pater 1984: 82)

Sebastian's desire for order is intimately connected to a desired escape from the stuff of life which does not submit to order, and it is given expression earlier in the story in terms as unmistakably Icarian as Stephen's. We are told that he 'enjoyed the sense of things seen from a distance, carrying us, as on wide wings of space itself, far out of one's actual surroundings' (68).

In sum, Joyce and Pater jointly recognise the perils of excess, either of self-release into the materials at hand or of self-curtailment in coping with them. They embody the opposition defined by Pater between classicists and romanticists, 'between', as he remarks in the 'Postscript' to *Appreciations*, 'the adherents in the culture of beauty, of the principles of liberty, and authority, respectively – of strength, and order or what the Greeks called [orderly behaviour]' (210). It is mostly thanks to the misleadings of Eliot, who all the while surreptitiously uses Pater's own standards, that criticism persists in putting Joyce and Pater into simple antithetical postures. In both Pater and Joyce, when it comes to the uses of language, this fear of excess means, in Pater's words, from 'Style' – and in Joyce's notorious practice – that 'the literary artist is of necessity a scholar'. And for what reason? Because 'the material with which he works' – it can be language and only language – 'is no more a creation of his own than the sculptor's marble' (107). The writer is required to know everything about the past association of words, all of their accumulated meanings and usages, if he is to use any of them with tact and propriety. Only then can he, in Eliot's apposite phrase, 'dis-locate if necessary, language into his meaning'. Pater's essay on 'Style' sounds again and again like a source for Eliot's 'The Metaphysical Poets' of 1921, notably when Eliot explains why 'poets in our civilization as it exists at present, must be *difficult* . . . more and more comprehensive, more allusive, more indirect . . .'. (Eliot 1978: 248) Pater had written in 1888:

That imaginative prose should be the special and opportune art of the modern world results from two important facts about the latter: first, the chaotic variety and complexity of its interests, making the intellectual issue, the really master currents of the present time incalculable – a condition of mind little susceptible to the restraint proper to verse form, so that the most characteristic verse of the nineteenth century has been lawless verse; and secondly, an all-pervading naturalism, a curiosity about everything whatever as it really is, involving a certain humility of attitude, cognate to what must, after all, be the less ambitious form of literature. (1984: 106)

Not to labour the point, Eliot's argument in 'Ulysses, Order, and Myth', to the effect that Joyce is 'classical in tendency' is but a version of Pater's claim that the writer must be a scholar if he is to deal properly with the incalculable resonances of language. To be 'classical in tendency', Eliot says, is not superficially to protect yourself by turning away from 'nine tenths of the material which lies at hand'. Rather, it is to do 'the best one can' with it. (Eliot 1975: 176–7) Again, what else is this if not a fulfillment of Pater's suggestion in the 'Postscript' to *Appreciations* that classicism and romanticism are 'tendencies really at work at all times in art, moulding it, with the balance sometimes a little on one side sometimes a little on the other' (Pater 1984: 212)? And the balance is needed, he says later, because the problem for literary art 'just now' (meaning 1876) is

to induce order upon the contorted, proportionless accumulation of our knowledge and experience, our science and history, our hopes and disillusions, and, in effecting this, to do consciously what has been done hitherto for the most part too unconsciously . . . . (220)

This says all that Eliot will say in 'Ulysses, Order, and Myth' about the necessity of Joyce's method, as a way of 'controlling, of ordering, of giving shape and significance to the immense panorama of futility and anarchy which is contemporary history'. And Pater says it, besides, without the accompanying operatics about the horrors of contemporary life and without the elevation of so called 'mythic method' – what else is Milton's? – to a 'scientific discovery' of such magnitude as to make the novel a form 'which will no longer serve' (Eliot 1975: 176–7). It is Eliot, at last, who clearly no longer serves as dependable guide to Pater or Joyce or, for that matter, to literary modernism.[2]

Notes

1. In addition to Kermode, the exceptions would include Graham Hough, *The Last Romantics* (1949); Harold Bloom, *Selected Writings of Walter Pater* (1984: 'Introduction'); Louis Menand, *Discovering Modernism* (1987); Perry Meisel, *The Myth of the Modern* (1987); Carolyn Williams, *The Transfigured World: Walter Pater's Aesthetic Historicism* (1989).
2. A version of this essay first appeared in the *James Joyce Quarterly* 26, 1, Fall 1988.

11

Of 'of': The Romance of a Preposition
John Hollander

For poetry in English, prepositions may be the most private parts of speech. They carry no manifest freight of reference, and thus cannot easily be misapplied for figuration without falling into the kind of solecism which even far-fetched tropes escape. For example, 'Give it back of me' – for 'Give it back to me' – sounds only like bungled English, whereas 'Give her back to the grass', say, or the notorious para-predication of Chomsky's, 'colourless green ideas sleep furiously', would not. They would only sound figurative. (In this latter instance, as Frank Kermode recently pointed out in the instance of an exemplary phrase used by John Searle (Kermode 1986), there are allusive dimensions to the total rhetorical activity of the sentence.) The romance of nouns, then of verbs, at various periods in the history of meditative grammar has been discussed by linguists,[1] and the implicit non-literal predications of adjectives and adverbs are acknowedged by rhetorical theory.

It is less common to observe that the senses of prepositions may be transferred to some of the same effect as those of other parts of speech. Dickens' celebrated zeugma in *The Pickwick Papers*, 'She went straight home, in a flood of tears and a Sedan chair', is not usually analysed, for example, as turning on two different senses of the preposition 'in'. And yet there is only one sense of 'went' employed here. (On the other hand, by that magnificently revisionary use of a mere comma – where a grosser spirit might have employed the rib-elbowing dash – in Norman Douglas' *South Wind* [*in re* a questionable priest] 'He was a fisher of men, and of women' the invitation is extended to take 'men' in its more limited, gender-bound sense; the prepositions remain fixed in their use.)

I have suggested elsewhere (Hollander 1989: 9–10, 13) that one of the great sources of difficulty in Emily Dickinson's poetry is her use of prepositions in ways that are, at more than merely first glance, quite opaque. Sometimes it is merely a matter of a sort of prepositional trope involving the substitution of one for another, as in poem #1745: 'Uncertified of scene / Signified of sound', where 'of' = 'by' at a first reading: the additional resonances of similar constructions ('neat of dress', 'tall of stature') only clouding the syntactic clarity later on. On the other hand, take the third line of poem #1569, 'A Vagabond for Genesis' (whether or not it is appositive of 'Some schism in the Sum' in the previous line – the syntax is quite ambiguous, too): the preposition is itself much more hard and unyielding than the elusive but inviting pairing of the nouns it relates. A vagabond *from* [the land of] Genesis? [Unwittingly] headed for it? Wandering within it? A vagabond aimlessly, or even methodically, revising or misdoing the work of genesis? Or again, the 'by' in 'Eternity by term' (#615): does this mean 'what is termed Eternity', whatever it is we call by that name or (perhaps necessarily), pseudonym? Does it designate a contingent Eternity, one which indeed has a finite term? Or do both readings command our attention in that strange way of great poetry, wherein the relation between the two (*what we call X is a contingent X*, or possibly even *because it's contingent we call it by the name of the real thing*, etc.) comes into play. One feels that Dickinson's *for*s and *by*s are being pressed into multivalent service of the kind which we often see at work with the preposition *of*.

This may be the most modest of our prepositions; like *by* and *for*, it lacks the active directedness of all those others which occur in pairs which help map their roles, *up/down, in/out, to/from, over/under, before/after, before/behind, for/against* etc., all of which provide fundamental categories for the construction of tropes of lyric and romance. Unlike *by* and another sense of *for*, its phonology is pale and unmarked: with no initial consonant, our most reduced vowel, unstressed *schwa*, and a final voiced labial fricative, it becomes easily elided in speech (thus slightly archaic *o'* as in 'Clock o' Clay', or, in modern American fiction's ad hoc mode of transcription, simply *a* as in 'cuppa cawfee', or the British Dairy Board's advertisment of twenty years ago, 'Drinka Pinta Milka Day', which plays wittily with it in the middle term).

But *of* is grammatically complex, both from a synchronic and a diachronic viewpoint. The sixty-odd types of sense that the OED distinguishes aside, in the paradigmatic English phrase, *the*

X of Y, it can serve the variety of conceptual masters – possessive, objective, qualitative, definitive, material, partitive – that the Latin genitive does, as well as a locative one. At the same time, it apes the French *de*, and provides a simple alternative to the purely Germanic construction, *Y's X*, and a whole range of more ambiguous ones to the equally Germanic mode of compound, *the YX* – thus the two different operations *of* performs in *piece of cake* and *peace of mind* can both potentially be handled by *cakepiece* and *mindpeace*, although the former feels much more awkward and less likely than the latter. At two different times in the history of our language (and in a more or less continuous way since the second one), *X of Y* was used as a calque on many French phrases, thus, e.g., 'the poison of choice' (say, for adolescent suicides) is a calque on the French *'[quelque chose] de choix'* – thus *'article de choix'* = 'choice article' or *'Hommes de choix'* = 'picked men' – whereas 'this is a matter of choice' is clearly not.

Sometimes this could have the result of further mystifying an English word with its cognate, but cognitively dissonant, ghost. Thus, in 'marriage of convenience', *of* derives its strange associative power – not possessive, locative, partitive, causative, etc. – from *'mariage de convenance'* (= 'arranged marriage'); but in no case does *of* work here as it does generally in English, as in, say, 'a marriage of convenience and elegance'. A more sensationally modish example, adduced by and in the name of modern Parisian theorising, is of the bivalent role of *de* in *'désir de* [X]*'*, where, say, *'le désir de Vénus'* could designate the goddess' wish for Mars, or Mars' wish for her (let alone with regard to the general term, desire, which is always 'of Venus', in some of the more complex allegorical English senses – Desire is her realm, her creation, her instrument, the consequences of her activity, she is of its essence or it is of hers). But in any case, the immense variety of *ad hoc* uses of *of* in idiomatic English helps to destabilise its precise operation in certain phrases even more, and to infect clearly marked and more regular ordinary uses of the preposition with strange auras. This is certainly not true of ordinary usage. But for the poet, whose relation to his or her native language is always one of wonder born both of the deepest familiarity and the most puzzling sort of estrangement, the fruitful ambiguities of the *X of Y* construction are a matter of intimate knowledge.

I don't want to suggest that no other English prepositions exhibit a variety of phrasal behaviours. *By* has instrumental and locative senses – 'Go by car, along the road by the brook' – but they rarely present ambiguities. *In*, as was observed in the example from Dickens cited earlier, has an interestingly bidirectional force; we might ourselves observe that old Dorrit was in despair, debt and a room in the Marshalsea prison. The sequence of locations moves outwards from an 'inner' state (although the despair is 'in' one), through a condition (debt) that feels more like an implicit physical confinement than the condition of the soul does, to a literal physical enclosure. When persons are *in* X, X can be, if a 'state' or 'condition', in the person, in our standard modern mythologies of the psyche. Milton's Satan, a great rhetorician full of the sense of 'The Hell within him, for within him Hell / He brings' melodramatises this dialectic of the inner/outer, formerly a fashionable topic of academic concern, in a powerfully poetic way. Internalisation is still contingent with him, and with Hell; whereas in the case of Adam's arisen form of 'Paradise within thee, happier far', there is no question of a dialectic: without Paradise, it can only lie within. It might be thought that the enrichment of *of* by means of various calques and analogies would lead to nothing more than the possibility of occasional witty zeugma as well – 'He was free of debt and spirit' (where *from* is meant in the first instance, and a linkage of compounding in the second), or 'I am of Ireland, and of dubious sobriety'.

But I believe that this is not the case. So many instances of *the X of Y* in our poetry depend for their force upon a simultaneous use of different prepositional modes, that it almost seems to be a characteristic trope-enacting scheme in English poetry from Milton on. Meredith's (not Milton's) Lucifer confronts 'The army of unalterable law' ('Lucifer in Starlight' 1. 14), and it is not that we must correctly construe the phrase to decide that 'unalterable law' is: (a) a domain; (b) a ruler; (c) a general; (d) the entire personnel and materiel of the army itself; (e) the characteristic behaviour of the troops. It is rather that just here we cannot reject any of them, and the encompassing power of the phrase is thereby underlined: the reader's resolution of the prepositional mode by some pernicious casuistry would be as interdicted by the unalterable law as would Satan's victory in dubious battle. Blake's 'Give me my bow of burning gold, / Give me my arrows of desire' follows the purely material genitive *of* in the first phrase with a mixture of (strangely) material, partitive, qualitative (arrows being generally desirous of their marks), possessive (the arrows were originally those of Classical Desire, or Cupid, although Blake might have wanted that thrown out with the rest of the rubbish of the Daughters of Memory). Bacon's 'Idols' of Cave, Marketplace, Theatre, etc. – however problematic the sense of 'idol' as *eidos* or graven image, or both, may be – instance a locative *of*, but strongly reinforced by possessive and qualitative senses.

Tennyson's title *Idylls of the King* employs only that special, most interesting, sense (OED class VIII = 'concerning, about') that I shall discuss later, but it is instructive to consider the way in which Wallace Stevens carefully cuts this sense away from a primarily partitative one in 'The poem is the cry of its occasion, / Part of the res itself and not about it' ('An Ordinary Evening in New Haven' XII), however complex 'cry' may be (= outcry or vendor's or huxter's cry). Stevens often depends upon the complex *of*, as in the resonant phrase from 'The Man Whose Pharynx Was Bad', 'The malady of the quotidian', wherein he invents, on the analogy of the archaic medical terms 'tertian fever' 'quartian fever', etc., a sort of 'quotidian fever' which peaks every day. (Indeed, the term is used by Izaak Walton in his life of Sir Henry Wotton.) But is this the malady that the quotidian brings with it? The malady that the quotidian suffers? (The quotidian fever, peaking at noon, say, which afflicts every day?) The malady that the quotidian *is*? Here the inability to choose among these constructions, and the fitful grasp of the presence and inter-relation of all their consequences in the elevated pulse of the humdrum, is analogous to the situation in the last line of Mere-dith's sonnet.

Another celebrated case – actually, two related instances will be cited here – of an intense ambiguity is usually considered in its epistemological context, but the muddying of its waters depends upon the fluidity of *of*. In 'The picture of the mind revives again' (from 'Tintern Abbey') the question is whether the mind is painter, collector, etc., or the *subject* (and hence, in another vocabulary, an *object*), but the possessive sense remains dominant; analogously, Mount Snowdon seen as 'The perfect image of a mighty mind' (*The Prelude* 1805, 13. 68–9) demands at first that the possessive be suppressed, only to return somewhat furtively after all.

For the poet's sense of language, words are not merely things, utensils, but beings, and those which relate are no less full of matter than those which designate. Since words live and move and have their being in phonology, it is a matter of poetic importance that (in a particular sort of non-genitive use), *of* and *love* rhyme. Moreover, the very relations enacted by, say, prepositions, themselves can be momentarily privileged in poetry. William James wrote most interestingly of this, in a passage pointed out by Richard Poirier (1987: 15–16):

> If there be such things as feelings at all, *then so surely as relations between objects exist* in rerum naturâ, *so surely, and more surely, do feelings exist to which these relations are known*. . . . We ought to say a feeling of *and*, a feeling of *if*, a feeling of *but*, and a feeling of *by*, quite as readily as we say a feeling of *blue* or a feeling of *cold*. (James 1983: 238)

Nathaniel Hawthorne fancied in his notebooks how he might personify even the meanest parts of speech ('To personify If – But – And – Though, etc.' (quoted in Mathiessen 1941: 244)) and Emily Dickinson comes close to doing just that with the modal auxiliaries (her acknowledgment of two senses of 'may' involving logical probability and social possibility being of particular interest):

> There are two Mays
> And then a Must
> And after that a shall
> How infinite the compromise
> That indicates I will?
>   (#1618)

And while there are no odes to *of* that I know of, its ability to play so many positions in the game of our speech becomes for the poet a resource for word play at another level. Whereas a French pseudo-philosopher might ascribe all sorts of universal situations to what he or she might call the epistemological consequences of the grammar of '*désir de*', a poet writing in English will make a strong point turn on an acute instance. The particular matter can be made even more complex, and, indeed, rendered far less arbitrary. Consider Pope's 'The love of Comfort, and the love of Sway', where women desire both of these and execute both, as in their love for men when they simultaneously give comfort and manipulate. Even more fruitful in this respect is the celebrated opening line of Shakespeare's Sonnet 144, 'Two loves have I of comfort and despair'. The original complexity comes from the formulation itself: I have two loves that, separately or because there are two of them, both comfort me and make me despair. On the other hand, they can be thought of as two loves, one that comforts, one that makes me despair, or is itself despair*ing* (as the other may be comfort*ing*). Yet again, the 'loves' are (a) faculties, in which case the French sort of *désire de* problem arises, and (b) the objects of those very faculties, jointly or respectively. And yet again once more, the comfort and despair may be the material of either the faculties or the objects.

It seems momentarily useful to invoke some conceptual pattern, like that of the scholastic four causes, in which to array the various operations of X *of* Y. For example,

Material Cause: 'cup of gold', 'cloth of gold' (but not, of course, 'mother-of-pearl').

Efficient Cause: 'cup of Cellini's', 'Toccata of Galuppi's'.

Formal Cause: 'cup of oval shape', 'coat of many colours'.

Final Cause: 'cup of vows' (but not, really, 'cup of tea', which caps purpose with fulfillment – this tends to be true in all cases where X is container and Y thing contained: the pattern is asymmetric with respect to the appropriate term here, 'teacup' (= cup for tea)).

On the other hand, these could easily be mapped on the modes of the Latin genitive, for example. The point, however, is that while ordinary discourse has no problem with these, and while wit can call sudden attention to the difference between the functions with, say, a clever zeugma, poetry may want to suggest, and perhaps to employ, two or more of them at once. The various functions exist for the poet, perhaps, as rhyming words and homonyms do – not just as potential material for wordplay, but with any one of them (pairs of homonyms, rhyming morphemes) being permanently affected by the existence of the other.

When *the* X *of* Y is further complicated by an X or Y with more than one sense, the grammatical functions can help deploy them

in the entire phrase. Britomart's spherical mirror, in Book III of
The Faerie Queene, in which she sees her future husband Artegall,
is like 'a world of glass' in several senses, some simple (where
'world' = 'terrestrial globe', for example, or where 'glass' is
simply material), some not (as when 'glass' = 'mirror').[2]
    The most celebrated example would perhaps be the title of
Leaves of Grass. This is a phrase so rich and strange to begin with
– it runs immediately counter to the idiom 'blades of grass' and
demands that 'leaves' be taken as 'pages' (perhaps taking a look
back at Wordsworth's 'Those barren leaves' with a view to green-
ing them?). The material, efficient and formal causes are all at
work here and, most particularly, the designative function (=
about) as well. But both X and Y invoke previous tropes: 'leaves'
= pages aside, the figure of leaves-as-lives that runs from Homer,
Virgil, Dante, and Milton to Shelley and after, and that originat-
ing in Isaiah and the Psalms, of human bodies as grass to be
mown in (and, later, by) time. Given these, there is a strong
implication in the title of what the poetry itself confirms as a
major trope, a sense of 'leaves (lives) *as* grass (bodies)'. That the
(botanic) leaves and the (codex) leaves are somehow proleptically
(although anachronistically) associated in the scattered prophecy
of the Cumaean Sybil comes only as long afterthought. So does
another resolution of the *unheimlich* quality of 'leaves' used for
'blades' of grass: the Old English root of our 'leaf', unlike the
more generally Germanic 'blade' (etymologically related to 'blos-
som', Latin *'folium'* and *'flos'* etc. with a central sense of 'bloom'),
may have an Indo-European origin with a basic sense of breaking
off (as if the essence of a leaf was to fall). Also, our sense of the
word, innocent of the etymon or the cognate, would lead us –
as it would the child who brings the poet the grass in section 6
of 'Song of Myself' – to think of grass blades as perhaps being
a transfer from sword blades (not as it is, of course, the other
way around). And although in other Germanic languages, leaves
are blades (German *Blätter*), in the English of Whitman's poem,
even the blades of grass are (falling) leaves renewing themselves.
    It may be argued here that the figurative over-determination
of the particular X and Y here, and the fact that leaves = pages
can easily be *of* Y by being *about* it, cloud the issue of the *of*. But
the subsequent section (or poem) title, 'Song of Myself' presents
similarly interesting problems. A 'Song of Y' could be about Y,
composed by Y, composed of Y, from (the land of) Y, etc.. In

this instance, 'of myself' resonates also with the idiomatic 'by myself'. It is as much the dynamic ambiguity of the phrase function as the recurrently fascinating problem of the relation among the senses of *ipse, se* and *ego* (or the French *le moi*) in the English word *myself* itself, that makes this title appropriate for a poem in which there are at least three 'selves' as major agents.

Sometimes, indeed, it may be useful to think of the preposition as playing an ancillary role, either placing the Y-noun on some figurative stage, or urging us immediately to search for another use (this may be another way of saying the same thing). Scott in *Guy Mannering* calls attention to this rather elegantly, referring to 'Hazlewood-House and the House of Hazlewood – meaning by the one, the mansion-house of my family, and by the other, typically, metaphorically, and parabolically, the family itself' (Scott 1877: II, 212) (whereas the literal or first sense of 'house' might enter grotesquely into the phrase here, such as 'My people built our house of hazlewood' or 'Our family house stands in the middle of Hazlewood forest' or even 'Sir Hazlewood rebuilt our house after the original one, the House of Sir Walter [Hazlewood] that he built of stone, was wrecked in a siege'). But perhaps this is only to say that the paradigmatic *House of Y* can itself be deployed in a variety of ways, from *House* (more literally) *of God*, *Houses of Parliament* to all of the immense array of allegorical *Houses of Y* in romance fictions. Whether these denote what, with regard to Spenser, Angus Fletcher has termed 'temples' or 'labyrinths', their use of *House* oscillates between two senses of *House*: what we encounter merely as 'Hazlewood House' becomes for us, after we enter it, 'the House of Hazlewood' itself. Moreover, in poetic topography, partially as the result of a scheme to be considered shortly, *Place of Y* tends to become allegorical ('House of Holiness', 'Bower of Bliss', 'Slough of Despond' help shade the senses of 'Hall of Justice', 'Land of Heart's Desire', perhaps even 'Houses of Parliament', where the Y almost evaporates into the 'parleying' of the legislative body).

But for an exhaustive taxonomy of the arrangements of what she calls 'The Genitive Link', the reader should turn to Christine Brooke-Rose's *A Grammar of Metaphor* (1958: 146–205, Chapters VII and VIII). Except to praise its incisiveness, I shall remark here only on the representative grammar of the book's own title. Were it used in the kind of English and American poetry I have in mind, the phrase might be deeply and systematically ambiguous.

It might partake not only of what its author calls a Double Genitive Link – in this case, a reciprocating one, of the kind that
might be underlined by a sort of Jakobsonian construction, *The
Grammar of Metaphor* and *The Metaphor of Grammar*. In addition,
all the senses of metaphoric 'grammars', an alternative sort of
grammar composed of metaphoric substitutions or displacements
or condensations or whatever, a grammar (= an abstract structure
to be inferred from the phenomena of utterance) of metaphoric
instances, a grammar (= a sort of analytic book about a language
which invites you to learn it, and of it) might be present, and
even working with, and not against, one other. Finally, I refer
the reader back to William Empson's fine pages on the paired
linkages in Shakespeare that he calls 'The A and B of C' (1947:
88–101) although it is primarily the interaction of *and* and a partitive sort of *of* that he discusses.

The case of Lysimachus' 'deeds of darkness' (*Pericles* IV.vi.30)
for 'dark deeds' (= copulating) presents another aspect of the
question of X *of* Y, one which involves the connection of an
abstract Y and a concrete X. This is ordinarily an instance of X
of Y = Y(*adj*) X. Frequently, though, there is great pressure on the
reading of Y to become genitive; it tends to become allegorised, to
develop an initial capital and preside over the X in a multiplicity
of ways. 'Dark deeds' are one thing; those 'of Darkness' – where
Darkness may be e.g. a kind of ultimate, necessary demon who
does one's dark deeds for one whenever one thinks one is doing
them oneself. The reason for this lies not merely in the variety
of colloquial uses of *of*, but in one particular textual tradition
which has permeated English usage, and which I now propose
somewhat briefly to consider.

It comes from the English Bible. I might have introduced it by
citing a line of Robert Frost's, from 'Directive' – 'A brook that
was the water of the house' (where a paraphrase of 'a brook that
was all the running water they had' will clearly not do). Why it
is that it won't not only involves the history of quasi-allegorical
instances of 'house' that lie behind the phrase, but Biblical commonplace as well. Or, again, Christina Rossetti's subtitle for her
'Monna Innominata', a group of fourteen sonnets: 'A Sonnet of
Sonnets'. Here the material genitive *of* names the poem as a sort
of super-sonnet, made up of sonnets for lines, as well as a sonnet
made up of the trope of sonneteering, but, as a sequence written
by a woman, the sex which is usually the clichéd sonneteer's

Muse, here 'drawn not from fancy but from feeling'. Or, it is a sonnet *about* sonnets. But however we construe the phrase, the sense of some sort of meta-sonnet inheres in the paradigm that lies behind it, *the X of Xs*. Which, again, is Biblical.

The particular prototype here, 'Song of Songs', is an instance of the standard translation of a common construction in Biblical Hebrew. A singular noun in the construct state with its own plural simply indicates a superlative: *X of X's* = Best of all X's. *Shir ha-shirim*, or 'Supreme Song' (Marvin Pope in his remarkable edition for the Anchor Bible gives 'Sublime Song').[3] Thus all of the other resonant occurrences which have become rhetorical commonplaces: 'King of Kings' (Daniel 2. 37); 'Vanity of vanities' (Ecclesiastes 1. 2); Canaan as 'servant of servants' (Genesis 9. 25) etc. The Vulgate translates these with the flexible genitive, whereas the Septuagint interprets this particular construction with a dative (e.g. *canticum canticorum*, but *asma asmatân; rex regum*, but *basieleus basileôn; servus servorum* but here, simply *oiketês* 'slave' etc.). But the English translations, using the multivalent *X of Y*, allow other senses of the construction to becloud the intended literal one. There is no sense of the partitive in the Hebrew (i.e. X of X = 'one of many Xs'), but it presents itself in the English as a sort of synecdoche. (It is amusing to note, however, that the commonplace 'Holy of Holies' (Exodus 26. 33), for the Hebrew *kodesh ha-kadashim*, occurs nowhere in the Authorised Version, which translates quite accurately 'most holy place'; the popular English phrase itself translates the Vulgate's '*sancta sanctorum*'.)

But it is the problem of nouns in the construct state in general, aside from this particular usage, which so enriches the English phrase that was drafted so early into its service. In general, two nouns in the construct state in Hebrew (in the form X *the* Y) may usually be most easily translated into English as the noun-noun compound, *the YX*. The construct binds nouns in a variety of ways like the Latin genitive, but it lacks a primary possessive sense. For example, the modern Hebrew word for school, *bet ha-sepher* ('house the book') should be rendered 'the bookhouse' (= 'school'). But the English Bible's inevitable construction, 'the house of the book' raises, and contributes to, all the complexities of *of* under consideration. The pressure on 'book' to become 'Book' and, particularly in American English, so shaped by radical protestantism, to invoke *the* Book, ('the Good Book' = Scripture), would be very strong. 'The House of [temple of?] the Book' – consecrated to? enclosing? belonging to? comprised of? it, perhaps – seems poised by its very grammar on the brink of allegory.

All of those wonderful cases where the simply adjectival sense of the Hebrew original becomes, in its English _X of Y_, another sort of creature, provide, for English writing up until the phasing out of the English Bible as a common text, a store of rhetorical matrices. The 'multitudes, multitudes in the valley of decision' (Joel 3. 14) are in the Hebrew _b'emek heḥarutz_ (in Septuagint, _en tê koilathi tês dikês_ – the ordinary construct is there translated, as in Latin, by the genitive; in Latin, _in valle concisionis_). In English it should be 'Decision Valley' (like 'Death Valley'); but what happens in AV is similar to what might happen if 'Customs-House' were ordinarily designated 'House of Customs', although it is partially the mythopoetic work of Hawthorne's introductory chapter to _The Scarlet Letter_ to work through just such a quasi-Spenserian conception. In the phrase from Joel, there is the lurking notion that to have to make certain kinds of crucial decisions is always somehow like being in a valley, with a lot of other people – too many, perhaps – having to do the same thing. The mountain of Decision is a _very_ different sort of place, and one would probably be up there alone, which would be more scary. And yet the Valley seems insufficiently comforting. Perhaps all Biblical valleys are infected with what ails the 'valley of the shadow of death' (Psalm 23. 4) which itself exhibits a complex doubling of the phrase that combines a [_place_] of Y with a [_representation_] _of_ Y, each of which has an allegorising thrust of its own. (I have discussed this particular figure elsewhere (Hollander 1987).)

And so with 'wine of astonishment' (_yayin tarelah_) of Psalm 60. 3; given the archaic 'astonishment' for 'staggering' (= intoxicating), we half expect an allegorical efficient cause (the wine brewed by a witch named Astonishment), or a formal one (the vintage pressed from the grapes of astonishment, rather than of wrath), etc. Or again, sometimes an accidental allusion can be pointedly engaged by the simultaneous prepositional functions, as in the frequently occurring phrase 'the apple of [his, thine] eye' (as in Deuteronomy 32. 10, where the Lord guarded Jacob _c'ishon eno_). It means, simply, 'eyeball', but 'apple' is so redolent in English Christian tradition of the original fruit of the Fall that it tends here to suggest 'the object of the eye's desire' to the unlearned but attentive ear, especially when it becomes a commonplace in quotation.

One of the most celebrated of such phrases arises from no translation of Hebrew – indeed it is a New Testament rubric – but remains current only in misconstruction: the designation 'The whore of Babylon' occurs as the running-head on Chapter XVII of Revelation in the Geneva Bible (fol. GGg. iiii[r]: the previous recto has the phrase 'The fall of Babylon', and, ramifying the paradigm, is the mutually invoked 'The tower of Babel'). Often misconstrued by a literalising temperament in popular homily as a locative (i.e. 'Babylonian whore') instead of the allegorical figure of Babylon as whore, derived from the prophetic trope of wicked city as harlot, it ends up pretty much that as a rhetorical commonplace. But the very construction of the rubric almost seems to have the translators' sense not of Greek, but of the Hebrew paradigm behind it.

Yet the very strength of Biblical English is often to iron out linguistic and rhetorical differences between the Old and New Testaments, as well as between their individual 'books'. So that in the 'pearl of great price' (Matthew 13. 46), the ordinary function of the Latin genitive of quality (used only when the quality is modified by an adjective) moves vaguely toward some attributive sublimity, as if in any Scriptural X *of* Y, the concrete X and the abstract Y formed a kind of recurring *figura* of their own.

It is interesting to consider, too, such permutations as X *of* Y, X *of* W, X *of* Z, etc., and to observe the shift of prepositional function as one moves from, say, 'work of thy hands' (Psalm 143. 5 and *passim*) to 'work of one day' (Ezra 10. 13), to modern colloquial 'work of art' (complex – a skilful act becomes its product) 'work of charity' (also as currently distinguished from 'labour of love'?).

But all these occurrences sing their various roles in a strange chorus of voices, and the cup of *of* is filled with possibility. It is a matter of verbal moments in Scripture receiving overlays, because of linguistic change and the colouring of analogies, that render them opaque and even slightly mysterious, somewhat in the way Kermode (1979: 23–47) has demonstrated for narrative moments. And even when Milton, fully aware of Hebrew grammar, uses the construction somewhat problematically, it is hardly a case of merely hoisting the stylistic standard of a Hebraism. Satan

> Led Eve our credulous Mother to the Tree
> Of prohibition, root of all our woe.
> 					(*Paradise Lost*, bk 9. 654–6)

Milton's implicit construct, 'tree the prohibited' (= 'prohibited tree') engages, as the language of *Paradise Lost* so often does, the true ambiguity it generates. The Tree is the sole focus and instance of Prohibition in Paradise; its ramifications, if misused (treated as if it were part of an orchard, rather than contemplated as an ever-present emblem), will reach into the realm of *all* myriad prohibitions that will test fallen virtue, particularly in the complex cross-predications of tree/prohibition: root/woe that Christopher Ricks (1963: 75f.) suggested so long ago. The Biblical 'tree of the knowledge of good and evil' itself, especially in contrast with the 'tree of life' (Hebrew *etz hachayim*) of Genesis, itself a complex term, presents its genitive possibilities. And Milton makes the most of these.

I have been suggesting that the Biblical formula provides, particularly for poetry, the bases for an array of *ad hoc* calques, mingling and co-existing with a host of others. The last one I shall consider occurs when, as evidenced previously, the X term names some discursive entity or representation in general (*Book of*, *Tale of*, etc.), so that the formula engages the use of *of* for *concerning*. That is, I should like to conclude the discussion of *of* with something about *about*.

The OED sense 7 of that preposition – not its locational meaning of 'around' – is designated as 'Touching, concerning, in the matter of, in reference or in regard to. The regular preposition employed to define the subject-matter of verbal activity, as in to speak, think, ask, dream, hear, know *about* . . .' (In all of these instances, it will be observed, *of* could be substituted; but the list continues:) '. . . to be sorry, pleased, perplexed *about*;' (where *of* can't be used) 'to give orders, instructions, information *about*:' (likewise?) 'to form plans, have doubts, feel sure *about*'. Here, in these last two cases, 'doubts *about* X' and 'doubts *of* X's Y' are different, and perhaps to be noted in connection with the general density of the functions of *of*.

The use of *of* for the Latin and Romance *de*, and for the *about* that seems almost a calque on the Greek *peri* (the German use of *über* for this purpose feels too lofty for discussion here), occurs in the absolute form *of* X in rubrics and titles. Bacon's essay-titles, ('Of Truth', etc.) probably following Montaigne's, give the feeling of a slightly different sense of aboutness from the one engaged by, say Hazlitt's. ('On Gusto', etc.; his 'Of Persons One Would Wish to Have Seen' is quite rare for him. But 'On Sitting for One's Picture' tends to suggest, as do perhaps most instances of *on* X when X is a present participle, an ellipsis of 'on the occasion of X'.)

Generally, the implication is that specifying 'the subject-matter of verbal activity', even of a piece of complex writing, is easy enough to do, and perhaps even that the claim to have done it is easily verifiable. This may indeed be true in some instances, and in some of these *of* and *about* might seem to function slightly differently. A.: 'He spoke of X.' B: 'No he didn't – I was there all night and he didn't mention her once.' This does indeed seem a case for verification. But then, A: 'He was talking about X.' B: 'Not actually – he was really talking about Y all the time.' Here it is a matter of validating an interpretation, and A can easily reply 'No he wasn't' without any hope of further confirmation either way. In short, 'X is about Y' most often behaves, as a proposition, like 'X is like Y': the answer of 'No it isn't' will not settle anything. Likeness surfaces in assertions in the form of similes, which look as if they might be open to question. When collapsed into tropes, their expository candidacy is withdrawn. And so, perhaps, with aboutness, which seems to point to some topicality, some essentiality, with an implicit sense that both the mode of essentiality and the immediate instance of it will be acknowledged. I dimly remember a remark of Paul de Man's, which I find rather puzzling in this respect, to the effect that language can only be about something, but that it can never know whether it is about anything at all including itself, since it is precisely the *aboutness*, the referentiality, that is in question. Forgetting that language can't be said to *know* anything, one might observe that there is much more to '*aboutness*', and even the aboutness of some strange abstract entity called 'language', in which I could mention and designate X, be arguably speaking 'of Y', and perhaps submit to the charge that I was really talking 'about' either Z, or 'myself', etc., than referentiality.

To claim that an utterance or text is 'about X', then, is more like a trope itself than our usual way of thinking of it admits. And an 'of X' that is synoynmous with it, particularly when it enters into an X *of* Y formula can be very figurative indeed. And from this perhaps derives some of the force of the most resonant 'of' in our literature. Milton could perfectly well have started out on *Paradise Lost* without a preposition: Virgil's accusative object of *cano* could have been matched by a nominal object of the Heavenly Muse's singing. Indeed, Milton's very English precursor in singing of first things, Caedmon, is commanded by his audition only to 'syng [me] frumsceaft' (in the Old English translation of Bede's Latin). The *of* of the openings of Italian romance had of course been attempted both in prose and rhyme, but Milton's presentation of his great argument as an *of X, and Y whose A did B until C . . . etc*, is as *peri*, as around and about as one can get. It can hardly be said to pinpoint a topic in any but contingent and expositorily incidental (but poetically substantial) ways – the spatial, syllabic centrality of 'disobedience' in the first line, for example. Its mere aboutness seems to get drowned in a flow of possibility: human subject, action, object, source, consequence, ultimate consequence of consequence, all run into each other. The Muse will, in the vocalisations of the poem, sing *of* all this, and the poem will be a poem *of* so much that a merely topical discourse *about* a subject – say, Sir John Davies' *Orchestra, or A Poem* of *Dancing* – could never be. Its opening 'Of' is full of itself.

Notes

1. See Edward Stankiewicz, 'The dithyramb of the verb in 18th and 19th century linguistics' in Hymes 1974; Anne Ferry (1988: 49–64) has some interesting comments on Elizabethan conceptions of parts of speech. My discussion which follows has benefited from observations by Emile Benveniste (1971)
2. Interesting in this connection is Emerson's quatrain, 'Nahant': 'All day the waves assailed the rock, / I heard no church-bell chime, / The sea-beat scorns the minster-clock / And breaks the glass of Time' (Emerson 1903–4: IX 345), where the pressure of the various *X of Y* possibilities makes the literal hour-glass double with its trope (glass used as mirror and perhaps even vessel).
3. Marvin H. Pope, *Song of Songs* (1977). See his discussion of this construction (294–95).

Bibliography

Accardo, P. (1987) *Diagnosis and Detection* (London and Toronto: Associated Universities Press).

Alter R. and Kermode F. (1987) (eds) *The Literary Guide to the Bible* (London: Collins).

Amussen, S. (1985) 'Gender, family and social order, 1560–1725', in A. Fletcher and J. Stevenson (eds), *Order and Disorder in Early Modern England* (Cambridge: Cambridge University Press).

Annas, J. (1981) *An Introduction to Plato's Republic* (Oxford: Clarendon Press).

Aristotle (1908–52) *The Works of Aristotle Translated into English*, ed. W. D. Ross, 12 vols (Oxford: Clarendon Press).

Auerbach, E. (1973) *Scenes from the Drama of European Literature* (Gloucester, Mass.: Peter Smith).

Baring-Gould, W. S. (1968) *The Annotated Sherlock Holmes*, 2 vols (London: Murray).

Barolsky, P. (1987) *Walter Pater's Renaissance* (University Park, PA, and London: Pennsylvania State University Press).

Barthes, R. (1963) *Sur Racine* (Paris: Editions de seuil).

Barthes, R. (1977) 'The death of the author', in his *Image-Music-Text* trans. S. Heath (London: Fontana).

Barzaghi, A. (1980) *Donne o cortigiane? la prostituzione a Venezia documenti di costume dal XVI al XVIII secolo* (Verona: Bertani).

Beckson, K. (1987) *Arthur Symons: A Life* (Oxford: Clarendon Press).

Bellamy, J. (1984) *Criminal Law and Society in Late Medieval and Tudor England* (New York: St Martin's Press).

Belsey, C. (1980) *Critical Practice* (London and New York: Methuen).

Bennett, A. (n.d.) *Literary Taste* (London: Hodder and Stoughton).

Benveniste, E. (1971) *Problems in General Linguistics*, trans. M. E. Meek (Miami: University of Miami Press).

Benvenuto (1887) *Benvenuti De Rambaldis da Imola Commentum super Dantis Aldigherii Comoediam*, ed. J. P. Lacaita, 5 vols (Florence: G. Barbèra).

Berenson, B. (1927) *Three Essays in Method* (Oxford: Clarendon Press).

Berkeley, G. (1910) 'Three dialogues between Hylas and Philonous', in *A New Theory of Vision and Other Writings*, ed. A. D. Lindsay (London and New York: Dent and Dutton, Everyman's Library).

Blackmur, R. P. (1955) *The Lion and the Honeycomb: Essays in Solicitude and Critique* (New York: Harcourt Brace).

Bloom, H. (1984) (ed.) *Selected Writings of Walter Pater* (New York: Columbia University Press).

Brooke-Rose, C. (1958) *A Grammar of Metaphor* (London: Secker and Warburg).

Brown, D. A. (1979) *Berenson and the Connoisseurship of Italian Painting* (Washington: National Gallery of Art).

Burckhardt, J. (1951) *The Civilization of the Renaissance in Italy* trans. S. G. C. Middlemore, ed. L. Goldscheider (London: Phaidon).

Buttigieg, J. (1987) *A Portrait of the Artist in a Different Perspective* (Athens, Ohio: Ohio University Press).

Callimachus (1949–53) *Callimachus*, ed. R. Pfeiffer, 2 vols (Oxford; Clarendon Press).

Carey, J. (1989) 'Creating canon fodder', *The Sunday Times* (Books), 26 November.

Carr, J. D. (1949) *The Life of Sir Arthur Conan Doyle* (London: Murray).

Chojnacki, S. (1976) 'La posizione della donna a Venezia nel cinquecento', in *Tiziano e Venezia* (Venice: Convegno internazionale di studi).

Coryate, T. (1611) *Coryat's Crudities . . .* , 2 vols (London: William Stansby; repr. 1905, Glasgow: James MacLeHose).

Crewe, J. (1986) *Hidden Designs* (London: Methuen).

Davis, N. (1988a) *Fiction in the Archives* (Cambridge: Polity Press).

Davis, N. (1988b) ' "On the Lame" ', *American Historical Review*, 93.

de Maisse H. (1931) *De Maisse: A Journal of all that was accomplished by Monsieur de Maisse Ambassador in England from King Henri IV to Queen Elizabeth Anno Domini 1597*, trans. G. B. Harrison and R. A. Jones (London: Nonesuch Press).

de Man, P. (1979) *Allegories of Reading: Figural Language in Rousseau, Nietzsche, Rilke, and Proust* (New Haven: Yale University Press).

Derrida, J. (1980) *Positions*, trans. A. Bass (London: Athlone).

Dollimore J. and Sinfield A. (eds) (1985) *Political Shakespeare* (Manchester: Manchester University Press).

Doyle, A. C. (1903) *The Stark-Munro Letters and Round the Red Lamp* (London: Smith, Elder).

Doyle, A. C. (1912) *Through the Magic Door*, (London: Smith, Elder).

Doyle, A. C. (1974) *The Memoirs of Sherlock Holmes*, ed. K. Amis (London: John Murray and Cape).

Doyle, A. C. (1981) *The Return of Sherlock Holmes* (London and Harmondsworth: Penguin).

Drakakis, J. (1985) (ed.) *Alternative Shakespeares* (London: Methuen).

Dunhill, R. C. (1976) '17th century invective: defamation cases as a source for word study', *Devon and Cornwall Notes and Queries*, 33.

Durham (1845) *Depositions and other Ecclesiastical Proceedings from the Courts of Durham, extending from 1311 to the reign of Elizabeth* (London: The Publications of the Surtees Society).

Edwards, O. D. (1983) *The Quest for Sherlock Holmes* (Edinburgh: Mainstream).

Eliot, T. S. (1975) *Selected Prose of T. S. Eliot*, ed. F. Kermode (New York: Harcourt, Brace, Jovanovich).

Eliot, T. S. (1978) *Selected Essays* (New York: Harcourt, Brace, Jovanovich).

Ellis, J. (1989) *Against Deconstruction* (Princeton: Princeton University Press).

Emerson, R. W. (1903–4) *The Complete Works of Ralph Waldo Emerson*, ed. E. W. Emerson, 12 vols (Boston and New York: Houghton, Mifflin; Centenary edition).

Empson, W. (1930) *Seven Types of Ambiguity* (London: Chatto and Windus; (1947) 2nd edn., New York: New Directions).

Erasmus, D. (1703–06) *Opera omnia*, 10 vols (Leyden: P. van der Aa).

Erasmus, D. (1974-) *The Collected Works of Erasmus*, eds R. J. Schoeck, B. M. Corrigan *et. al.*, vols in progress (Toronto and Buffalo: University of Toronto Press).

Ferguson, M. W., Quilligan, M. and Vickers, N. J. (1986) (eds), *Rewriting the Renaissance: The Discourses of Sexual Difference in Early Modern Europe* (Chicago: University of Chicago Press).

Ferry, A. (1988) *The Art of Naming* (Chicago: University of Chicago Press).

Fish, S. (1982) 'Professional anti-professionalism', *The Times Literary Supplement*, 10 December.

Fish, S. (1988) 'No bias, no merit: the case against blind submission', *Publications of the Modern Language Association of America*, 103.

Foster, R. (1962) *The New Romantics: A Reappraisal of the New Criticism* (Bloomington: Indiana University Press).

Galinsky, G. K. (1975) *Ovid's Metamorphoses: An Introduction to the Basic Aspects* (Oxford: Basil Blackwell).

Genette, G. (1972) *Narrative Discourse: An Essay in Method* trans. J. E. Lewin (Ithaca, New York: Cornell University Press).

Gill, C. (1979) 'Plato's Atlantis story and the birth of fiction', *Philosophy and Literature*, 3, 1.

Gombrich, E. H. (1969) *In Search of Cultural History* (Oxford: Clarendon Press).

Gombrich, E. H. (1970) *Aby Warburg: An Intellectual Biography* (London: Warburg Institute).

Goode, J. (1979) 'The decadent writer as producer' in I. Fletcher (ed.), *Decadence and the 1890's* (London: Edward Arnold, Stratford upon Avon Studies No. 17).

Greenblatt, S. (1988) (ed.), *Representing the English Renaissance* (Berkeley: University of California Press).

Hahn, T. (1978) 'Indians East and West', *Journal of Medieval and Renaissance Studies*, 8.

Haigh, C. A. (1975) 'Slander and the church courts in the sixteenth century', *Transactions of the Lancashire and Cheshire Antiquarian Society*, 78.

Hair, P. (1972) *Before the Bawdy Court: Selections from Church Court and other Records relating to the Correction of Moral Offences in England, Scotland and New England 1300–1800* (London: Elek).

Handelman, S. (1987) 'Jacques Derrida and the heretic hermeneutic', in Krupnick, M. (ed.) *Displacement: Derrida and After* (Bloomington: Indiana University Press).

Harrison, B. (1991) *Narrative and Reality: Literature and the Limits of Theory* (New Haven: Yale University Press).

Heath, S. (1972) *The Nouveau Roman: A Study in the Practice of Writing* (London: Elek).

Heraclitus (1922) *Dei Fragmente der Vorsokratiker*, ed. H. Diels. vol 1 (Berlin: Weidmannoche).

Herbert, G. (1941) *The Works of George Herbert*, ed. F. E. Hutchinson (Oxford: Clarendon Press).

Herrup, C. B. (1987) *The Common Peace: Participation and the Criminal Law in Seventeenth-Century England* (Cambridge: Cambridge University Press).

Hexter, J. H. (1952) *More's Utopia: The Biography of an Idea* (Princeton: Princeton University Press).

Hollander, J. (1987) 'Psalms' in D. Rosenberg (ed.), *Congregation: Contemporary Writers Read the Jewish Bible* (New York: Harcourt, Brace, Jovanovich).

Hollander, J. (1989) 'Emily Dickinson', *PEN Newsletter*, 68, May.

Hough, G. (1949) *The Last Romantics* (London: Duckworth).

Hughes, D. O. (1986) 'Distinguishing signs: ear-rings, Jews and Franciscan rhetoric in the Italian renaissance city', *Past and Present*, 112.

Hymes, D. (1974) (ed.) *Studies in the History of Linguistics* (Bloomington: University of Indiana Press).

Ingram, M. (1976) 'Ecclesiastical Justice in Wiltshire 1600–1640 with special reference to cases involving sex and marriage', unpublished D. Phil. thesis, University of Oxford.

Ingram, M. (1985) 'Ridings, rough music and mocking rhymes in early modern England', in B. Reay (ed.) *Popular Culture in Seventeenth Century England* (London: Croom Helm).

Iser, W. (1960) *Walter Pater: Die Autonomie des Asthetischen* (Tubingen: Niemeyer); English translation (1987) *Walter Pater: The Aesthetic Moment*, trans. D. Wilson (Cambridge: Cambridge University Press).

James, W. (1983) *The Principles of Psychology* (Cambridge, Mass.: Harvard University Press).

Jardine, L. (1983) *Still Harping on Daughters: Women and Drama in the Age of Shakespeare* (Brighton: Harvester).

Jardine, L. and Swindells, J. (1989) *What's Left? Women in Culture and the Labour Movement* (London: Routledge).

Johnson, S. (1905) *Lives of the English Poets*, ed. G. Birkbeck Hill, 3 vols (Oxford: Clarendon Press).

Josipovici, G. (1988) *The Book of God: A Response to the Bible* (New Haven and London: Yale University Press).

Joyce, J. (1957) *A Portrait of the Artist as a Young Man* (New York: Viking Press).

Jung, C.G. (1953) *Psychology and Alchemy*, trans. R. F. C. Hull (London: Routledge and Kegan Paul).

Kahn, C. (1981) *Man's Estate: Masculine Identity in Shakespeare* (Berkeley and London: University of California Press).

Kappeler, S. (1986) *The Pornography of Representation* (Cambridge: Polity Press).

Kautsky, K. (1927) *Thomas More and his Utopia*, trans. H. J. Stenning (London: A. & C. Black).

Kermode, F. (1952a) (ed.) *English Pastoral Poetry: From the Beginnings to Marvell* (London: Harrap).

Kermode, F. (1952b) 'The argument of Marvell's "Garden" ', *Essays in Criticism*, 2, 3.

Kermode, F. (1954) (ed.) *The Tempest*, The Arden Shakespeare (London and New York: Methuen).

Kermode, F. (1957) *Romantic Image* (London: Routledge and Kegan Paul).

Kermode, F. (1960) (ed.) *The Living Milton* (London: Routledge and Kegan Paul).

Kermode, F. (1962) *Puzzles and Epiphanies* (New York: Chilmark Press).

Kermode, F. (1967) *The Sense of an Ending: Studies in the Theory of Fiction* (London, Oxford, & New York: Oxford University Press).

Kermode, F. (1968) *Continuities* (London: Routledge and Kegan Paul).

Kermode, F. (1971a) *Renaissance Essays* (London: Routledge and Kegan Paul).

Kermode, F. (1971b) 'Poet and dancer before Diaghilev', in *Modern Essays* (London: Fontana).

Kermode, F. (1975a) *The Classic* (London: Faber and Faber). (See 1983b for 2nd edn.)

Kermode, F. (1975b) (ed.) *Selected Prose of T. S. Eliot* (London and New York: Faber and Faber; Harcourt, Brace, Jovanovich).

Kermode, F. (1979) *The Genesis of Secrecy: On the Interpretation of Narrative* (Cambridge, Mass.: Harvard University Press).

Kermode, F. (1981) 'Embers from Newcastle' in *The Times Higher Education Supplement*, 30 January.

Kermode, F. (1983a) *Essays on Fiction: 1971–82* (London: Routledge and Kegan Paul).

Kermode, F. (1983b) *The Classic: Literary Images of Permanence and Change* (Cambridge, Mass.: Harvard University Press). (2nd edn. of 1975a)

Kermode, F. (1985a) *Forms of Attention* (Chicago and London: University of Chicago Press).

Kermode, F. (1985b) 'The decline of the Man of Letters', *Partisan Review*, 52, 3.

Kermode, F. (1986) 'The plain sense of things', in G. H. Hartman and S. Budick (eds) *Midrash and Literature* (New Haven and London: Yale University Press).

Kermode, F. and Alter R. (1987) (eds) *The Literary Guide to the Bible* (London: Collins).

Kermode, F. (1988) *History and Value* (Oxford: Clarendon Press).

Knox, R. A. (1954) 'Studies in the Literature of Sherlock Holmes', in his *Essays in Satire* (London and New York: Sheed and Ward).

Krupnick, M. (1987) (ed.) *Displacement: Derrida and After* (Bloomington: Indiana University Press).

Langbein, J. (1974) *Prosecuting Crime in the Renaissance: England, Germany, France* (Cambridge, Mass.: Harvard University Press).

Langbein, J. (1977) *Torture and the Law of Proof* (Chicago: University of Chicago Press).

Levin, R. (1979) *New Readings vs. Old Plays: Recent Trends in the Reinterpretation of English Renaissance Drama* (Chicago and London: University of Chicago Press).

Lilly, J. (1867) *A Collection of Seventy-Nine Black-Letter Ballads and Broadsides, Printed in the Reign of Queen Elizabeth, Between the Years 1559 and 1597* (London: Joseph Lilly).

Lucian (1913–67) *Lucian*, trans. A. M. Harmon and others (Cambridge, Mass. and London: Harvard University Press and Heinemann, Loeb Classical Library).

Macherey, P. and Balibar, E. (1978) 'Literature as an ideological form', *Oxford Literary Review* 3.

Mallarmé, S. (1945) *Oeuvres complètes* (Paris: Gallimard).

Mandeville, J. (1919–23) *Mandeville's Travels*, ed. P. Hamelius (London: Early English Text Society, Original Series, vols. 153/154).

Marchant, R. A. (1969) *The Church under the Law: Justice, Administration, and Discipline in the Diocese of York, 1560–1640* (Cambridge: Cambridge University Press).

Mathiessen, F. O. (1941) *American Renaissance: Art and Expression in the Age of Emerson and Whitman* (London and New York: Oxford University Press).

Meisel, P. (1987) *The Myth of the Modern* (New Haven: Yale University Press).

Menand, L. (1987) *Discovering Modernism: T. S. Eliot and his Context* (New York and Oxford: Oxford University Press).

Menander (1880–8), *Comicorum Atticorum Fragmenta*, ed. T. Kock, 3 vols (Leipzig: Teubner).

Menander (1921) *Menander*, trans F. G. Allison (London: Heinemann, Loeb Classical Library).

Montaigne, M. (1603) *The Essayes of Morall, Politike and Militarie Discourses of Lo: Michaell de Montaigne*, trans. J. Florio (London: V. Sims).

Montaigne, M. (1872–1900) *Les Essais de Montaigne*, ed. E. Courbet and C. Royer, 5 vols (Paris: Lemerre).

Montrose, L. (1983) ' "Shaping Fantasies": figurations of gender and power in Elizabethan culture', *Representations* 2; reprinted in Grenblatt, S. (1988) (ed.) *Representing the English Renaissance* (Berkeley: University of California Press) and in shortened form in Ferguson M. W., Quilligan, M., and Vickers, N. J. (eds) (1986), *Rewriting the Renaissance: The Discourses of Sexual Difference in Early Modern Europe* (eds) (Chicago: University of Chicago Press).

Moore, E. (1896) *Studies in Dante*, first series (Oxford: Clarendon Press).

More, T. (1931) *The English Works of Sir Thomas More*, eds W. A. Campbell and A. W. Reed, 2 vols (London: Eyre and Spottiswoode).

More, T. (1965) *The Complete Works of St. Thomas More*, vol. 4, ed. E. Surtz and J. H. Hexter (New Haven: Yale University Press).

More, T. (1978) *The Complete Works of St. Thomas More*, vol. 8, ed. L. A. Schuster, R. C. Marius, J. P. Lusardi and R. J. Schoeck (New Haven: Yale University Press).

Mullaney, S. (1988) *The Place of the Stage: License, Play, and Power in Renaissance England* (Chicago: University of Chicago Press).

Nagel, A. F. (1973) 'Lies and the limitable inane: contradiction in More's *Utopia*', *Renaissance Quarterly*, 26.

Nietzsche, F. (1956) *The Birth of Tragedy*, trans. F. Golfing (New York: Doubleday).

Nuttall, A. D. (1983) *A New Mimesis* (London and New York: Methuen).

Olsen, S. H. (1987) *The End of Literary Theory* (Cambridge: Cambridge University Press).

Orwell, G. (1970) 'The art of Donald McGill' in *The Collected Essays, Letters and Journalism of George Orwell* (London and Harmondsworth: Penguin).

Otis, B. (1970) *Ovid as an Epic Poet* (Cambridge: Cambridge University Press).

Pater, W. (1889) *Appreciations* (London: Macmillan).

Pater, W. (1980) *The Renaissance. Studies in Art and Poetry*, ed. D. L. Hill (Berkeley, Los Angeles and London: University of California Press).

Pater, W. (1984) *Selected Writings of Walter Pater*, ed. H. Bloom (New York: Columbia University Press).

Pater, W. (1986) *Walter Pater: Three Major Texts*, ed. W. E. Buckler (New York: New York University Press).

Pennington, D. H. and Thomas, K. (1978) (eds) *Puritans and Revolutionaries: Essays in Seventeenth-Century History Presented to Christopher Hill* (Oxford: Clarendon Press).

Plato (1517) *Platonis opera*, ed. M. Ficino (Venice: F. Pincio).

Plato, (1930) *Republic*, trans. P. Shorey, 2 vols (New York and London: Putnam and Heinemann, Loeb Classical Library).

Plato (1961) *The Collected Dialogues of Plato*, eds E. Hamilton and H. Cairns (New York: Bollingen Foundation).

Plutarch (1960–9) *Moralia*, trans. F. C. Babbitt and others, 16 vols (Cambridge, Mass. and London: Harvard and Heinemann, Loeb Classical Library).

Poe, E. A. (1984) *Poetry and Tales*, ed. P. F. Quinn (New York: Library of America, Literary Classics of the United States).

Poirier, R. (1987) *The Renewal of Literature* (New York: Random House).

Pope, M. H. (1977) *Song of Songs* (New York: Doubleday).

Pound, E. (1917) 'James Joyce', *Egoist*, 2 February.

Prevost-Paradol L. A. (1855) *Élisabeth et Henri IV (1595–1598): Ambassade de Hurault de Maisse en Angleterre au sujet de la paix de Vervins* (Paris: Durand).

Rankin, H. D. (1964) *Plato and the Individual* (London: Methuen).

Read, F. (1968) (ed.) *Pound/Joyce* (London: Faber and Faber).

Richards, I. A. (1974) *Beyond* (New York: Harcourt, Brace, Jovanovich).

Richards, I. A. (1977) *Complementarities: Uncollected Essays*, ed. J. P. Russo, (Manchester: Carcanet).

Ricks, C. (1963) *Milton's Grand Style* (Oxford: Clarendon Press).

Ricoeur, P. (1981) *Essays on Biblical Interpretation*, ed. L. S. Mudge, (London: SPCK).

Roper, L. (1985a) 'Discipline and respectability: prostitution and the Reformation in Augsburg', *History Workshop*, 19.

Roper, L. (1985b) ' "Going to church and street": weddings in Reformation Augsburg', *Past and Present*, 106.

Rossiter, A. P. (1961) *Angel with Horns and other Shakespeare Lectures*, ed. G. Storey (London: Longmans, Green).

Rowse, A. L. (1974) *Sex and Society in Shakespeare's Age: Simon Forman the Astrologer* (New York: Scribner).

Sacks, J. (1989) 'A challenge to Jewish secularism', *The Jewish Quarterly*, 36, 2.

Said, E. W. (1984) *The World, the Text, and the Critic* (London: Faber and Faber).

Said, E. W. (1987) 'The horizon of R. P. Blackmur', in E. T. Cone, J. Frank and E. Keeley (eds) *The Legacy of R. P. Blackmur: Essays, Memoirs, Texts* (New York: Ecco Press).

Salusinszky, I. (1987) *Criticism in Society* (New York and London: Methuen).

Sansovino, F. (1578) *Del Governo et Amministratione di Diversi Regni et Republiche* (Venice).

Santore, C. (1988) 'Julia Lombardo, "somtuosa meretrize': a portrait by property', *Renaissance Quarterly*, 41.

Sartre, J.-P. (1938) *La Nausée* (Paris: Gallimard).

Scott, W. (1877) *Guy Mannering* (New York: Hurd and Houghton: Riverside edition).

Shakespeare, W. (1954) *The Tempest*, ed. F. Kermode, The Arden Shakespeare (London and New York: Methuen).

Shakespeare, W. (1965) *Othello*, ed. M. R. Ridley, The Arden Shakespeare (London and New York: Methuen).

Shakespeare, W. (1982) *Troilus and Cressida*, ed. K. Palmer, The Arden Shakespeare (London and New York: Methuen).

Sharpe, J. A. (1980) *Defamation and Sexual Slander in Early Modern England: The Church Courts at York* (York: Universities of York and St Andrew's, Borthwick Papers 58).

Sharpe, J. A. (1984) *Crime in Early Modern England 1550–1750* (London: Longman).

Shweder, R. A. and LeVine R. A. (1984) (eds) *Culture Theory: Essays on Mind, Self, and Emotion* (Cambridge: Cambridge University Press).

Singleton, C. S. (1967) *Journey to Beatrice* (Cambridge, Mass: Harvard University Press).

Sontag, S. (1967) *Against Interpretation and Other Essays* (London: Eyre and Spottiswoode).

Spufford, M. (1984) *The Great Reclothing of Rural England: Petty Chapmen and their Wares in the Seventeenth Century* (London: Hambledon).

Steiner, P. (1984) *Russian Formalism: A Metapoetics* (Ithaca and London: Cornell University Press).

Stevens, W. (1955) *The Collected Poems of Wallace Stevens* (London: Faber and Faber).

Stokes, J. (1989) *In the Nineties* (Hemel Hempstead: Harvester-Wheatsheaf).

Swindells, J. and Jardine, L. (1989) *What's Left? History, Literature and the Labour Movement* (London: Routledge).

Symons, A. (1909) *The Romantic Movement in English Poetry* (London: Constable).

Symons, A. (1916) *Figures of Several Centuries* (London: Constable).

Symons, A. (1958) *The Symbolist Movement in Literature*, ed. with an introduction by R. Ellmann (New York: Dutton).

Tennenhouse, L. (1986) *Power on Display: The Politics of Shakespeare's Genres* (New York: Methuen).

Thomas, K. (1978) 'The puritans and adultery; the act of 1650 reconsidered', in Pennington, D. H. and Thomas, K. (eds) *Puritans and Revolutionaries: Essays in Seventeenth-Century History Presented to Christopher Hill* (Oxford: Clarendon Press).

Thomas, K. (1988) 'The past in a clearer light, a beacon on our future', *Times Higher Education Supplement*, 2 December.

Turner, V. W. and Bruner, E. M. (1986) (eds), *The Anthropology of Experience* (Champaign, Illinois: University of Illinois Press.

Veeser, H. A. (1989) (ed.) *The New Historicism* (London: Routledge).

Vespucci, A. (1894) *The Letters of Amerigo Vespucci*, trans. C. R. Markham (London: Hakluyt Society).

Warner, F. (1758) *Memoirs of the Life of Sir Thomas More . . . To which is added his History of Utopia* (London: L. Davis and C. Reymers).

Waugh, E. (1962) *Brideshead Revisited* (London and Harmondsworth: Penguin).

Wilde, O. (1966) *Complete Works of Oscar Wilde* (London: Collins).

Williams, C. (1989) *The Transfigured World: Walter Pater's Aesthetic Historicism* (Ithaca: Cornell University Press).

Wölfflin, H. (1888) *Renaissance und Barock* (Munich: Ackermann).

Wrightson, K. (1982) *English Society 1580–1680* (London: Hutchinson).

Wuletich-Brinberg, S. (1988) *The Rationale of the Uncanny*, Studies in Romantic and Modern Literature 2, ed. W. S. Johnson (New York: Lang).

Yesimin-Volpin, A. S. (1961) *A Leaf of Spring*, trans. G. Reavey (London: Thames and Hudson).

Index